QUALITATIVE RESEARCH
THROUGH CASE STUDIES

INTRODUCING QUALITATIVE METHODS provides a series of volumes which introduce qualitative research to the student and beginning researcher. The approach is interdisciplinary and international. A distinctive feature of these volumes is the helpful student exercises.

One stream of the series provides texts on the key methodologies used in qualitative research. The other stream contains books on qualitative research for different disciplines or occupations. Both streams cover the basic literature in a clear and accessible style, but also cover the cutting edge issues in the area.

SERIES EDITOR
David Silverman (Goldsmiths College)

EDITORIAL BOARD
Michael Bloor (University of Wales, Cardiff)
Barbara Czarniawska-Joerges (University of Gothenburg)
Norman Denzin (University of Illinois, Champaign)
Barry Glassner (University of Southern California)
Jaber Gubrium (University of Florida, Gainesville)
Anne Murcott (South Bank University)
Jonathan Potter (Loughborough University)

TITLES IN SERIES
Doing Conversational Analysis: A Practical Guide
Paul ten Have

Using Foucault's Methods
Gavin Kendall and Gary Wickham

The Quality of Qualitative Evaluation
Clive Seale

Qualitative Evaluation
Ian Shaw

Researching Life Stories and Family Histories
Robert L. Miller

Categories in Text and Talk: A Practical Introduction to Categorization Analysis
Georgia Lepper

Focus Groups in Social Research
Michael Bloor, Jane Frankland, Michelle Thomas, Kate Robson

QUALITATIVE RESEARCH THROUGH CASE STUDIES

Max Travers

⑤SAGE Publications
London ● Thousand Oaks ● New Delhi

First published 2001. Reprinted 2002, 2004, 2006

SAGE Publications Ltd
1 Oliver's Yard
55 City Road
London EC1Y 1SP

SAGE Publications Inc
2455 Teller Road
Thousand Oaks, California 91320

SAGE Publications India Pvt Ltd
B-42 Panchsheel Enclave
Post Box 4109
New Delhi 100 017

British Library Cataloguing in Publication data

A catalogue record for this book is available
from the British Library

ISBN-10 0-7619-6805-9
ISBN-10 0-7619-6806-7 (pbk)
ISBN-13 978-0-7619-6805-4 (hbk)
ISBN-13 978-0-7619-6806-1 (pbk)

Library of Congress Control Number 2001 131812

Typeset by Mayhew Typesetting, Rhayader, Powys
Printed and bound in Great Britain by Athenaeum Press Ltd.,
Gateshead, Tyne & Wear

Contents

Preface

Qualitative research has been one of the big growth areas in social science in the postwar period. There are now a vast number of books covering all aspects of qualitative research. These range from general introductions, to practical guides on how to use different methods, to texts which advocate a particular vision of the history and practice of qualitative research through critical discussion of underlying issues.

Despite this large literature, there are many undergraduates who still feel far more comfortable conducting a survey, or analysing a quantitative data set, than doing qualitative research. Most find no difficulty in collecting qualitative data: after all, anyone can carry out a few interviews, describe some events in a particular social setting, or tape-record and transcribe a conversation, without specialist training. The difficulty lies in turning this into a rigorous, theoretically informed analysis of some well-defined question or problem. Here students often do very badly, and are unable to relate the approaches and traditions they cover in theory courses to their own experience of doing research.

Another way of expressing this problem is that few methods texts explain the distinction between method and methodology. Methods are the techniques used in collecting data. Methodology, on the other hand, refers to the assumptions you have as a researcher, which can be epistemological or political in character, or mean that you support the view of the world promoted by a particular theoretical tradition. Whether they are acknowledged or not, or even whether you are fully aware of them, these assumptions will influence how you research any topic. You will be challenged to defend and explain them in your viva interview to obtain a PhD, if you get that far in your studies, and by academics reviewing your work who may be highly critical towards your theoretical perspective. However, even at undergraduate level, you can achieve a higher standard in research projects or dissertations by thinking and writing about methodological issues.

There are two things that have to be taught on any social science programme where more than lip-service is paid to the idea that students should learn about qualitative methods. The first is that every student should get first hand experience in at least one of the techniques used by researchers. There is usually little space for this on the average sociology degree, and even less for those studying in a department of law, business or nursing. However, it makes little sense that students are expected to learn about interviewing, ethnographic fieldwork, or discourse analysis, without there being an opportunity to collect some data.

However, simply knowing what an interview is, or how to make a tape-recording, are not in themselves enough either to appreciate or conduct qualitative research. There are different ways of teaching qualitative research methods, but, in my view, the only way to acquire real competence is to understand the methodological basis of classic studies, and to emulate the things you like about them in your own work (see also Mills 1959, p. 215). I have, therefore, chosen to organize this text around summaries of a number of well-known or exemplary studies. I would also recommend reading as many actual studies as possible, in order to get a feel for what qualitative research looks like, even if they have no direct relevance to your own degree or research topic. In short, there is no substitute or shortcut to reading and thinking about a large number of studies, if you want to improve the quality of your own work.

The other feature of this text which is unusual is that I have chosen to introduce different ways of conducting qualitative research, through reviewing a number of different research traditions. Here it is important to recognize that most qualitative research in the human sciences is conducted by different traditions or schools, and that graduate students in departments of sociology, anthropology and linguistics learn their craft from communities of researchers who share similar epistemological and methodological assumptions.

My main objective in this text is to introduce these communities, and enable you to appreciate their objectives, and how they write about the social world. Although I cannot address every tradition, I will be covering a wider range of approaches than most introductory texts, including 'interpretive' traditions like symbolic interactionism and ethnomethodology, and 'critical traditions' like feminist qualitative research and critical discourse analysis.

My decision to present qualitative research in this way creates the risk that this will become a text in sociological theory rather than qualitative research methods. It is, for example, difficult explaining how Marxist and post-Marxist traditions interpret qualitative data, without also having to discuss theoretical debates and developments within structural-conflict sociology. It is also difficult explaining something like postmodern ethnography without spending some time talking about different responses to positivism in the human sciences.

There are some who will feel that making connections between debates in sociological theory and qualitative research is inappropriate or ambitious for students who may never have studied sociology at degree level. However, my own experience suggests that this is not the case. I am regularly approached by postgraduate students outside sociology departments seeking advice on how to develop a theoretically informed approach in their own research projects. These students are already well aware that one cannot use postmodern methods, or grounded theory, or ethnomethodology, in any meaningful sense, in researching topics like the legal process, schools or business organizations, without knowing something about sociological theory.

This is not to say that there is no place for viewing qualitative research as a set of uniform procedures for producing facts that are of practical use to organizations like corporations or government agencies, or that it may not always be appropriate to include a lengthy discussion about methodological or epistemological issues when presenting findings to these audiences. I will, however, be trying to show that the best studies (by which I mean the most interesting, useful and persuasive) always have a well-defined theoretical focus.

My answer to this potential objection is, therefore, that this text must necessarily have to explain sociological theory, and to some extent the philosophy of social science, in introducing qualitative research methods. However, my focus throughout will be on how it is possible to find out things about the world using these traditions. The point of theory, it seems to me, lies in how it can inform and enrich our understanding of the world, by stimulating us to conduct empirical studies.

In an ideal world, anyone interested in qualitative research would have the opportunity to take a survey course which reviewed a wide range of methodologies and approaches, followed by a range of options taught by specialists in different fields. Similarly, every doctoral student would be part of a large graduate school in which small groups met regularly to share the problems they experienced in collecting and analysing data. This may be the experience of some, but many students may only get a few lectures about interviewing, and never have the opportunity to take a specialist course.

This text is intended to form the basis for a survey course, but it also offers a self-help guide for students who may want to learn more about different traditions. Each chapter introduces the history of a particular approach, and the methodological assumptions of practitioners. It then illustrates these by looking at several case studies: classic or exemplary studies which illustrate how the approach can be used in researching particular topics.

The chapters also contain a guide to further reading, and a practical exercise in which students are encouraged to use ideas and techniques from the approach. Most of these exercises are based on the kind of access that undergraduates can obtain to public settings, or to groups based on a university campus. However, students doing work placements, or taking masters courses, particularly in applied disciplines, are encouraged to make use of whatever opportunities are available in researching particular occupational settings, such as criminal justice agencies, businesses, hospitals or schools. In each case, the exercise involves collecting a small amount of data, through either interviewing, observation, tape-recording or looking at documents. You are then asked to develop a preliminary analysis using ideas and resources from different research traditions.

I begin in an introductory chapter by starting with the basic, if surprisingly difficult, question: what is qualitative research? I review the main methods used by qualitative researchers, and explain the importance of foundational debates about epistemology in the social sciences for how one collects and analyses qualitative data. These debates revolve around different responses to positivism, a set of assumptions that continue to inform a great deal of empirical work in the human sciences. I also review different reasons why one might wish to do qualitative research, ranging from a commitment to science or a desire to make a political or epistemological statement, to an interest in providing a service to public or private sector organizations.

The first part of the book introduces a range of methodologies informed by interpretivism, the view that social science must address the meaningful character of human group life. This part contains chapters on the fieldwork tradition in symbolic interactionism, grounded theory, dramaturgical analysis, ethnomethodological ethnography and conversation analysis. In each I try to show, through examples, the methodological basis of the approach, and how it can be used in studying a range of topics.

The second part introduces what I will be calling 'critical perspectives', which are influenced by a different set of epistemological responses to positivism. I begin by looking at a number of critical traditions in ethnography and discourse analysis, and distinguish them from how the same methods are employed in the interpretive tradition. These traditions view research as a way of doing politics, which can be contrasted with the interpretive objective of addressing meaning. I then discuss feminism as an example of a critical tradition that has become highly influential in the academy, but is not always discussed in introductory methods texts. I also review the postmodern turn in ethnography, and discuss the implications of poststructuralism for qualitative researchers.

In the conclusion of the book, I look at some of the practical issues that arise in doing qualitative research, including how to obtain funding for qualitative projects, and what is involved in publishing academic books and journal articles. I also return to the question of why one might wish to do qualitative research, and how you can tell the difference between 'good' and 'bad' work. I suggest that one can obtain a great deal of pleasure from trying to do rigorous work within a particular school or tradition, in which one has to satisfy the demands and expectations of other academics working in that field. However, there are many varieties of qualitative research, and another test of adequacy is whether your work can address practical problems inside commercial and public sector organizations.

Although this text is written for undergraduates on sociology degrees, I hope that it will also be relevant for students in a range of disciplines who are often expected to pursue qualitative projects using sociological methods. These disciplines include social policy, politics, psychology, socio-legal studies, criminology, business and management, leisure and tourism, media studies, cultural studies, geography, education, nursing, science and technology studies and environmental science. There are, of course, specialist methods texts which apply some of the traditions I will be reviewing to specific subject areas. This book is intended to supplement these texts, by showing how a wide range of approaches, ranging from grounded theory to critical discourse analysis, can be used in studying any topic or social setting.

Acknowledgements

I would like to thank David Silverman, the editor of this series, Simon Ross, Michael Carmichael and Beth Crockett at Sage, and the anonymous reviewers who supplied critical and informed comments at different stages of the project. I would also like to thank my colleagues, and the other people I have worked with in the Department of Human Sciences, Buckinghamshire Chilterns University College for their support over the last ten years, and particularly Chris Crowther and Julian Matthews (for many pleasant evenings in The Falcon during 1999), Kevin Stenson and Paul Watt.

The author and the publishers wish to thank the following for permission to use copyright material.

In Chapter 2: Table of Contents from Paul Cressey (1932), *The Taxi-Dance Hall*, p. xxi. Reprinted with permission of University of Chicago Press.

Figure 3.1, diagram from Anselm Strauss (1985) *Qualitative Analysis for Social Scientists*, p. 254. Reprinted with permission of Cambridge University Press.

In Chapter 3 Table of Contents from Barney Glaser and Anselm Strauss, *Awareness of Dying*. Reprinted with permission of Aldine de Gruyter. Copyright © 1965. Renewed 1993.

Diagram in Chapter 5 from Lucy Suchman (1987) *Plans and Situated Actions: The Problem of Human-Machine Communication*, p. 116. Reprinted with permission of Cambridge University Press.

Dialogue extract in Chapter 6 from an interview between Michael Charlton and Margaret Thatcher, BBC Radio 3, 17th December 1985. Reprinted with permission of the British Broadcasting Corporation. Interview reproduced in N. Fairclough (1993) *Language and Power*, pp. 172–3. London: Longman.

Extract in Chapter 8 from Richardson, Laurel, *Fields of Play: Constructing an Academic Life*, copyright © 1997 by Laurel Richardson. Reprinted by permission of Rutgers University Press.

1

What is Qualitative Research?

CONTENTS

Before looking at research in different qualitative traditions, it is necessary to cover some general issues about the nature and purpose of qualitative enquiry. I begin with an overview of the methods used in qualitative studies, and explain the distinction between method and methodology. I then discuss the distinction between qualitative and quantitative research by considering two classic sociological studies: Emile Durkheim's *Suicide*, and Max Weber's *The Protestant Ethic*. I also explain the importance of epistemology by reviewing four positions which can inform how you collect and analyse qualitative data (positivism, interpretivism, realism and poststructuralism). I conclude by reviewing some reasons why you might wish to pursue qualitative research.

The methods of qualitative enquiry

There are five main methods employed by qualitative researchers: observation, interviewing, ethnographic fieldwork, discourse analysis and textual analysis. Each is simple to do, and requires little, if any, specialist training. In this section, I want to consider some issues that arise in using these methods, and the relationship between them, before one even starts to think about methodological issues, or developing a theoretical position. Another way of putting this is that I am interested in the practical issues that arise in collecting data, which are equally relevant to all the traditions reviewed in this text. I will do this by considering how the five methods can be employed in researching a magistrates' court, the lowest tier of the criminal courts in England and Wales. They could also, however, be used to study any topic. One might, for example, want to employ the same methods in researching a business corporation, a street gang, a doctor's surgery or a police station.

Observation

I have been teaching a methods course for a number of years, based on visiting the local magistrates' court in High Wycombe (a town about mid-way between London and Oxford in England). There is probably a similar institution near your own campus. If you have never been, it would be worth spending a morning in the public gallery. You will observe a lot of guilty pleas, applications for bail and adjournments, but, if you are lucky, you may see a full trial.

Some of the best sociological studies about courtrooms have been based on observing hearings. The ones I teach on my course include Pat Carlen's (1976) *Magistrates' Justice*, a politically engaged, Marxist study which employs ideas from Erving Goffman in analysing the spatial organization of hearing rooms, and Mary Eaton's (1986) feminist ethnography *Justice for Women?* These studies interpret what takes place in magistrates' courts from a particular theoretical point of view, and I will be discussing some of these traditions in later chapters. However, they are all based on observing and making contemporaneous notes of hearings from the public gallery.

It might be necessary to observe many hearings over a few weeks or months to obtain enough examples for the kind of analysis conducted in these studies. You can, however, also learn a great deal simply by spending a morning in this social setting. Even without taking notes, you should be able to come away with a reasonable understanding of the role played by different occupational groups, and the type of cases being heard, and develop a number of research questions that you might wish to pursue using different methods.

Interviewing

One thing you will learn from observing legal hearings is that a number of occupational groups work in the courts. These include judges, lawyers, probation officers, police officers and journalists who each have a different perspective on the proceedings. The quickest way to learn about any one of these perspectives might be to interview people about their day-to-day tasks. Another kind of data-collection technique, the focus group, involves interviewing people in groups, or getting them to talk amongst themselves about particular topics.

There is no hard and fast rule for how many people you need to interview, since it will partly depend on the time available to collect, transcribe and analyse your data. Evaluation researchers working for large organizations routinely conduct a hundred or more interviews, and computer software packages now make it much easier to retrieve and manipulate large amounts of data. Howard Becker's doctoral dissertation about school teachers' careers (which I discuss in Chapter 2) was based on interviewing sixty contacts in a range of schools in the Chicago area. Some of the best life-history studies have been based on a series of interviews with one respondent.

For an undergraduate project, you will only have time to conduct a few interviews. It is, however, worth noting that it is always possible to learn a lot from very little data. If you ask open-ended questions, follow up particular topics in a second interview, and give the interviewee the opportunity to comment on your interpretation of the answers, you are likely to obtain some rich, original data. You will understand far more about what takes place in the courtroom (at least from the interviewee's perspective) than simply by observing hearings from the public gallery.

Few undergraduate students will be able to conduct an interview-based study of groups like lawyers or probation officers, although there is no harm in trying, and some may already have access through a relative or family friend. If you approach an institution like the magistrates' courts or the probation service cold, you will need to explain why you are conducting the study, and perhaps also give managers the opportunity to read drafts of anything you plan to publish. Obtaining this kind of access always takes a great deal of time (maybe even a year), and if you want to conduct an interview study, you will have to plan accordingly.

Ethnographic fieldwork

Ethnography as a general term includes observation and interviewing. It is, however, often used in the more specific sense of a method which requires a researcher to spend a large amount of time observing a particular group of people, by sharing their way of life (Hammersley and Atkinson 1995). This is known as doing fieldwork. One could use this method to study a magistrates' court by getting access to a particular occupational group, and spending a long time observing their day-to-day activities.

Anthropologists typically spend a year trying to make sense of another culture, but it also takes time acquiring an adequate understanding of how people work in a particular occupational setting. My own study of work in a firm of radical lawyers (Travers 1997) was based on four months of fieldwork. Ideally, the ethnographer should be able to observe a wide range of activities, but also ask questions to draw out how practitioners understand their routine activities. Ethnographers normally write up their observations as fieldnotes at the end of each day; they use these notes to produce a more developed analysis after they leave the field.

Most undergraduates will not have much opportunity to obtain hands-on experience in conducting a lengthy piece of ethnographic research, although it should be possible to conduct studies based on work placements, or participation in student societies, including religious and political groups.

Discourse analysis

Most of the business of magistrates' courts, and the occupational groups working in this setting, is conducted through talk. This may be stating the obvious, but none of the methods I have reviewed so far involve paying close attention to how we communicate through language. The general name for approaches concerned with language is discourse analysis (see van Dijk 1996; Jaworski and Coupland 1999).

Once you become sensitive to language, the hearings themselves become interesting as multi-party conversations. There will be other conversations taking place in and around the court building. When the magistrates retire to make a decision, they will have a short conversation in a room adjoining the court. You might also see lawyers meeting their clients in interview rooms or in the corridor outside the court. Probation officers will also meet defendants in the court buildings, as part of their work in preparing social enquiry reports for the magistrates. All kinds of administrative meetings will be taking place to co-ordinate activities and ensure the smooth running of the courts.

If you want to conduct this type of analysis, you will need to tape-record some activity, and use the tape-recording as your principal source of data. It is possible to spend a long time analysing a single conversation (it could even be an interview in which you are one of the speakers). However, it is more usual for researchers to collect a small corpus of data: for example, ten episodes in which a doctor advises a patient, or a social worker deals with a request from a client. In either case, you can expect to spend a lot of time listening to tape-recordings again and again, and carefully transcribing what you hear on the tapes.

Recording legal hearings in the United Kingdom is illegal, but it is still possible to make contemporaneous notes, using shorthand, which preserve the detail of many exchanges between magistrates, lawyers and defendants. Another strategy for a research project might be to look at the publicly available data about courtrooms which is available in America. This includes celebrity trials like the O.J. Simpson case, but it is also possible to obtain recordings of routine cases from Court TV. If you approach an organization requesting permission to tape-record meetings, or professional–client interaction, you will need to explain why you require this kind of data.

Textual analysis

Qualitative researchers have always known that one can learn a lot about the world by looking at documents. An early example is the first volume of Thomas and Znaniecki's (1958) *The Polish Peasant in Europe and America* which examines the correspondence between immigrants and their families. This extends qualitative research into what is more usually called cultural studies – the study of all kinds of textual and multi-media products, ranging from television programmes to websites on the internet. It is also worth noting, however, that texts of all kinds form an important part of everyday life: one can learn a great deal about organizations simply by studying the messages pinned on notice boards (Watson 1997a). More profoundly, much of the interaction that takes place in modern societies is mediated by different kinds of texts.

In the case of the magistrates' courts, a textual project might involve trying to obtain copies of the files kept about defendants by different organizations. One might want to ask how these files are used, or analyse the contents using different techniques. It might also be interesting to collect any brochures or guides produced by the public relations department of your local court, or by the central government department which has ultimate responsibility for managing the legal system. What do these reveal about the official objectives of the courts, and how managers understand the problems they face in providing this service to the public?

The distinction between method and methodology

This review of different approaches to researching a magistrates' court has only been concerned with method – with some of the main techniques that you could employ in researching any group or social setting. I will include some discussion of the practical issues involved in using different techniques in later chapters, and there are a large number of books and manuals you could consult about all these methods. This, however, is not my main objective in writing this text. Instead, I wish to focus on the distinction between method and methodology. What do you have to do, having collected some data, to produce an interesting, theoretically informed analysis? The rest of this book is intended to answer this question, through examining how researchers in a number of theoretical traditions collect and analyse qualitative data. Before doing so, however, I want to use the rest of this chapter to discuss some general issues which are often raised about qualitative research.

The qualitative/quantitative divide

It should be no cause for surprise that academic life is divided into communities which specialize in particular approaches or research techniques with little communication between them. When I started graduate school, I was asked to make a choice in the first fortnight between specializing in quantitative or qualitative methods. Given the limited time one has in graduate school, it made sense to specialize in this way. It takes time to learn how to do regression analysis, or a qualitative method like conversation analysis or grounded theory. There are, therefore, good practical reasons why sociologists specialize in a theoretical school or tradition at an early stage in their academic careers.

There is, however, more to this debate than simply a choice between methods, or that people who did well at mathematics at school are most likely to enjoy doing quantitative work. Some have argued that quantitative and qualitative research are based on fundamentally different epistemological assumptions, and that making a choice commits you to a particular way of understanding social science, and studying human beings.

These debates go back a long way, and are set out most clearly in the writings of Emile Durkheim and Max Weber. Their two most famous studies – *Suicide* (1951) and *The Protestant Ethic* (1958) – can be used to illustrate the key assumptions, and why this remains an important debate.

Durkheim's Suicide

Many writers have argued, and remain committed to the view, that the best hope for sociology is that it becomes a science like natural science. This is ultimately a philosophical viewpoint, but it has become important in terms of research methods, in that quantitative methods are usually held out as being more 'scientific'.

Perhaps the most forceful advocate of this view was Emile Durkheim, who argued that sociology must become a science, and employ quantitative methods in making causal connections between variables in the same way as natural science. His best known study *Suicide* is worth looking at as an example of how quantitative methods (what we now call variable or multivariate analysis) can be used in addressing a research problem. It is based on comparing official statistics of suicide rates in different European countries, and relating these to other variables like type of religion or family structure. From this data, Durkheim derives causal laws, with a similar form to natural scientific laws, which explain why different groups commit suicide.

There are two reasons why Durkheim's study poses a challenge for qualitative researchers. Firstly, it argues that sociology should be concerned with large-scale 'macro' processes or phenomena; and, to this day, qualitative studies are criticized for only dealing with local or 'micro' social settings, which make only a limited contribution to our understanding of society as a whole. More fundamentally, it suggests that sociology should not be concerned with common-sense knowledge: what people understand about their own activities should be more or less irrelevant for the sociologist. Durkheim sets out this view in the preface to his *The Rules of Sociological Method*:

> We are still so accustomed to solving questions according to common-sense notions that we find it difficult to dispense with them in sociological discussions. When we believe ourselves to be free of common-sense judgements they take us over unawares. Only long and specialized experience can prevent such failings. We would ask the reader not to forget this. He should always bear in mind that his usual ways of thinking are more likely to be adverse rather than favourable to the scientific study of social phenomena, and he must therefore be wary of his first impressions. (1985, p. 63)

From this point of view, conducting interviews, or doing ethnographic fieldwork, does not address real scientific issues or problems. This criticism is not often made in such direct terms today, but one sometimes hears echoes in the comments of referees who share this way of thinking on grant proposals, and see little value in qualitative methods.

Weber's The Protestant Ethic

There have always been philosophers fiercely opposed to the view that social science should emulate natural science. Nineteenth century German writers in the idealist or romantic traditions argued that there are fundamental differences between human beings and inanimate objects in the natural world: they think, can experience emotion, and have free will.

Weber himself believed that sociology as a science had to address the meaningful character of social action, using interpretive methods. In contrast to Durkheim, he argued that the sociologist had to get inside the heads of those being studied. *Verstehen* or understanding, rather than the quantitative techniques used by natural scientists, should be the principal method used in social science.

Weber's most famous study, *The Protestant Ethic and the Spirit of Capitalism*, illustrates how this method can be used in researching the social world. The first part of the study is an attempt to address what it meant to be a member of a Protestant religious sect in the seventeenth century, drawing on historical records. This might be seen as equivalent to a contemporary ethnographic study in which one tries to understand what it means to be a member of a particular social group, by conducting interviews, or becoming a participant observer. The methodological argument is that the inner life of the Protestants is only available using interpretive methods. Although Weber did not directly engage with Durkheim in his methodological writings, he was proposing a different conception of social science.

Bridging the divide?

Is it then the case that only interpretivists can do qualitative research? Fiona Devine and Sue Heath complain that this view is widely held in sociology:

> A distinction is usually drawn between positivist, and anti-positivist or interpretive positions. The positivist view aligns itself with a particular view of the mechanisms and assumptions of the natural sciences, underpinned by a belief that only that which is grounded in the observable can count as valid knowledge. In contrast, the interpretive paradigm – associated with intellectual traditions such as phenomenology, symbolic interactionism and ethnomethodology – stresses the dynamic, constructed and evolving nature of social reality. It rejects the positivist notion of knowledge being grounded in the objective and tangible, and instead seeks to understand social reality through the eyes of those being studied. (1999, p. 202)

Devine and Heath make the point that interpretive sociologists do not have a monopoly when it comes to conducting ethnographic research, which will also be evident from the second part of this book. There are still, however, important differences between the epistemological assumptions which inform work in these different qualitative traditions. Interpretivists, following Weber, adopt a non-competitive, explicatory stance towards how people understand their own actions. Critical theorists, on the other hand, believe with Durkheim that they can obtain a superior, scientific understanding of society which can *explain* people's actions. From an interpretive perspective, the critical ethnographies discussed by Devine and Heath do not adequately address how their subjects understand the world. On the other hand, the critical theorist might legitimately complain that interpretive ethnographies are either conservative or apolitical because they never rise above common-sense notions and judgements.

Other writers believe that this kind of philosophically driven debate about methods should be avoided, since it is possible to combine quantitative and qualitative methods in researching the social world (see, for example, Hammersley 1989; Silverman 1993). These arguments need to be taken seriously, but they are unlikely to settle debates about the nature of social science, which have, if anything, intensified, given the rise of intellectual movements like poststructuralism and postmodernism. This is not because of the stubbornness of different proponents, or their inability to reach a reasonable compromise, but because the underlying philosophical issues, by their very nature, cannot easily be resolved. One might note, for example, that Durkheim seems to be suggesting that there are sure and objective grounds for knowledge, as in natural science. Weber's position, on the other hand, seems to lead towards the view that we can only describe or appreciate different viewpoints. It is only one further step to the position of poststructuralists (who are often proponents of qualitative methods): there is no truth, and the purpose of qualitative enquiry is to question this philosophical idea, and celebrate different viewpoints.

The importance of epistemology

It may already be apparent that 'methods talk', to use Jaber Gubrium and James Holstein's (1997) phrase, can easily become a lengthy discussion about epistemology – different philosophical views on how or whether (in the case of poststructuralism) it is possible to obtain certain or objective knowledge about the world. On the other hand, it is important to recognize that every researcher brings some set of epistemological assumptions into the research process (even if you are unaware of them!), and that these influence how you understand and interpret qualitative data. It is, therefore, desirable to become self-conscious about these issues, and the way they are understood by different traditions.

I have so far introduced two epistemological positions, positivism and interpretivism. Positivists, like Durkheim, favour the use of quantitative methods in researching large-scale phenomena. Interpretivists, like Weber, employ qualitative methods in order to address the meaningful character of human group life. I have, however, suggested that one can pursue qualitative research while holding a variety of epistemological assumptions, so that researchers working in different critical traditions as well as interpretivists, can conduct ethnographic research. To further complicate matters there are, in fact, two additional epistemological positions, and there are also epistemological debates *within* particular theoretical traditions: so there is, for example, a continuing tension between 'positivists' and 'interpretivists' inside the interpretive tradition

of symbolic interactionism (grounded theory versus postmodern ethnography). This will become clearer in later chapters, but for the moment
I will summarize the four positions, and explain their relevance for
qualitative research.

Positivism

There are numerous varieties of positivism, and arguably so many that
the term has very little value, and is often used unhelpfully as a term of
abuse. A central assumption is that it is possible to describe the world
objectively, from a scientific vantage point. Qualitative researchers who
share this assumption often favour building techniques into studies
modelled on the procedures used by natural scientists or quantitative
researchers. They might, for example, want to count the instances they
observed, in order to make claims about the representativeness of their
findings. They are also likely to favour collecting large amounts of data.
Evaluation researchers working for large organizations routinely
conduct a hundred or more interviews, and computer software packages
now make it much easier to retrieve and manipulate large amounts of
data (see, for example, Dey 1993).

Proponents of positivist styles of ethnography include Martyn
Hammersley (1991) who argues that all studies should be judged by a
set of scientific criteria, which include reliability and representativeness
(the same criteria used in quantitative research). This is also the 'language of method' (again Gubrium and Holstein's phrase) used by government departments, and other public agencies, when they commission
or conduct qualitative research. It has also been influential within
symbolic interactionism (which is usually associated with the interpretive tradition), and this will become apparent when I look at Becker et
al.'s (1961) study *Boys in White* in the next chapter, and the grounded
theory tradition in Chapter 3.

Interpretivism

Interpretivists believe that the objective of sociological analysis should be
to address how members of society understand their own actions. This
includes the issue of representativeness, so whereas a positivist would
spend a lot of time devising a sampling procedure, an interpretive
sociologist might want to know how members of society understand the
issue of representativeness. Wes Sharrock and Rod Watson (1989) have
observed that one does not usually need to conduct a survey, or spend
three months sampling activities on different days of the week, to come
to a judgement that something is typical or unusual in an occupational
setting: it should be obvious simply from looking at the faces, and
demeanour, of the people working there. If something unusual happens,
then people will talk about it.

David Sudnow's (1967) ethnomethodological study *Passing On*, which looks at how hospital staff understood death and dying in two hospitals, illustrates how 'unusualness' or 'typicality' can be investigated from an interpretive perspective. One of the chapters compares the way in which new members of the nursing team, and old hands, talked about the number of people who had died that week. For the new members, a death was an unusual, newsworthy event, something one talked about and counted by, for example, saying 'We had four deaths this week.' Old hands had, however, stopped counting deaths. They were simply something that happened as part of the job. Here different groups understood the same event as being 'unusual' or completely ordinary and typical. A positivist study which simply noted that there was an average of four deaths a week, or even that four deaths was unusually low for that week, would not be addressing how people in that setting counted deaths.

From an interpretive perspective, there are no benefits in working with large data sets, since these encourage a positivist mentality towards analysing interviews. It becomes all too easy to present very short decontextualized extracts from interviews, rather than exploring how interviewees understand their activities in any depth. The objective of a positivist study would be to make comparisons, and perhaps develop some kind of causal theory, based on measuring variables in different settings. An interpretivist, however, might want to know how people in a particular setting make comparisons between 'insiders' and 'outsiders' in the course of their daily affairs. For this reason, there is a preference for conducting in-depth ethnographies in one social setting, rather than comparative studies based on spending smaller periods in a number of sites.

Realism

The most popular position informing enquiry in the human sciences is realism, which involves looking behind appearances to discover laws or mechanisms which explain human behaviour. This becomes important when one interprets what people say about their own activities. Interpretivists usually take members' accounts at face value, or contrast these to the perspectives of different groups in society. Realists, however, are likely to view them as incomplete or deficient.

Marxist and feminist ethnographies about social class in Britain have, for example, found that members of the working class do not view their activities in class terms (see, for example, Skeggs 1997). The objective of these ethnographies is, however, to challenge these understandings, which they explain by pointing out the fact that people are often made to feel ashamed of belonging to the working class. Many of the critical traditions reviewed in the second part of this book are informed by this epistemological assumption. The goal of their studies is to reveal a reality concealed from ordinary members of society.

Poststructuralism

Positivism, interpretivism and realism all share the assumption that it is possible to obtain valid knowledge about the world, and that the studies we write can represent social reality. Poststructuralism is a radical philosophical movement which seeks to challenge these assumptions. Philosophers like Jacques Derrida and Jean Baudrillard have questioned the idea that it is possible to represent the world unproblematically through texts. This has become highly influential in the human sciences in recent years, although mainly at a theoretical level. It has, however, led some anthropologists and symbolic interactionists to challenge the idea of representation in traditional texts. This is often called 'postmodern ethnography' and I will be reviewing some of these studies in a later chapter.

Why do qualitative research?

Before you read further, it is also worth thinking about the different reasons why one might wish to pursue qualitative research. They are not necessarily mutually exclusive, and it is possible to use the same data for different purposes, or to address a range of audiences.

The practical value of research

The current emphasis of government policy towards universities, and higher education generally, both in Britain and elsewhere, is that it should contribute something of economic value to society. In Britain, the Dearing Report emphasized the acquisition of transferable skills, rather than the pursuit of knowledge for its own sake. All subjects have to demonstrate to assessment committees that they have vocational and practical value, including those one might previously have felt had no practical application, such as philosophy or English literature.

The moment you leave higher education it becomes clear that funding is usually only available for projects that have some practical value. The Economic and Social Research Council, which replaced the more academically oriented Social Science Research Council in the early 1980s as the main source of funding for social science research in Britain, has a narrowly utilitarian remit. Research has either to improve the economic position of the country, or contribute to the efficiency and effectiveness of public and private sector institutions. Research funded by public and private sector organizations similarly requires academics to employ research techniques in ways that are useful to those institutions.

There have always been opportunities for qualitative researchers to obtain funding for projects which involve describing processes within organizations. This has, however, been especially the case for the traditions reviewed in the first part of this book. Symbolic interactionists in the grounded theory tradition have, for example, played a large part in developing the sophisticated qualitative techniques (mainly involving the computer-assisted analysis of large data sets) which are now used, in combination with quantitative measures, to evaluate many government programmes in America. Ethnomethodologists and conversation analysts have been employed by corporations to describe activities in the workplace, and the social effects of technology. I review some of the practical applications of these traditions in Chapters 4 and 5.

Research as a form of politics

Even prior to the 1960s, the university played a central role as a site for political and moral debate. Max Weber (1949) noted that lecturers were most likely to obtain promotion in Germany in the early years of the twentieth century for advancing their political views to students and wider audiences. In liberal affluent societies like Britain and America, the university campus has become a home for the intellectual wings of different old and new social movements. These include different varieties of Marxism, feminism, gay liberation, environmental pressure groups, and organizations representing disadvantaged or minority groups, such as prisoners, the mentally ill, victims of crime or disabled people.

The university is not separate from society but very much part of the social, political and economic challenges that face everyone in the contemporary world. Students, as well as academics, often want to understand how their own experiences relate to a wider social context. It is, therefore, inevitable that many will want to address political or moral issues, through conducting qualitative research. I will be discussing some of the ways this can be done in the second part of the book.

Research – entirely for its own sake!

Writing in the early years of the twentieth century, Weber argued that research should ultimately be pursued for its own sake, as part of a commitment to science. It could also be argued that there is a value in humanistic enquiry, in the sense of any intellectual activity that makes us think about what it means to be a human being.

This may not be a fashionable view to express in the contemporary academy, but it is worth remembering that there is a great deal of pleasure to be gained from belonging to an intellectual community, and attempting to do rigorous research within that tradition. This has nothing to do with how many people read your published work, or whether your findings are of any practical value to government or industry, but arises entirely from the activity itself, just as one might get pleasure from playing music, or making a film. Gubrium and Holstein

(1997) present the craft of qualitative research as being similar to learning a language: a set of ways of talking about the world. To want to learn these languages requires a curiosity about social life, and an interest in writing about human activities. I would recommend approaching qualitative research in this spirit.

Further reading

For discussion about the quantitative/qualitative issue

Devine, F. and Heath, S. (1999) *Sociological Research Methods in Context.* Macmillan, Basingstoke.
Bryman, A. (1988) *Quantity and Quality in Sociological Research.* Unwin Hyman, London.
Denzin, N. (1989a) *The Research Act,* 3rd edn. Prentice-Hall, Englewood Cliffs, NJ.

For an introduction to epistemological issues

Hughes, J. and Sharrock, W.W. (1990) *The Philosophy of Social Research,* 2nd edn. Longman, London.
Halfpenny, P. (1979) 'The analysis of qualitative data', *Sociological Review,* 21 (1): 799–825.

For alternative conceptions of qualitative research

Silverman, D. (1993) *Interpreting Qualitative Data.* Sage, London.
Silverman, D. (ed.) (1997) *Qualitative Research.* Sage, London.
Gubrium, J. and Holstein, J. (1997) *The New Language of Qualitative Method.* Oxford University Press, New York.
Seale, C. (ed.) (1998) *Researching Society and Culture.* Sage, London.

EXERCISES

1   Choose any social setting that interests you, and make a case for using one of the following methods in an undergraduate project:
   interviewing
   fieldwork
   discourse analysis
   textual analysis.
2   How would your epistemological assumptions be relevant to this research project?
3   Write a 500 word grant proposal for your project, bearing in mind that your findings have to improve the competitiveness of British industry or the effectiveness of public services.

Part I

THE INTERPRETIVE TRADITION

The traditions in the first part of this book are all faithful to the Weberian injunction that it is important to take meaning seriously. This means that their aim is unashamedly descriptive: they seek to stay close to how social actors understand their own activities. They can, therefore, be contrasted with the traditions in Part II which all share the Durkheimian assumption that there are underlying structures which shape and constrain our actions, but which are hidden from ordinary members of society.

Although the idea of interpretive sociology originated in Europe, most of the sociologists I will be concerned with are American, and the approaches are most used in the English speaking world, Western Europe and Japan. The first two chapters are concerned with symbolic interactionism, a tradition that has deep roots in American academic life. In the early stages of American sociology, qualitative researchers, based at the University of Chicago, were the largest organized intellectual group in the discipline. The *American Journal of Sociology* was, for example, founded and edited for many years entirely by sociologists working in this tradition. During the 1950s and 1960s, symbolic interactionism was supplanted by structural functionalism and conflict theory. However, it remains highly influential in American sociology and further afield. Chapter 2 discusses the roots of qualitative research in Chicago, and how it was developed into a research programme by Herbert Blumer in the 1950s. Chapter 3 examines how it has diversified into a number of distinct traditions, including grounded theory and dramaturgical analysis.

Ethnomethodology is a smaller research tradition, founded by Harold Garfinkel and a group of sociologists working at the University of California at Los Angeles in the 1960s, which has also been extremely influential. Chapters 4 and 5 look at two traditions in ethnomethodology. Researchers in the studies-of-work tradition use ethnographic methods in studying organizational processes and decision-making. Conversation analysis has developed into a distinctive discipline in its own right, which investigates everyday and institutional talk.

As well as introducing the history and methodological assumptions of each tradition, the chapters also summarize a number of exemplary studies, and contain suggestions on how you can employ these qualitative approaches in your own work. There is, of course, a big difference between the kind of study you are able or equipped to pursue as an undergraduate, and the more developed studies one can read in the academic literature. The basic assumption common to these approaches is, however, that you can observe everyday things in the world around you (for example, what people say, or what they do), and describe them carefully in the same way as scientists describe events and activities in the natural world. In my experience, some people are better observers than others, or can achieve more in employing a particular approach. However, given practice, anyone should be able to explain the assumptions of these approaches in an undergraduate project, and employ them in collecting and analysing qualitative data.

2

Addressing Lived Experience: Symbolic Interactionism and Ethnography

CONTENTS

Researchers influenced by symbolic interactionism have produced a large number of empirical studies motivated by an interest in getting close to human beings and describing how they understand their own activities and social worlds. I will begin by providing a brief overview of symbolic interactionism as a research tradition, and summarize the methodological assumptions and objectives of analysts focusing on statements by Herbert Blumer and Robert Prus.

I will then illustrate applications of the approach by reviewing four case studies. Paul Cressey's *The Taxi-Dance Hall* is a classic study, published in 1932, which is instructive reading for anyone who wishes to study an institutional setting using ethnographic methods. Everett Hughes, Howard Becker and Blanche Geer's *Boys in White* is an example of how ethnography can be used to investigate the relationship between individuals and organizations. Elliot Liebow's *Tally's Corner* is a study of an ethnic group, based on gaining access through a key informant. Tom Weinberg's *Gay Men, Gay Selves* is an example of how interview data can be analysed from a symbolic interactionist perspective in studying how one acquires a gay identity.

I conclude the chapter by suggesting how you might want to approach conducting an ethnographic study for an undergraduate dissertation, or as a postgraduate project. One requirement is that you will need to obtain access to a social setting, and share in the world and activities of a particular occupation or community group. You may then need to learn to live with the uncertainties and anxieties that many ethnographers experience in the field.

Symbolic interactionism as a research tradition

There are a number of good historical accounts of symbolic interactionism that go into the detail of the often complicated relationship between people, ideas and institutions. I will not be attempting to go over this ground, or to advance a distinctive interpretation of how the approach has diversified and developed. Instead, I simply want to give an overview of some important figures and studies, before looking at a few of these in more detail later in the chapter.

The term 'symbolic interactionism' was first coined by Herbert Blumer in the 1950s, but the roots of the approach can be traced a long way back in American intellectual culture. The original theoretical impetus for naturalistic sociology, based on observing how human beings talk and act in ordinary settings rather than in laboratory conditions, came from the theoretical writings of the pragmatist philosopher Charles Horton Cooley and social psychologist George Herbert Mead. The fieldwork tradition itself originated with a group of academics associated with Robert Park, the head of the Sociology Department at the University of Chicago from 1913 to 1933. Since then it has been passed on through two students of Park, Herbert Blumer and Everett Hughes, to their own students, and become an academic field with its own journals, the *Journal of Contemporary Ethnography* (which used to be called *Urban Life*), *Qualitative Sociology* and *Symbolic Interaction*, and professional association, the Society for the Study of Symbolic Interactionism (SSSI).

The university is home to many intellectual traditions, which are passed on to new generations through the curriculum. At the core of academic life lies the teacher–student relationship. Students develop an interest in different approaches, or a competence as researchers, not simply by reading books and articles, but through coming into contact with teachers who are actively engaged in promoting particular ways of understanding the social world. The development of symbolic interactionism can be viewed in terms of a number of key figures, who have trained their students to do ethnographic research, and encouraged them to pass on the tradition to their own students. There are now a number of distinctive traditions and styles of work associated with symbolic interactionism. This will be evident by considering how the approach has developed, and diversified, through three generations.

The Chicago School

The first substantial piece of qualitative research in sociology was conducted by William Thomas (W.I. Thomas) and Florian Znaniecki in the Department of Sociology of the University of Chicago between 1908 and 1920. They published a five volume study which examined the experiences of Polish immigrants in America (Thomas and Znaniecki 1958, first published 1918–20). The method they employed was not ethnography, although Thomas would have been aware of the anthropological work being conducted by Hans Boas at the time, but documentary analysis of several hundred letters which immigrants sent to friends and relatives back home reporting their experiences of America. Thomas and Znaniecki also obtained a number of diaries kept by immigrants, and worked with one informant in publishing a hundred page autobiographical account of the problems he experienced in adapting to American society.

Robert Park joined the Department of Sociology at Chicago in 1913. He was an ex-journalist who became an advocate for employing ethnographic methods to investigate social processes and understand social problems. Other figures at Chicago who influenced the development of this tradition were Ellsworth Faris (who replaced Thomas in 1918) and Ernest Burgess. Their students conducted a number of studies based on ethnographic fieldwork, documentary analysis and life-history interviews.

The best known participation-observer ethnographies are *The Hobo* (1923) by Nels Anderson, which drew on his own experience as a 'homeless man' before becoming a sociologist, and *The Taxi-Dance Hall* (1932) by Paul Cressey, which looks at the perspectives of patrons, workers and managers in dance halls where men could pay to spend time with the dancer of their choice. Other studies include *The Gang* (1927) by Frederick Thrasher, *The Woman Who Waits* (1920) and *The Saleslady* (1929) by Frances Donovan, *Hotel Life* (1936) by Norman Hayner, and *The Strike* (1928) by E.T. Hiller. All these were based on sociologists spending large amounts of time with particular groups, or in a particular institutional setting.

Another type of research pioneered by students of Park and Burgess was the urban ethnography which documented styles of life in different parts of the city. These include Louis Wirth's (1928) *The Ghetto* and Harvey Zorbaugh's (1929) *The Gold Coast and the Slum*. Other researchers conducted life-history studies, based on extended interviews with a single informant. The best known of these is *The Jack-Roller* (1930) by Clifford Shaw which is the autobiographical account of a 'juvenile delinquent'. Finally, there were studies based on qualitative interviewing. Herbert Blumer's (1933) *Movies and Conduct*, and Herbert Blumer and Philip Hauser's (1933) *Movies, Delinquency and Crime*, look at the influence of films on young people (viewed as a serious social problem in the 1930s). Willard Waller's (1930) *The Old Love and the New* is based on interviews with people who had been divorced or widowed.

The second Chicago School

After Park retired in 1933, the main figures who remained interested in ethnographic research at Chicago were his students Herbert Blumer and Louis Wirth. Blumer graduated in the department in 1928 and taught there until 1952, when he moved to the University of California at Berkeley, San Francisco. Another ex-student of Park, Everett Hughes, joined the department in 1938 (after spending ten years at McGill University in Canada). However, it was only in the period from about 1946 to 1960 when large numbers of graduate students, supervised by Blumer, Hughes and Wirth, surpassed the achievements of the first Chicago School by producing a large body of empirical work. One condition for this was the expansion of American higher education during this period, which allowed the university to take on graduate students, and made it possible for them to obtain academic posts. Another was that a group of academics were working at Chicago, including the anthropologist W. Lloyd Warner, who were strongly committed to qualitative research, at a time when it was losing ground to the Durkheimian conception of sociology as a science being promoted by Talcott Parsons in Harvard and Paul Lazarsfeld at Columbia. John Gusfield reports that different members of the Chicago faculty 'all contributed to a skeptical orientation toward the emergent mainstream of a quantitative sociology, heavily dependent on survey, questionnaire or official records as data, or, alternatively, wedded to the quest for abstract general theory that was then attracting attention and dominance' (Fine 1995, p. xi).

Hughes and Blumer, like Park himself, did not conduct many empirical studies. Both were, however, responsible for creating the intellectual and institutional conditions for symbolic interactionism to develop as a research tradition. Blumer published a number of articles during the 1950s, which gave ethnographers a coherent, methodological basis for doing qualitative research, drawing on the theoretical writings of George Herbert Mead (1934). I will be looking at Blumer's conception of symbolic interactionism in the next section. Hughes encouraged a new generation of researchers to conduct ethnographic projects, particularly by studying work and occupations.

Students of Hughes included Howard Becker, Blanche Geer and Anselm Strauss, who worked with him on *Boys in White* (1961), a three year ethnographic study of a medical school. Becker and Geer also collaborated with Hughes on *Making the Grade* (1968), a study of a liberal arts college. Other students conducted studies of a range of occupations including factory workers, estate agents, doctors, local government officers, nurses and janitors. However, this hardly does justice to the number of students awarded doctorates from Chicago during this period, who went on to employ interactionist methods in researching a range of topics. These also include Robert Dubin, Orrin Klapp, Tamotsu Shibotani, Ray Gold, Fred Davis, Donald Roy, Ralph Turner, Morris Schwartz, Eliot Freidson, Erving Goffman (an anthropology student supervised by Lloyd Warner), John C. Scott, Joseph Gusfield and Jerome Carlin.

A third generation

The three most influential sociologists who were supervised at Chicago were Anselm Strauss, Erving Goffman and Howard Becker. Strauss has made a major contribution to medical sociology, and the research tradition of grounded theory. Goffman developed a distinctive approach to studying face-to-face interaction which has become known as dramaturgical analysis. Becker is best known for *Outsiders* (1963), which draws on his own background in describing the social world of the jazz musician, and also looks at the process of becoming a marijuana smoker. He has maintained this interest in culture in *Artworlds* (1982), a study which looks at the different occupational groups concerned with the production and distribution of art.

Symbolic interactionism is now no longer associated with Chicago, and is based mainly in smaller universities in North America, although there are also interactionists in Europe, especially in Germany (Flick 1998) and the United Kingdom. The December 1999 special double issue of the *Journal of Contemporary Ethnography* contains a number of articles about the past and future of ethnography by well-known contemporary practitioners. North Americans identifying with the Chicago School tradition include Patricia and Peter Adler (University of Denver), Robert Prus (University of Waterloo, Canada) and Gary Fine (Northwestern University). British ethnographers include Paul Atkinson (University of Cardiff), Martyn Hammersley (Open University), Robert Burgess (University of Leicester), Paul Rock (London School of Economics) and Robert Dingwall (University of Nottingham).

Symbolic interactionism has diversified since the 1950s in that separate schools have developed around different understandings of epistemology and method. The grounded theory tradition, founded by Strauss, has taken on a positivist flavour, in the sense that it presents qualitative research as a scientific method. The Illinois School around Norman Denzin is a postmodern version of symbolic interactionism. Dramaturgical analysis is another sub-tradition which grows out of the work of Erving Goffman. On the other hand, most symbolic interactionists continue to practise, and conceptualize, fieldwork in much the same way as Herbert Blumer or the Chicago School. I will look at some examples from this core tradition in this chapter, but will discuss grounded theory, dramaturgical analysis and postmodern ethnography in later chapters.

Methodological assumptions

A common source of anxiety for students doing empirical work is what to put in the 'methodology chapter' in a dissertation or doctoral thesis, which normally follows a review of the previous literature on a given topic, and leads into some empirical analysis. The methodology chapter should be a statement of your theoretical position, reviewing issues and debates in that tradition, and setting out how you have employed methods to address a particular research question. Because of the argumentative nature of sociology (which remains the case if you are drawing on sociological approaches in a school of education, law or business), setting out a position also requires defending it against possible criticisms. It is difficult to do a good piece of research, even if it is a report written for non-academic audiences, without being aware of how the same topic could be approached by someone with a different conception of epistemology, theory and method.

There are a number of ways of giving your work more theoretical bite, and ideally a perspective should be introduced on the first page of a project, and then developed in the methodology chapter. One technique that will keep you on the right lines (although it is not intended to be prescriptive) is to maintain a strong contrast between different theoretical traditions, and how they would approach your topic. Methodological statements by sociologists tend to combine a defence of the approach against possible criticisms, with a vigorous critique of other approaches. Two examples by symbolic interactionists that are worth consulting are a paper called 'Sociological analysis and the variable' by Herbert Blumer (1969, first published 1956), based on his presidential address to the American Sociological Society in that year, and a recent essay by Robert Prus (1996b) called 'Betwixt positivist proclivities and postmodern propensities'.

Herbert Blumer's critique of variable analysis

The main method that students learn on undergraduate courses in social science, and the only method often taught in psychology degrees, involves measuring two or more variables, and finding a statistical relationship between them using a computer package called SPSS-X. This first became a central part of the curriculum in the 1950s, mainly through the success of positivist methodologists like Paul Lazarsfeld, and theorists like Talcott Parsons, in promoting a Durkheimian conception of sociology in America.

A simple example of a variable analysis project would be a study intended to identify the factors causing educational success or failure in schools. The first step would be to select a representative sample of 1000 children (1000 is usually regarded as a big enough sample for a positive correlation to be statistically significant). The next step would be to measure a number of variables for each child. One variable would be how that child had performed in examinations. Others might be the annual salary of the child's parents (one way of measuring social class), or the child's gender or ethnic background. The objective would be to find a positive correlation between a dependent and an independent variable. Researchers have found, for example, that examination performance usually varies with social class.

This is only the beginning of a scientific investigation, which would involve measuring many other variables, and establishing the relationship between them (so one might find, for example, that the average time each child spent doing homework was a significant independent variable). To make a strong causal claim, it is necessary to identify other factors which might also have an effect on the dependent variable. The most sophisticated forms of multivariate analysis require serious computing power to handle large numbers of variables in increasingly sophisticated statistical tests.

Blumer's argument against variable analysis, as a symbolic interactionist, is that it does not address 'the process of interpretation or definition that goes on in human groups'. He explains this in the following way:

All sociologists – unless I presume too much – recognize that human group activity is carried on, in the main, through a process of interpretation or definition. As human beings we act singly, collectively and societally on the basis of the meanings which things have for us. Our world consists of innumerable objects – home, church, job, college education, a political election, a friend, an enemy nation, a tooth brush, or what not – each of which has a meaning on the basis of which we act toward it. In our activities we wend our way by recognizing an object to be such and such, by defining the situations with which we are presented, by attaching a meaning to this or that event, and where need be, by devising a new meaning to cover something new or different. This is done by the individual in his personal action, it is done by a group of individuals acting in concert, it is done in each of the manifold activities which together constitute an institution in operation, and it is done in each of the diversified acts which fit into and make up the patterned activity of a social structure or a society. We can, and I think must, look upon human group life as chiefly a vast interpretative process in which people singly and collectively guide themselves by defining the objects, events and situations which they encounter. (1969, p. 132)

This view of the social world sees meaning not as residing in the heads of individuals, but as shared by members of a society, or by particular social groups. Meaning, therefore, has an intersubjective rather than a subjective character; the theoretical writings of George Herbert Mead are an attempt to explain how intersubjectivity works, and how individuals are part of society. A key feature of the theory is that individuals are influenced by other people, but that they are also active in interpreting, and responding to, the people and objects they encounter in the world.

Blumer wants sociologists to conduct ethnographic studies that address this interpretive process, rather than reducing social life to a set of statistical relationships between variables. These should 'approach the study of group activity through the eyes and experience of the people who have developed the activity' and require 'an intimate familiarity with this experience and with the scenes of its operation' (1969, p. 139).

In the case of educational achievement, a symbolic interactionist study would involve spending a long time with teachers, parents and pupils, and trying to address their perspective on examination results, rather than measuring the relationship between variables. One advantage in adopting this approach is that one might discover an additional independent variable that seems to be important in addition to social class or ethnic background. Some classroom ethnographies have, for example, found that the way teachers categorize and treat pupils from different class backgrounds is a key factor in explaining outcomes (Rist 1970). The point that Blumer is making is not, however, simply that one can identify more variables through conducting an ethnography, which can then be measured, for example, by an attitude questionnaire, and tested statistically for significant correlations in a variable analysis study. Instead, he is making the more radical interpretive epistemological point that the ethnography will always produce a deeper insight into 'the real operating factors in group life, and the real interaction and relations between factors' (1969, p. 138).

If you conduct a project based on symbolic interactionist assumptions, it would help to review some quantitative studies about your topic in a methodology chapter, and contrast these with the ethnographic approach you have employed in collecting and analysing data. Your aim should be to show what is theoretically distinctive about your approach to the topic, and also how your choice of methods has been dictated by theoretical considerations.

Robert Prus's critique of postmodernism

Although variable analysis is still widely practised in the social sciences (especially in psychology), it is no longer the dominant method of conducting research. Robert Prus defined the challenge for sym interactionists in the 1990s as defending their conception of ethnograp. research against both positivists and the new challenge of 'postmodern' styles of analysis:

> Over the past century, the social sciences have been dominated by an overarching set of positivist/structuralist agendas, with the interpretivists providing backbench opposition of sorts. Despite deeply embedded resistance, some significant inroads have been made in the social sciences by those pursuing an intersubjectivist viewpoint, and qualitative viewpoints have become more accepted overall. Still, there is considerable resistance to interpretive viewpoints in mainstream social science and since the 1980s the position has become complicated further by the proliferation of 'postmodernist' (poststructuralist et al.) thought within the social sciences. Postmodernism shares some affinities with symbolic interaction and other interpretive approaches, but postmodernist skepticism violates essential features of intersubjectivity and the human struggle for existence, and thus poses another set of problems for those wishing to build a social science based on human lived experience. (1996b, p. 204)

I will be reviewing the work of qualitative researchers influenced by the epistemological assumptions of postmodernism and poststructuralism in Chapter 8. Like many symbolic interactionists in the Chicago tradition, Prus is very much opposed to these new varieties of ethnography. He argues that these, like variable analysis, do not adequately address 'human lived experience'.

An alternative way of constructing a methodology chapter in a symbolic interactionist research project might, therefore, be to discuss this debate and justify your own approach to collecting and analysing data. There is, however, no set way of writing a methodology chapter. Your main objective should be to explain your own objectives and assumptions as a qualitative researcher. The easiest way to do this, however, is by making a contrast between your own position and at least one other research tradition, through reviewing a few studies of relevance to your topic. Writing a methodology chapter should force you to think more deeply about your own assumptions, and result in a stronger and more developed piece of research.

Four case studies

The type of ethnographic research favoured by Blumer and Prus requires a long period developing an 'intimate familiarity' with some group or social setting. I will look at some practical issues relating to this variety of ethnography at the end of the chapter. My central objective, however, is to convey something of a feel for how sociologists in this tradition have conducted research, by encouraging you to read some exemplary studies. It is impossible to appreciate what a term like 'human lived

experience' means, or evaluate Blumer's claim that symbolic interactionism supplies a richer insight into social processes than variable analysis,
or produce something that reads like a symbolic interactionist ethnography, without reading a lot of previous studies. I have only room to
discuss four studies, but they illustrate some of the main methods used
by sociologists in this tradition, and how they can be used to address a
wide range of topics.

The Taxi-Dance Hall

This Chicago School ethnography by Paul Cressey (1932) is almost
seventy years old, and you may find that it requires handling with care,
if you have a copy in your library, or obtain it through an inter-library
loan. In some British institutions, older texts which are not regularly
used are removed from the shelves to make way for newer materials,
and are only saved if an academic happens to notice this happening and
makes a case for keeping it in the library. This text deserves to be read
today, as a good example of how to conduct an occupational ethnography, even though the institution Cressey writes about has gradually
disappeared from American cities.

The taxi-dance hall was an institution that developed during a period
of mass immigration to America at the end of the nineteenth century. It
was a dancing club in which men could pay for dances with young
women. Cressey worked in the equivalent of the city social services
department and was asked to conduct the study since it was feared that
the halls were a route to prostitution. In the language of our own times,
the study was aimed at a policy audience, although very few ethnographies of this kind are commissioned today by government agencies.

Cressey employed four research assistants (three men and two
women) to collect data, who went to dances as participant observers, and
later interviewed taxi-dancers and their clients, and the businessmen
who ran the halls. We learn very little about how they conducted the
study, such as the length of the project, or the ethical and practical issues
encountered in the research process (which only became a standard part
of monographs relatively recently). We do learn, however, a great deal
about 'lived human experience' in this setting, which is conveyed by
observational accounts of what happened at dances, and numerous,
lengthy extracts from interviews (the distinctive feature of many symbolic interactionist ethnographies).

The contents page of *The Taxi-Dance Hall* is worth reproducing since it
illustrates the clear, matter-of-fact way in which Chicago School
ethnographers present and organize their data:

PART I. THE TAXI-DANCE HALL: WHAT IT IS
I. A night in a taxi-dance hall
II. The taxi-dance hall as a type

The first chapter of the book presents an account of a night out in 'The Eureka Dancing Academy'. This is 'lodged unimpressively on the second floor of a roughly built store building' near 'an important street-car intersection'. There is a 'dully-lighted electric sign flickering forth the words "Dancing Academy"', and a 'portable signboard on which is daubed the announcement, "Dancing Tonight! Fifty Beautiful Lady Instructors"' (1932, p. 4). There are few ethnographers today who could match the quality and precision of the writing in this account, which vividly describes the kind of people who visit and work in taxi-dance halls. Here are two extracts about the arrival of patrons, and the demanding nature of the taxi-dancer's work:

> Before long the patrons and taxi-dancers begin to arrive. Some patrons come in automobiles, though many more alight from street cars. Still others seem to come from the immediate neighborhood. For the most part they are alone, though occasionally groups of two and three appear. The patrons are a motley crowd. Some are uncouth, noisy youths, busied chiefly with their cigarettes. Others are sleekly groomed and suave young men, who come alone and remain aloof. Others are middle-aged men whose stooped shoulders and shambling gait speak eloquently of a life of manual toil. Sometimes they speak English fluently. More often their broken English reveals them as European immigrants, on the way toward being Americanized. Still others are dapperly dressed little Filipinos who come together, sometimes even in squads of six or eight, and slip quietly into the entrance. Altogether the patrons make up a polyglot aggregation from many corners of the world. (1932, pp. 4–5)

> The taxi-dancer's job is an arduous one. The girl must have almost unlimited stamina to stand up indefinitely to the many forms of physical exercise which the patron may choose to consider dancing. As a matter of fact, dancing is

anything but uniform in the taxi-dance hall. Some couples gallop together over the floor, weaving their way in and around the slower dancers; others seek to obtain aesthetic heights by a curious angular strut and a double shuffle or a stamp and a glide. Still others dance the 'Charleston', and are granted unchallenged pre-emption of the center of the floor. Still others are content with a slow, simple one-step as they move about the hall. At times certain dancers seem to cease all semblance of motion over the floor, and while locked tightly together give themselves up to movements sensual in nature and obviously more practiced than spontaneous. These couples tend to segregate at one end of the hall where they mill about in a compressed pack of wriggling, perspiring bodies. It is toward such feminine partners that many of the men rush at the end of each dance; these are the taxi-dancers who, irrespective of personal charm, never seem to lack for patrons. 'It's all in a day's work, and we are the girls who get the dances', would seem to be their attitude. (1932, pp. 7–8)

This first chapter gives an intriguing taste of the taxi-dance hall, through the first impressions of an outside observer. It concludes by raising a number of questions that anyone with a curiosity about human behaviour would come away with after visiting this setting. These are then explored systematically in later chapters, drawing on interview data, and personal recollections supplied by the fieldworkers. We learn, for example, in Chapter IV that many girls see dancing as a glamorous and well-paying alternative to an early marriage, or to working in a factory or office. Chapter V looks at the pressures which lead them to dress and dance more provocatively, to attract patrons, or to accept dances from low-status ethnic groups like Filipinos. Chapters VI and VII look at the backgrounds and expectations of different types of patrons, who are portrayed sympathetically as 'detached or lonely people . . . who have failed to find a place in the more conventional groups and institutions of the city, and who yet need the satisfactions which inclusion in such groups affords' (1932, p. 240). There is also some discussion of the language or argot used in dance halls: patrons were, for example, often described by dancers as 'suckers', 'fruit' or 'fish'. The result is a revealing and intimate portrait of this social world, built up through a careful study of different group and individual perspectives.

Boys in White

Perhaps the best known ethnography to have come out of the second Chicago School is *Boys in White* (1961), which is based on a team of three researchers, directed by Everett Hughes, spending three years in an American medical school. The faculty allowed Hughes to conduct this study, partly in the interests of advancing knowledge, but also because they were concerned about the level of effort expended by students, what they were learning, and their uncaring attitudes towards some patients. In today's language, *Boys in White* might be described as an 'evaluation study', although one that explained why students did not do what their teachers wanted, rather than making any recommendations on how the school should change.

Boys in White is a more conceptually developed study than *The Taxi-Dance Hall*, in that the researchers set out with the idea, which derives from the writings of George Herbert Mead, that 'their conduct, whatever it might be, would be a product of their interaction with each other when faced with the day-to-day problems of medical school' (Becker et al. 1961, p. 11). The central theme is how medical students begin their studies with idealistic expectations about learning everything about medicine, but by the end of the first year they have learnt collectively to direct their efforts towards learning only what is required to get through assessments and examinations. Becker, Hughes and Geer went on to conduct a similar study about the student experience in a liberal arts college called *Making the Grade* (1968). The reason why this perspective develops is because students feel overwhelmed by the subject-matter, and are terrified of failing. They, therefore, make every effort to tie their lecturers down to specifying what they need to know, and revise accordingly.

Boys in White is also methodologically more developed than *The Taxi-Dance Hall*, not in the sense that it employs more advanced methods, but because it explains how these were employed in considerably more detail. It is significant that there is a separate first section entitled 'Backgrounds and Methods', which explains the theoretical approach that informed the development of a research question, and how they collected and analysed their data. The practical demands of fieldwork are described in the following passage:

> In participant observation . . . the researcher participates in the daily lives of people he studies. We did this by attending school with the students, following them from class to laboratory to hospital ward . . . We went with students to lectures and to the laboratories in which they studied the basic sciences, watched their activities, and engaged in casual conversation with them. We followed students to their fraternity houses and sat with them while they discussed their school experiences. We accompanied students on rounds with attending physicians, watched them examine patients on the wards and in the clinics, and sat in on discussion groups and oral exams. We had meals with the students and took night call with them.
>
> We observed the participants in the daily activities of the school – which is to say that we were not hidden; our presence was known to everyone involved, to the students, their teachers and their patients. Participating in the ordinary routine, we did so in the 'pseudo-role' of student. Not that we posed as students, for it was made clear to everyone that we were not students; but rather it was the students we participated with. When a lecture or class ended, we left with the students, not the teacher; we left the operating or delivery room when the student did, not when the patient or surgeon did, unless these happened to coincide. We went with the students wherever they went in the course of the day. (1961, pp. 25–6)

One significant difference in the way data was collected is that the researchers set out to find 'positive' and 'negative' cases to test a preliminary observation, and review all their data systematically when presenting their findings and conclusions. *The Taxi-Dance Hall* was probably produced in the same way, but Hughes and his team were conscious that critics might regard their findings as unpersuasive or anecdotal. The study was, therefore, intended as an 'experiment in being more explicit about the modes of proof involved in analysis of this kind' (1961, p. 30). The procedures they used are described in the following passage:

> We have tried to lessen our readers' dilemma by stating the nature and extent of our evidence on points under discussion in such a way that it will explain our own reasons for putting a certain degree of confidence in a conclusion, and give the reader ample opportunity to form his own judgment; that is, we describe all the items of evidence that bear on a given point (although usually in summary form) and the degree to which they seem to us to confirm the proposition. A technical problem arises in considering how can one be sure that all the items of evidence have been considered; it would clearly be impracticable to search through 5,000 pages of notes every time one wished to check a proposition. To avoid this, we indexed our fieldnotes and labeled each entry with code numbers referring to major topics under which the given item might be considered. These entries were then reassembled by code number so that we had in place all the facts bearing on a given topic, thus making possible a relatively quick check of our data on any given point. (1961, pp. 31–2)

A good example of how this method was used is in their analysis of how students used the term 'crock' to refer to patients who were not suffering from a clearly identifiable physical illness. When this first came up in an interview, the research team deliberately set out to find other examples. These are presented systematically in a chapter entitled 'Students and Patients'. They concluded that students adopted an instrumental attitude towards patients, which was a continuation of the collective perspective developed in their first two years at the school. A patient was only considered 'interesting' if students could learn something new which would help them become better doctors. When someone died this reminded 'them less of medicine's tragic inability to control disease' than 'the autopsy they will have to attend' (1961, p. 329). Writing an autopsy report was regarded as a tedious and time-consuming task which took them away from the wards.

Tally's Corner

This book by Elliot Liebow (1967) became a best-seller, through providing a compelling human portrait of a group of black 'street corner men' living in an inner-city district of Washington. It is the first in a series of ethnographies which have received critical acclaim by politicians and journalists for addressing what remains America's biggest social problem, which include Elijah Anderson's (1976) *A Place on the Corner*, Jay MacLeod's (1976) *Ain't No Makin' It*, and most recently Michael Duneier's (1999) *Sidewalk*. The *Washington Star* review was typical: 'This is a sharp, hard-hitting observation of a segment of life and society in action. And the hope here is that there will be more books like it.'

It is not strictly speaking a symbolic interactionist study, since Liebow was an anthropologist, working in the tradition of urban ethnography represented by William Foote Whyte's (1943) *Street Corner Society*. However, there had always been a close relationship between the Departments of Sociology and Anthropology at Chicago. Thomas had been influenced by the work of Hans Boas, and Hughes had a close relationship with W. Lloyd Warner. The affinity between the two traditions is evident from the fact that Liebow cites Becker and Hughes along with anthropological studies in his bibliography.

Tally's Corner is methodologically distinctive in resulting from the collaboration between Liebow and a key informant, 'Tally', who helped him obtain research data and develop an understanding of this particular social world. Whyte obtained access to the Italian community he wrote about in *Street Corner Society* through a similar friendship with 'Doc'. A methodological appendix (which has become a standard part of many ethnographies) describes how Liebow first met Tally through accidentally striking up a conversation about a puppy with four men outside a carry-out store (a combination of a take-away restaurant selling hamburgers and hot dogs, and a late night grocery store).

One question which Liebow anticipates is whether he found it difficult as a white man (from an immigrant Jewish background) to gain the trust of black Americans, given that he was 'an outsider not only because of race, but also because of occupation, education, residence and speech' (1967, p. 252). The answer is simply that he had grown up in a mixed, low-income neighbourhood and, after he helped Tally raise money to get a friend bailed from a murder charge, people were happy to accept him as an observer in their social world. Liebow provides the following account of how he spent his time during the project:

> By April, the number of men whom I had come to know fairly well and their acceptance of me had reached the point at which I was free to go to the rooms or apartments where they lived or hung out, at almost any time, needing neither an excuse nor an explanation for doing so. Like other friends, I was there to pass the time, to hang around, to find out 'what's happening'.
>
> I switched my day around to coincide with the day worker's leisure hours: from four in the afternoon until late at night, according to what was going on. Alone, or with one, two or half a dozen others, I went to pool rooms, to bars, or to somebody's room or apartment. Much of the time we just hung around the Carry-out, playing the pinball machine or standing on the corner watching the world go by. Regularly at five, I met my five 'drinking buddies' when they

came off from work and we went into a hallway for an hour or so of good drinking and easy talk.

   Friday afternoon to Sunday night was especially exciting and productive. I'd go to Nancy's 'place' (apartment) where, at almost any hour, one could get liquor, listen to music, or engage in conversation. Or perhaps seven or eight of us would buy some beer and whisky and go up to Tonk's apartment near the Carry-out where he lived with his wife. Occasionally, I'd pair up with one or two men and go to a party, a movie, or a crap game, which might be in almost any part of town. Sunday afternoon was an especially good time to pick up news or happenings of the preceding forty-eight hours. People were generally rested up from the night before, relaxed, and ready to fill one another in on events which involved the police, breakups of husband-and-wife relations and bed-and-board arrangements, drink stimulated brawls, sex adventures, and parties they had witnessed, heard about or participated in over Friday and Saturday'. (1967, pp. 246–7)

Liebow produced this study while employed 'to collect field material about low-income adult males' in a project funded by the National Institute of Mental Health about child-rearing practices in low-income families. Like most anthropologists, he spent a full year in the field, which enabled him to present an insider account which challenged how other social scientists and politicians portrayed the group he was studying. The American government viewed black street corner men as a deviant group, who did not want to work, and shirked their family responsibilities. Exactly the same views are expressed about the underclass today. However, what Liebow shows is that these attitudes only arose because they could not obtain decent jobs. The second chapter in the study, entitled 'Men and their Work', makes this point particularly well by starting with the view an outsider might have of the street corner men by observing them loitering outside the carry-out, and then taking us inside their experience of doing a series of casual, badly paying jobs. It remains a powerful critique of the way in which many middle-class Americans still view black, urban poverty.

Gay Men, Gay Selves

This study by Tom Weinberg (1983) illustrates how it is possible to conduct a qualitative project based on a number of in-depth interviews. It explores the nature of gay identity from a symbolic interactionist perspective. There is a large literature, which includes Mead's (1934) *Mind, Self and Society*, about how we develop a sense of self through interacting with others. Weinberg was interested in how gay men came to see themselves as being gay, and the difficulties they experienced in view of the fact that, in contemporary America, 'heterosexuality is taken as ideal, and homosexuality is considered criminal, pathological or even sinful' (1983, p. vii).

Weinberg interviewed thirty men who responded to the following advertisement placed in the magazine of a local gay society:

> WANTED: GAY MEN – to participate in a study of gay identity. The objectives are (1) to learn more about how people come out, the kinds of problems they encounter, and how they solve them; (2) to use this information for counselling purposes . . . to help counsellors to aid people to come out more easily and smoothly.
> IF INTERESTED – Contact Prof. Tom Weinberg at . . . Dept. of Sociology [Eastern City College]. (1983, p. 305)

Even if you have no interest in the topic, or in symbolic interactionist ideas about the self, this study is worth reading as an example of how to analyse qualitative data systematically using a set of theoretical concepts and categories. To give one example of this, Weinberg knew from the literature that one can engage in same-sex behaviour without suspecting, or coming to see, oneself as a homosexual. He analyses his interviews by considering the following questions:

> (a) Do people first come to suspect themselves as a result of feedback that they get from other people, or does the individual himself begin the process? (b) If a person develops self-suspicion on his own, what factors or criteria . . . arouse self-suspicion? (c) Why does the person think that these factors that cause him to suspect himself are 'signs' of homosexuality . . .? (d) How does the person feel about his suspicion, and what does he do about these feelings? (1983, p. 79)

Each question or theme is illustrated by short extracts from the interviews. The rest of the book looks systematically at the 'work' involved in acquiring or resisting a gay identity (which can involve choosing a reference group, such as 'bisexuals', in which same-sex sexual behaviour does not mean becoming a homosexual), and at the pace at which this happens. The result is a remarkably detailed and informative analysis about the experience of a particular social group, in which the theoretical observations are grounded in qualitative data.

Some practical issues

There are a large number of texts which provide a practical introduction to doing ethnographic research in the traditions of symbolic interactionism, or urban anthropology as represented by Whyte and Liebow. Some of these contain detailed advice on how to obtain access (Lofland and Lofland 1995), conduct interviews (Spradley 1979), write fieldnotes (Emerson et al. 1995) or deal with relationships in the field (Coffey 1999). They tend to draw both on the authors' own experiences in conducting studies, and examples of how other researchers overcame similar problems.

This secondary literature on research methods is now so large that some have complained that it threatens to overwhelm the ethnographies that still get published (Atkinson et al. 1999). It is worth remembering here that few ethnographers learn their trade by reading research methods texts, or even by taking courses on fieldwork methods. This is not intended to suggest that research methods training in ethnography is pointless, since it encourages students to think about methodological issues, and to develop a professional identity as fieldworkers. It is not, however, necessary to do much more than read one or two classic studies, along with some of the general literature on your research question, before starting a fieldwork project. Liebow describes how he was introduced to fieldwork in the following terms:

> I spent the first week in familiarizing myself with the project and with the work that had already been done. I had several informal discussions with Dr. Hylan Lewis, the director of the project, and gradually gained a feeling for the kind of material that was wanted. Importantly, he laid down no hard-and-fast ground rules on the assumption that the job could best be done if I were free to feel my way around for a few weeks and discover for myself the techniques that were most congenial to me. His one prescription was that the work be securely anchored in the purposes of the project, remembering, too, that 'everything is grist for our mill'. As I think back on this now, I see a clear connection between his instructions and his fondness for the quotation, 'The scientific method is doing one's darndest with his brains, no holds barred.'
>
> Having partially digested the project literature, I told the director that I was ready to get started. He suggested a neighborhood that might be 'a good place to get your feet wet'. His instructions were: 'Go out there and make like an anthropologist. (1967, pp. 234–5)

The casual way in which Liebow talks about research methods is also characteristic of most studies published by first and second generation symbolic interactionists. There is, for example, no discussion of research methods in *The Taxi-Dance Hall*. The methodological essays of Herbert Blumer are almost entirely concerned with issues of theory and epistemology, rather than with employing specific techniques. At one point he notes that there are all kinds of methods one can use in researching human group life. These include 'direct observation, field study, participant observation, case study, interviewing, use of life histories, use of letters and diaries, use of public documents [and] panel discussions' (Blumer 1969, p. 50). He suggests that students should take advantage of any training that is available in these areas. However, he also warns against the dangers of any technique acquiring 'a standardized format'.

There is much to be said for the view that fieldworkers learn their craft by doing studies rather than reading texts on research methods. Nevertheless, it is worth giving a few practical hints on how to get started. I will begin by summarizing some comments made by Erving Goffman, and then say something briefly about studies based on interviews, how to design a smaller project, and how to write up ethnographic research.

Erving Goffman on fieldwork

Perhaps the best advice for aspiring fieldworkers is contained in some remarks made by Erving Goffman which were surreptitiously tape-recorded by one of his students during a session organized by John Lofland at the Pacific Sociological Association in 1974. Goffman begins by repeating Lofland's warning that all you get in attempting to specify methods are 'rationalizations': and, of course, anyone who has completed a PhD knows that the methodology chapter is always written after doing the analysis. However, he does make some useful observations which are worth conveying to a wider audience.

Goffman begins with a definition of participant observation that conveys the particular demands it places on the researcher:

> [It requires] . . . subjecting yourself, your own body and your own personality, and your own social situation, to the set of contingencies that play upon a set of individuals, so that you can physically and ecologically penetrate their circle of response to their social situation, or their work situation, or their ethnic situation, or whatever. So that you are close to them while they are responding to what life does to them . . . To me, that's the core of observation. If you don't get yourself in that situation, I don't think you can do a serious piece of work. (Although if you've got a short period of time, there are all kinds of reasons why you wouldn't be able to get into that situation.) But that's the name of the game. You're artificially forcing yourself to be tuned into something that you then pick up as a witness – not as an interviewer, not as a listener, but as a witness to how they react to what gets done to and around them. (1989, pp. 125–6)

Goffman notes that it requires a lot of discipline to be a good fieldworker:

> you have to open yourself up in ways you're not in ordinary life. You have to open yourself up to being snubbed . . . Then you have to be willing to be a horse's ass. In these little groups, the world consists of becoming very good at doing some stupid little thing, like running a boat, or dealing, or something like that, you see. And you're going to be an ass at that sort of thing. And that's one reason why you have to be young to do fieldwork. It's harder to be an ass when you're old. (1989, p. 128)

Doing fieldwork also requires great political skills, since it is inevitable that any institution will comprise classes of people with different interests and perspectives (and these may well be divided into subgroups). Anyone who has gained access to an institutional setting, such as a school, a hospital or even a small business, will be familiar with what Goffman calls the 'affiliation issue':

> You can't move down a social system. You can only move up a social system. So, if you've got to be with a range of people, be with the lowest people first. The higher people will 'understand', later on, that you were 'really' just studying them. But you can't start at the top and move down because then the people at the bottom will know that all along you really were a fink – which is what you are. (1989, p. 130)

Although Howard Becker (1967) has suggested that the researcher always has to make a moral choice of siding with dominant or sub-ordinate groups during fieldwork (see also the discussion in Hammersley 2000), there is nothing to prevent you from trying to address a range of perspectives in any institutional setting, through adopting Goffman's method of starting at the bottom, and working your way up to senior management.

Goffman recommends that you should take notes when you can, and write these up at the end of each day. You will need to spend most effort on writing notes during your first few days in the field:

> There is a freshness cycle when moving into the field. The first day you'll see more than you'll ever see again. And you'll see things that you won't see again. (1989, p. 130)

He also suggests, however, that you should take care not to take too many notes, since there will be too much to read and analyse by the end of the study. This still remains true if you have the time to type your fieldnotes into a computer data-base. You will only have the time and concentration to use a fraction of the materials you can collect in even a short ethnographic study.

Finally, Goffman advises that you need to spend at least a year in the field in order to fully exploit your access:

> Otherwise you don't get the random sample, you don't get a range of unanticipated events, you don't get deep familiarity. It's deep familiarity that is the rationale – that, plus getting material on a tissue of events – that gives the justification and warrant for such an apparently 'loose' thing as fieldwork. (1989, p. 130)

Doing an interview study

Many postgraduate students will not want to expose themselves to the heavy emotional and physical demands of doing fieldwork, which Goffman suggests also involves stripping the rest of your life 'to the bone' (1989, p. 127). It has also become increasingly difficult to secure the opportunity to spend a long time in the field, at least in the United Kingdom, given that most students need to teach throughout their doctorate, to improve their chances of obtaining a lecturing post, or simply to make ends meet.

One alternative way of doing a symbolic interactionist project, which is equally demanding but does not pose the same practical difficulties, is to conduct a study based on interviews. Exemplary studies include the research by Tom Weinberg on acquiring a homosexual identity, based on thirty interviews, reviewed earlier in this chapter. It would also be worth obtaining a copy of Howard Becker's (1951) doctoral thesis, through inter-library loan, which is based on interviews with sixty high school teachers in Chicago. It is often easier to obtain permission to collect interview data rather than to conduct ethnographic fieldwork, and you should obtain a rich set of materials about the perspective of a particular social group.

There is no fixed rule on how many interviews you need to conduct, other than that you will need enough data to explore and document a range of themes. Robert Prus has conducted studies, over a two or three year period, which can involve interviewing a few hundred people (see, for example, Prus and Styllianos 1980; Prus 1989). Weinberg, on the other hand, notes that it is usually only possible to conduct a small number of interviews, if the objective is to analyse these in any detail:

> Although [interviewing thirty men] would be an inadequate sample for some kinds of research such as large-scale social surveys, it is an average size for intensive, probing, in-depth studies, because of the great amount of material that must be analysed. In this study . . . the researcher was working with over one hundred hours of tape-recordings. Full transcriptions of an average three-hour interview took from forty to fifty hours, eventually necessitating the development of a technique by which only partial transcriptions were made of the bulk of the interviews. Given the fact that the researcher was limited in terms of his resources and that his was really an interest in the quality of the gay experience, he decided that it made more sense to concentrate his efforts on an in-depth examination of a small sample rather than on a cursory examination of a larger one. (1983, p. 307)

Designing a smaller project

Most undergraduates will only have a limited amount of time to arrange interviews, or conduct fieldwork. Nevertheless, without too much effort, it should be possible to find something interesting to study which is close at hand. Students often have access to work settings, youth subcultures, class and ethnic cultures, and religious and sporting groups, many of which have never been investigated using ethnographic methods. This could form the basis for a third year dissertation which is based on original research. It is also worth noting that there is a great deal one can learn from a single interview, or a day spent observing work in a particular occupational setting. There is no reason to be ashamed of conducting a short investigation that raises some preliminary questions about a setting or topic.

Writing up ethnographic research

A central argument in this book is that the difficult task begins once you have collected your data, since there is a difference between simply reporting your observations, or presenting extracts from interviews, and developing a coherent analysis informed by a particular theoretical tradition or perspective. In the case of symbolic interactionism, the central objective is to address 'human lived experience' in a more thoroughgoing way than quantitative studies, or research informed by poststructuralist thought or critical theory.

There are many different ways in which you can present and organize qualitative data. You can address different perspectives like *The Taxi-Dance Hall* or *Boys in White,* or divide up what you observed into analytic themes derived from symbolic interactionist theory like Tom Weinberg. There is no correct way of writing up your data, but, however you do it, you will be judged by other symbolic interactionists on the extent to which you meet the standards of the classic studies reviewed in this chapter.

This may seem like a tall order, especially if you are an undergraduate working with very little data. It should be remembered, however, that writing should always be the most enjoyable part of any project. This is because even if you only collect a small amount of data, it is likely that you will discover something interesting that complements the findings made by other researchers. You may even be the first person to write about that particular topic! A good symbolic interactionist project should make a strong contrast between the assumptions and objectives of symbolic interactionists and other research traditions in the human sciences. It should also contain some discussion of your reasons for choosing this particular topic, and the practical problems you encountered in collecting data. Your main aim, however, should simply be to report, in as much detail as possible, what you observed in the field.

Further reading

For general guides to symbolic interactionism

Prus, R. (1996a) *Symbolic Interaction and Ethnographic Research.* State University of New York Press, New York.
Blumer, H. (1969) *Symbolic Interactionism: Perspective and Method.* University of California Press, Berkeley, CA.
Rock, P. (1979) *The Making of Symbolic Interactionism.* Macmillan, London.

For practical introductions

Lofland, J. and Lofland, L. (1995) *Analyzing Social Settings: a Guide to Qualitative Observation and Analysis,* 3rd edn. Wadsworth, Belmont, CA.
Spradley, J. (1979) *The Ethnographic Interview.* Holt, Rinehart and Winston, New York.

Hammersley, M. and Atkinson, P. (1995) *Ethnography: Principles and Practice*, 2nd edn. Routledge, London.
Emerson, R., Fretz, R. and Shaw, L. (1995) *Writing Ethnographic Fieldnotes*. University of Chicago Press, Chicago.

EXERCISES

1   This is designed to be completed by a group of four students. Each should tape-record and transcribe a twenty minute interview with two first, second or third year students. The interview should focus on any difficulties they have encountered in completing assessed work.
    The group should then use the data to write an account of how students change during the three years of a degree course, drawing upon the conceptual framework in *Boys in White* and other symbolic interactionist studies about adult socialization.

2   The second chapter of Liebow's *Tally's Corner* makes a contrast between how a particular group is viewed from the outside, and how it understands its own activities.
    Conduct a similar study about any group that interests you, by interviewing members of that group.

3   Write a proposal for conducting an ethnographic study of a particular group or occupational setting. This should review previous ethnographic studies of similar settings, and discuss any relevant methodological issues.

3

Varieties of Symbolic Interactionism: Grounded Theory and Dramaturgical Analysis

CONTENTS

Like most of the research traditions reviewed in this text, symbolic interactionism has generated a range of sub-traditions, which have distinctive approaches towards the study of social life. The most important have developed as researchers have become more self-conscious about their epistemological assumptions, and have written more explicitly about methodological issues. This crystallized in the 1990s in a debate between what might loosely be called positivist and poststructuralist wings in the symbolic interactionist community, with interpretivists (who see themselves as upholding the original Chicago School tradition) occupying the middle ground.

The grounded theory tradition, founded by Barney Glaser and Anselm Strauss, is a more rigorous, scientific version of symbolic interactionism, which is widely taught, especially in departments of medicine and education. I will provide an introduction to the approach in the first half of this chapter, and contrast it with the poststructuralist wing of symbolic interactionism in a later chapter about postmodern ethnography. In the rest of this chapter, I will look at another distinctive tradition which has emerged out of the work of Erving Goffman, and has become known as dramaturgical analysis. I will then consider some criticisms of each tradition.

Grounded theory

The grounded theory tradition was developed by Barney Glaser and Anselm Strauss, while they were working in the Department of Nursing at the University of California in San Francisco in the late 1950s. Strauss had been a student of Hughes at Chicago, and had done three months of background research for the *Boys in White* study, before conducting a two year study of a psychiatric hospital on a project funded by the National Institute for Mental Health. Glaser had been trained in the Department of Sociology at Columbia University which had pioneered the quantitative methods of analysis criticized by Blumer under the leadership of Paul Lazarsfeld. Strauss and his students have subsequently done much to develop and promote the approach, through a number of studies, teaching manuals and methodological statements. Computer packages, such as The Ethnograph and NUD•IST, designed specifically for this kind of analysis, have introduced an even wider international group of students to this way of conducting qualitative research.

The development of a methodology

Glaser and Strauss wrote *The Discovery of Grounded Theory* (1967) at a time when most American sociologists had become Durkheimians. Ethnographies, of the kind practised by the Chicago School, were viewed as impressionistic or anecdotal; as little more than 'soft science or journalism' (Blumer 1969, p. 38). It was generally believed that the objective of sociology should be to produce scientific theory, and to test this using quantitative methods. Many realized that grand theory (for example, of the Parsonian variety) often seemed to have little connection with what one could discover through empirical studies (Merton 1967; C. Wright Mills 1959). Nevertheless it was accepted that natural science should be the model for sociological research. Ethnographies would only have a place to the extent to which they developed questions which could be tested using statistical methods.

Herbert Blumer's response in essays like 'Sociological analysis and the variable' was to criticize the epistemological basis and assumptions of quantitative studies from an interpretivist perspective. He not only defended the right of ethnographers to be unscientific, as judged by the standards of quantitative analysis, but argued that quantitative methods could not address the complexity of human action. This echoes similar criticisms by interpretivist thinkers, including Weber and Mead, about the inappropriateness of using scientific methods and styles of reasoning to understand human beings, given that we live in a meaningful social world.

In marked contrast to Blumer, Glaser and Strauss accepted that the study of human beings should be scientific, in the way understood by quantitative researchers. This meant that it should seek to produce theoretical propositions that were testable and verifiable, produced by a clear set of replicable procedures, and could be used to predict future events. Glaser and Strauss defined theory in the following terms:

> theory in sociology is a strategy for handling data in research, providing modes of conceptualization for describing and explaining. The theory should provide clear enough categories and hypotheses so that crucial ones can be verified in present and future research; they must be clear enough to be readily operationalized in quantitative studies when these are appropriate. (1967, p. 3)

In contrast to studies which simply aim to produce rich or 'thick' descriptions, research using grounded theory seeks to produce theory: a set of interrelated categories that describe or explain some phenomenon. Strauss and his collaborators specifically note at the end of *The Social Organization of Medical Work* (1985) that there is little point in supplying the lengthy extracts from interviews or field observations one finds in ethnographies like *The Taxi-Dance Hall, Boys in White* or *Tally's Corner*:

> we do not follow the practice of frequently quoting chunks of material drawn from interviews or fieldnotes, as is the standard practice in qualitative-research publications. Back in 1967. . .[*The Discovery of Grounded Theory* made] a forceful argument for theoretical formulation based on the qualitative analysis of data. Then and now, much that passes for analysis is relatively low-level description . . . Then and now, many quite esteemed and excellent monographs use a great deal of data – quotes or field note selections. This procedure is very useful when the behavior being studied is relatively foreign to the experiences of most readers or when the factual assertions being made would be under considerable contest by skeptical and otherwise relatively well-informed readers. Most of these monographs are descriptively dense, but alas theoretically thin. If

you look at their indexes, there are almost no new concepts listed, ones that have emerged in the course of the research. (1985, p. 204)

'Theory' in this tradition is understood as formal generalizations, of the kind used by Georg Simmel who had taught Robert Park. Simmel's conception of theory-building in sociology involved the identification of general processes in social life, such as 'conflict' or 'sociation', and the exploration of their dimensions and the relationship between them. There might, for example, be seven general types of conflict (with sub-categories), so that any particular instance of a conflict could be placed in one of these categories. Hughes employed this technique in a remarkable series of essays which explored different aspects of work (including 'making a mistake' and the distinction between 'good' and 'dirty' work), drawing on examples from a range of occupations. Glaser and Strauss turned this into a method that could be used for generating a more systematic body of theory.

An important principle in grounded theory is that the analyst should use a 'codified procedure for analysing data . . . which allows readers to understand how the analyst obtained his theory from the data' (1985, p. 229). Developing these procedures was a response to the standard charge made by quantitative researchers that ethnographic enquiry is 'impressionistic' or 'anecdotal'. They include searching for negative cases, through the 'constant comparative method'.

Strauss accepted that it is possible to make useful practical recommendations that are taken seriously, 'with no data collection or coding', simply through obtaining direct experience of a particular social group or setting. However, he suggests that in the best research studies, 'knowledge is likely to be generalized and systematically integrated into a theory' (1985, p. 227).

Doing grounded theory research

In contrast to the almost deliberately casual and careless way in which ethnographers like Liebow or Goffman talk about method, the grounded theorist follows a set of systematic procedures for collecting and analysing data. Whereas the novice ethnographer is often sent out into the field with little more than a copy of William Foote Whyte's *Street Corner Society*, the trainee in grounded theory works through a manual with a research group in a series of structured workshops. These are led by an instructor who is likely to have been trained, using the same method, either by Glaser and Strauss or by one of their students.

The main manual used by grounded theory researchers is the (1998) second edition of Strauss and Corbin's *Basics of Qualitative Research: Techniques and Procedures for Producing Grounded Theory* which was published shortly after Strauss's death. This is a shorter, user-friendly version of his (1987) *Qualitative Analysis for Social Scientists*. Each contains not only a guide on how to do grounded theory analysis, but also transcripts of data-analysis sessions, showing how students developed an understanding of the approach guided by other students and the instructor.

A distinctive feature of the method is that the collection of data and the analysis take place simultaneously, with the aim of developing general concepts to organize data and then 'integrating' these into a more general, formal set of categories. The research process involves students progressing through the following stages.

Microscopic examination of data   At an early stage, students are asked to bring a short piece of data to the class, which the instructor goes through line by line, with the aim of stimulating them to think about developing theoretical categories. Strauss and Corbin summarize what happens in these sessions:

> First, we ask the class to scan a section of an interview. Then we follow up with questions such as 'How would you interpret what the interviewee is saying?' and 'What is in this material?' Generally, the students easily name many themes, for their personal and disciplinary experiences have made them sensitive to a range of issues and 'problems'. We write each of these on a blackboard and eventually point out their considerable range. But we also note that connections among the issues, problems or themes, as actually stated, are only implicit and certainly not systematically worked out. (1998, p. 59)

The next stage is to look at the first sentence of a piece of interview data given to the students in considerable detail:

> Our discussion/examination usually begins with the very first word of the quotation. 'What does this word seem to mean, or what could it mean?' . . . Usually, the discussion of this first quoted word takes many minutes, perhaps as much as an hour, depending on the richness of the discussion and the range of the word's possible meanings explored in it. (1998, p. 60)

They give examples of how a colour term like 'red' can lead to all kinds of reflections about the meaning of the colour in different circumstances (for example, blood or lipstick), and the phrase 'when I heard the diagnosis' to a discussion drawing on the students' knowledge about the timing of announcements to different categories of patients in hospitals.

Coding   The most important procedure used in grounded theory research is to organize data into a set of themes or codes. This is done firstly by 'open coding', but students are then encouraged to think about different dimensions of these categories ('dimensionalizing') and to find links between categories ('axial coding'). Different events and situations are observed to build up a complete picture of the variations within any theoretical category ('theoretical sampling'). Eventually, categories are refined so that a theoretical framework emerges ('selective coding'). It is suggested that students should use diagrams to represent the complex relationship between categories.

Using the computer Grounded theory particularly lends itself to the analysis of qualitative data using computer software packages. Many readers will already have hands-on experience, since they already form a standard part of research methods training at undergraduate and postgraduate level. It is particularly easy to teach the approach, since it is possible to generate theoretical categories from very small amounts of data (see, for example, Dey 1993).

Heiner Legeiwe, who was one of the developers of ATLAS, describes how the computer can help in conducting a grounded theory analysis:

> Before starting your analysis, you have to store your data in the computer memory, for example, transcribed fieldnotes and interviews . . . In *open coding*, you display and scroll each document on screen, mark relevant text passages, and assign *codes* and *memos* to them . . . Later on, mouse-clicking an item in the code or memo list will retrieve all text passages indexed of that code or memo within their respective contexts, facilitating *constant comparisons* of all indicators of a given code or concept . . . Furthermore, the code and memo lists allow different *sorting*, for example, according to the *groundedness* (number of text passages of a code or memo) or *conceptual density* (number of other codes connected with a code).
>
> On the *conceptual level* (working mainly with concepts), the steps of *axial* and *selective coding* are supported by different functions. One set would be to join codes and memos to *families* like the family of all conditions or consequences. For *theory building*, you have to define concepts consisting in codes of higher order, which are no more connected to text passages but [rather] to other codes. The most powerful support on this level is achieved by *graphic representations* of text segments, codes, and memos . . . By these graphic tools, the analyst is easily able to construct his or her own semantic networks, that is to *build theories out of text segments, codes, and memos.* (Strauss and Corbin 1998, pp. 277–8)

Packages like The Ethnograph or NUD•IST teach a scientific way of thinking about qualitative data, informed to some extent by positivist assumptions about the nature of theory and explanation, which can be contrasted to the very different understanding of research held by qualitative traditions informed by different epistemological assumptions, such as interpretivism, realism or poststructuralism. This is because the goal, stated clearly in this passage and in other methodological statements, is to produce an objective, verifiable account of the world, with the aim of producing formal theory which can be tested using quantitative methods.

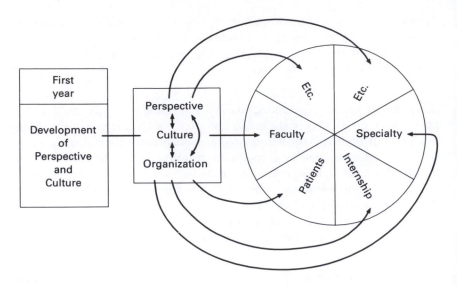

FIGURE 3.1   Diagramming Howard Becker et al.'s *Boys in White* (in Strauss, 1985)

Diagrams   Another technique used by grounded theory researchers is to represent the relationship between theoretical categories in the form of diagrams. Strauss suggests that this encourages theory-building, and describes workshops in which students develop a clearer understanding of their own data, through producing a 'succession of operational, integrative diagrams' (1987, p. 170).

Perhaps the clearest example relates to a study I have already summarized, Becker et al.'s (1961) *Boys in White*. Strauss admires this study, but believes that it could be conceptually denser and more developed. He suggests that this is evident from Figure 3.1, which represents the main findings. Strauss argues that the sections of the circle on the right (the different ways in which medical students develop a perspective towards different aspects of the medical school) are not fully developed in the subheadings in particular chapters, or in the index to the book. Diagramming (relating categories together systematically) makes this visible:

> In short, [*Boys in White*] is carefully ordered around core categories – integrated well – but is not especially dense in its conceptualization, not even in dimensionalizing and subdimensionalizing its core categories. That part of the conceptualization tends, as the diagram hints, to be more implicit than explicit; and in that regard is not very different than many other excellent qualitative analyses. The implicit character of much of the analysis, but then again its underdevelopment, was once underlined for me by two readers of this monograph when it was first published. A physician friend said that reading the book made him uncomfortable because 'these outsiders got to know so much!' By contrast, a sociologist, highly sympathetic to this kind of research,

nevertheless finished it with a sense of disappointment: 'It has so few *ideas*, really, in it.' (1987, p. 255)

Two case studies

This short summary of the epistemological assumptions and objectives of grounded theory researchers, and the procedures used in conducting research, will still leave some readers confused about what a grounded theory analysis looks like, and how qualitative data is presented in a research report. I suggest throughout this book that the best way to develop an appreciation for how research is conducted by any particular tradition is to read as many well-known studies as possible, and emulate what you like about them in your own work.

Strauss and Corbin (1997) have published a collection which illustrates how grounded theory can be used in researching a range of topics, including the work of scientists, recruitment firms and social workers dealing with abusive relationships. Most grounded theory research has, however, so far been conducted in medical settings. Two of the best known studies are Glaser and Strauss's (1965) *Awareness of Dying*, and Strauss et al.'s (1985) *The Social Organization of Medical Work*.

Awareness of Dying   The data for this study was collected over a period of three years, through interviewing practitioners and observing routine work in a number of hospitals in the Bay Area of San Francisco. The central concept developed in the book is the 'awareness context': what a set of people know in relation to a person who is dying, and how they act in those circumstances.

Strauss became interested in this topic through caring for his dying mother, and later participating 'in what he perceived as "an elaborate collusive game" designed to keep a dying friend unaware of his impending state' (Glaser and Strauss 1965, p. 287). Later, he and Glaser developed an 'integrated theory', or systematic set of categories which address the different contexts which arise when someone is dying. These categories were refined and elaborated using the constant comparative method, as the research team collected data to test and develop the theory.

The central concept developed by Glaser and Strauss, which enabled them to organize a large amount of material, was the 'awareness context'. They identified three variations: where a patient was unaware (a closed context), where both patient and carers were aware (an open context), and where both concealed their awareness (a mutual pretence context). In each situation, participants were faced with the problem of what to say or do, for example, when everyone knew that death was inevitable and 'there was nothing more to do'.

The systematic character of the way Glaser and Strauss work through these possibilities is evident from the contents page, which is worth reproducing in full:

Each of the substantive chapters develops a particular theme, through drawing on examples observed during the fieldwork. The chapter about the mutual pretence awareness context contains the following passage, about how patients and doctors rely on props to maintain the pretence that the patient will recover from a terminal illness:

Patients dress for the part of the not-dying patient, including careful attention to grooming, and to hair and make-up by female patients. The terminal patient may also fix up his room so that it looks and feels 'just like home', an activity that supports his enactment of normalcy. Nurses may respond to these props with explicit appreciation – 'how lovely your hair looks this morning' – or even help to establish them, as by doing the patient's hair. We remember one elaborate pretense ritual involving a husband and wife who had won the nurse's sympathy. The husband simply would not recognize that his already comatose wife was approaching death, so each morning the nurses carefully prepared her for his visit, dressing her for the occasion and making certain that she looked as beautiful as possible.

The staff, of course, has its own props to support its ritual prediction that the patient is going to get well: thermometers, baths, fresh sheets, and meals on time! Each party utilizes these props as he sees fit, thereby helping to create the pretenses anew. But when a patient wishes to demonstrate that he is finished with life, he may drive the nurses wild by refusing to cooperate in the daily routines of hospital life – that is, he refuses to allow the nurses to use their props. Conversely, when the personnel wish to indicate how things are with him, they may begin to omit some of those routines. (1965, p. 72)

This passage employs the same analytic techniques found in the work of Erving Goffman to reveal something interesting about the problems that arise in caring for the dying patient. However, the distinctive feature of the grounded theory tradition is the way the individual sections form part of a general scheme that compares different types of patients, and different dimensions of the nurse–patient relationship. Glaser and Strauss claim that the systematic character of the theory, and the fact that it is illustrated through examples which practitioners will recognize from their own experience, mean that it can be used to improve medical practice. Although they do not make any recommendations in the book, they suggest that this kind of detailed, analytically driven description can help policy-makers make better decisions:

> In utilizing these types of concepts in our book, we have anticipated that readers would almost literally be able to see and hear the people involved in terminal situations – but see and hear in relation to our theoretical framework. It is only a short step from this kind of understanding to applying our theory to the problems that both staff and patients encounter in the dying situation. For instance, a general understanding of what is entailed in the mutual pretense context, including consequences which may be judged negative to nursing and medical care, may lead the staff to abandon its otherwise unwitting imposition of medical pretense upon a patient. Similarly, the understanding yielded by a close reading of our chapters on family reactions in closed and open contexts should greatly aid a staff member's future management of – not to say compassion for – those family reactions. A good grasp of our theory also, will help hospital personnel to understand the characteristic problems faced on particular kinds of hospital services, including their own, as well as the typical kinds of solutions that personnel will try. (1965, p. 264)

The Social Organization of Medical Work   This project was completed over five years by three researchers working with Anselm Strauss. The central concept used to analyse data was the 'trajectory' of an illness. This is not simply the 'physiological unfolding of a patient's disease', but 'the total organization of work done over that course, plus the impact on those involved with that work and its organization' (Strauss et al. 1985, p. 8).

Strauss et al. recommend their concept as 'a means for analytically ordering the immense variety of events that occur – at least with contemporary chronic illnesses – as patients, kin and staff seek to control and cope with those illnesses' (1985, p. 9). At an early point in the book they present two case studies which illustrate the distinction between a routine and problematic trajectory. The routine case

> illustrates such phenomena as: (a) multiple trajectories, (b) emergency (acute) hospital care, (c) initial steps in diagnosing or mapping of a major trajectory (heart failure), (d) the complexity of divisions of labour, including that among trajectory managers as well as among various technical specialists from

different departments, and (e) the several kinds of work involved in trajectory management. (1985, p. 12)

This is then contrasted with a problematic trajectory which causes problems for all concerned. Distinctive features of this case include:

(a) . . . multiple trajectories [because more than one illness was diagnosed], (b) the multiplicity of trajectory managers and the confusion over coordination of their efforts, (c) the number of medical and technical departments drawn upon as resources, (d) the sheer difficulty of predicting outcomes of the medical interventions and deciding which to utilize, (e) the patient's active role both in reacting to staff decisions and making her own daily decisions, and (f) the cumulative impact on everybody, including frustration because of the great difficulty in gaining and maintaining control over the various courses of illness, anger and upset over the patient's 'uncooperative' behavior, conflict and resulting anger among the staff members themselves, and dismay and upset over the issue of dying. (1985, pp. 15–16)

Having described general features of the illness trajectory, the study then looks at different aspects or dimensions of the work in any illness. These are discussed in chapters about 'machine work', 'safety work', 'comfort work', 'sentimental work' and 'articulation work'. Strauss gives an insight into how some of these categories were developed in weekly meetings in his (1987) *Qualitative Analysis for Social Scientists*. The result is a study which shows in great detail how medical work gets done, by organizing qualitative materials into a set of categories, and integrating these into a general theory.

Dramaturgical analysis

Dramaturgical analysis offers an interesting contrast to grounded theory in that many would associate it with a unique style of qualitative research invented by Erving Goffman, but which never developed into a method or school. This is true to the extent that Goffman did not write manuals on how to do qualitative research, and probably viewed the craft of ethnography as more art than science. Nevertheless, students supervised by Goffman have used his ideas in their own ethnographic research, and it has developed into a sub-tradition of symbolic interactionism known as dramaturgical analysis. It provides a range of concepts and way of looking at the world that can usefully be applied in studying any social setting.

Erving Goffman and the interaction order

Goffman was awarded a doctorate in anthropology with W. Lloyd Warner at the University of Chicago in 1953, and taught at the University of California at Berkeley between 1961 and 1967, and at the University of Pennsylvania until he died at the age of sixty from cancer in 1982 (for a fuller account of his career, see Manning 1992, pp. 3–4). He conducted three ethnographic studies: a year-long study of a community in the Scottish Shetland Isles; a year-long study of a psychiatric hospital funded by the National Institute of Mental Health, in which he collected data while working as 'the assistant to the athletics director' in St Elizabeth's Hospital in Washington, DC; and a study of casinos in Las Vegas in which he worked periodically as a card-dealer. The only ethnography he published was *Asylums* (1961a), based on the study of St Elizabeth's. He also published a large number of books and articles, including *Encounters* (1961b), *Strategic Interaction* (1970), *Relations in Public* (1971) and *Frame Analysis* (1974), which drew on material from these studies, but also on a much wider range of sources about how people behave in everyday life, including newspaper reports, comic books, etiquette manuals, novels and autobiographies.

Goffman's objective in all these studies was to reveal a dimension to social life that had never been studied by sociologists: what he calls the interaction order (Goffman 1983). This concerns the way people interact when they are in face-to-face contact. Like Strauss, he organized examples from different settings into general themes such as face-work, or impression management, so one could view his whole work as concerned with producing a body of formal theory. Although they are both influenced by Simmel, Goffman's work has, however, a very different character to a grounded theory analysis. This is because it takes the form of a series of brilliant, but only loosely connected, observations in an essay style which was probably partly influenced by the work of Everett Hughes. There is no attempt to turn these observations into systematic theory in the way favoured by Strauss.

Rod Watson (1999) has suggested that the key to understanding Goffman's analytic interest in the interaction order, and his distinctive writing style, is a technique which the literary theorist Kenneth Burke has termed 'a perspective by incongruity'. Hughes used this when he made a running comparison in his essays between the work of high- and low-status groups, such as doctors and prostitutes, who are not usually viewed as sharing the same problems. The objective here was to reveal something interesting about work by making a deliberate comparison between two incongruous groups. Watson shows how Goffman does much the same thing by using a series of metaphors and similes to reveal features of face-to-face interaction which we normally take for granted. These include talking about people as if they were players in a team game, espionage agents seeking to avoid discovery, or confidence tricksters. The central, and most powerful, metaphor he develops is to compare people in everyday situations to the actors in a theatrical performance. This has become known as dramaturgical analysis.

The best way to learn this perspective, and with it a way of doing sociological analysis, is to read *The Presentation of Self in Everyday Life* (1959). Goffman introduces the perspective in the preface in the following terms:

> I mean this report to serve as a sort of handbook detailing one sociological perspective from which social life can be studied, especially the kind of social life that is organized within the physical confines of a building or plant. A set of features will be described which together form a framework that can be applied to any concrete social establishment, be it domestic, industrial or commercial.
>
> The perspective employed in this report is that of a dramaturgical performance; the principles derived are dramaturgical ones. I shall consider the way in which the individual in ordinary work situations presents himself and his activity to others, the ways he guides and controls the impression they may form of him, and the kinds of things he may or may not do while sustaining his performance before them. (1959, p. xi)

This is developed in a systematic way, through chapters on 'performances', 'teams', 'regions and region behaviour', 'discrepant roles', 'communication out of character' and 'the arts of impression management'. Here are a few examples which illustrate how Goffman develops a dramaturgical perspective, and uses it to make sense of social institutions.

Presenting a good impression   Goffman seeks to persuade us that any individual, in any social situation, is engaged in something like a theatrical performance since the people he encounters will be trying 'to acquire information about him', such as 'his general socio-economic status' or 'his attitude toward them' (1959, p. 1). This is, incidentally, a good example of how it was common to use 'he' to refer to both genders before this became a political issue during the 1960s. Everyone tries to present a good impression, and here Goffman supplies the example of a sociological study about dating behaviour which found that female college students arranged for themselves to be phoned several times in order to impress other students in their hall of residence. Later in the book, he applies the same approach to looking at the performances of street beggars and 'members of the higher professions'. He suggests, for example, that anyone who has undergone the extensive period of training required to become a doctor or a lawyer is required 'to foster the impression that the licensed practitioner is someone who has been reconstituted by his learning experience and is now set apart from other men'. He also notes that 'executives often project an air of complacency and general grasp of the situation, blinding themselves and others to the fact that they hold their jobs partly because they look like executives, not because they can work like executives' (1959, pp. 46–7).

The distinction between 'doing' and 'being'   In the second chapter, Goffman makes a distinction between actors who believe the part they are playing, and the individual who has 'no belief in his own act' (1959, p. 18). This distinction between 'doing' and 'being', between your position in society and how you see yourself in relation to that position, is a recurring theme in symbolic interactionism (and a central concern of Mead and Park). Goffman suggests that this should be seen as a process, in which some people start out as idealistic performers but become cynical over time, while others are initially cynical but later come to believe in the part they are playing. This is a useful analytic device one can use in studying occupational careers, but is also useful in studying social stratification. Goffman gives the following example from his ethnographic study of a Shetland Isles community:

> For the last four or five years, the island's tourist hotel has been owned and operated by a married couple of crofter origins. From the beginning, the owners were forced to set aside their own conceptions as to how life ought to be led, displaying a full round of middle-class services and amenities. Lately, however, it appears that the managers have become less cynical about the performance that they stage; they themselves are becoming middle-class and more enamored of the selves their clients impute to them. (1959, p. 20)

Team performances   Goffman notes that most people are not just performers in their own right, but members of teams which are engaged in giving a joint performance. He gives the example of middle-class family life in 1950s America in which 'the wife may demonstrate more respectful subordination than she may bother to show when alone with him or when with old friends' (1959, p. 79). The concept is again particularly useful in analysing the conduct of the professions. Goffman observes that 'when a member of the team makes a mistake in the presence of the audience, the other team members often must suppress their immediate desire to punish and instruct the offender, until, that is, the audience is no longer present'. Teachers will, for example, rarely criticize a colleague in front of pupils or their parents; but in the privacy of the staffroom, 'violent criticism may and does occur' (1959, pp. 89–90).

Frontstage and backstage regions   From a dramaturgical perspective, all social settings consist of a backstage, where individuals prepare for a performance, and a frontstage where they are on display. Goffman notes that 'in many service trades, the customer is asked to leave the thing that needs service and to go away so that the tradesman can work in private'. This 'conceals the amount and kind of work that had to be done . . . and other details the client would have to know before being able to judge the reasonableness of the fee that is asked of him' (1959, pp. 114–15). Another example is the behaviour of teachers and pupils in a high school:

When pupils leave the schoolroom and go outside for a recess of familiarity and misconduct, they often fail to appreciate that their teachers have retired to a 'common room' to swear and smoke in a similar recess of backstage behaviour. (1959, p. 132)

More generally, backstage areas are necessary for people to relax before the demands of their next performance. In most institutions, formal or informal backstage areas exist or are temporarily created where people can engage in 'profanity, open sexual remarks, elaborate griping, smoking, rough informal dress (for male executives, this might involve loosening one's tie), "sloppy" sitting and standing posture, use of dialect or sub-standard speech [or] mumbling and shouting' which are not permitted before audiences (1959, p. 132).

Two case studies

Like all the traditions reviewed in this book, dramaturgical analysis is best viewed not as a research method, but as an analytic tradition that offers one way of interpreting and organizing qualitative data. To use the perspective requires being able to explain and elaborate upon the central concepts, and apply these systematically to some social setting. The perspective also identifies the kind of data one might want to collect in an empirical project, and makes visible features of social life that one normally takes for granted. If you find it difficult thinking about qualitative data in theoretical terms, it might be worth trying your hand at a Goffmanian analysis of a social setting. Most people, in my experience, find the concepts easy to use and can generate an elaborate analysis simply by thinking about individual and team performances, and the distinction between frontstage and backstage behaviour.

Although ideas and concepts from Goffman are often employed in qualitative studies, relatively few people have used the perspective systematically in analysing social settings. The following studies are worth reading, because they demonstrate how a relatively simple idea, which Goffman never claims is more than a useful metaphor, can be used to reveal something interesting about institutions.

An abortion clinic ethnography   This study by Donald Ball (1967) describes the work of practitioners in an abortion clinic on the California–Mexico border, at a time when abortion was still illegal in California. After setting the scene, Ball uses three concepts from Goffman ('setting', 'appearance' and 'manner') to select, organize and interpret qualitative data obtained by observing medical procedures in the clinic and interviewing practitioners about their work. The overall argument is that the clinic used a series of devices (a 'rhetoric of legitimation') to create a good impression for patients.

Ball notes that the 'medical wing' of the clinic was a 'far cry from the shabby and sordid image of the "kitchen table abortionist" drawn in the popular press'. The abortions were carried out in a room designed to give the impression of 'modern scientific medicine'. This contained 'familiar . . . medical paraphernalia' such as 'surgical tools' and 'hypodermic syringes'. Staff in the clinic wore 'white tunics', and 'ostentatiously' put on surgical gloves 'at the beginning of the procedure'. Even the manner in which operations were conducted was designed to reinforce the impression that this was a normal hospital. Everyone used medical terminology when referring to 'operations', and the word 'abortion was never used in the presence of a patron' (1967, pp. 297–8). There were even elements from normal medical practice built into the procedures such as taking a 'pre-operative medical history', and recording these 'upon a standard multi-carboned form', and having a 'post-operative consultation'.

The success of the clinic lay in presenting an image that reduced the anxieties of patients, and also gave staff a positive self-image, even though everyone knew that it was not a proper hospital. Although they gave the appearance of being proper doctors, the practitioners were not, in fact, medically qualified. Moreover, although the equipment in the operating room looked impressive, it was used in breach of normal medical rules about hygiene:

It should be pointed out that, aseptically, tunics are no substitute for full surgical gowns; that full precautionary tactics would also include items such as face masks, caps, etc.; and that it is highly irregular for an operating room to lack an autoclave (for the sterilization of instruments) and changeable covering for the table, and for surgical instruments to stand on display, exposed to the air for long periods of time. Additionally it may be noted that the portion of the pre-operative medical history which is taken by the senior practitioner is recorded by him after his elaborate display of putting on surgical gloves – a less than ideal practice for sterility. (1967, p. 299)

One reaction to this study might be to feel that it is about a particular kind of medical institution, which can only attract patients through some degree of deception. Goffman, however, believed that the same approach could be used in studying any organization or institutional setting. One might, for example, want to look at the routine things that doctors and lawyers do to present a professional image of competence and respectability to clients. This includes the framed diplomas one finds on the wall in their offices, and the careful preparation that takes place before meeting patients or clients. It can also include the strategies used by companies and public institutions to develop a suitable image, and the manner in which trainees have to acquire the right manner and appearance to succeed in a professional career.

Becoming an accountant Symbolic interactionists have always been interested in the topic of 'adult socialization': the way in which individuals are influenced by the people they meet, and how they are shaped by different kinds of institutions. This is particularly easy to research if you already belong to a particular occupational or professional group. You can observe the behaviour of work colleagues, draw on your own experience of socialization, and interview a range of people at different stages of their careers.

A paper by Richard Harper (1987) illustrates how it is possible to analyse the process of professional socialization from a dramaturgical perspective. Harper had trained as an accountant, and obtained permission to conduct research as a participant observer in the audit division of 'one of the "Big Seven" multinational chartered accountancy firms' (1987, p. 2). In addition to observing people at work, he also conducted interviews and tape-recorded 'talk about work'. The main theme is how people were required to change, by developing the right professional appearance and manner, if they wanted to succeed in accountancy.

Harper begins by describing the frustrations experienced by trainee accountants, who were required to do boring, menial tasks in their first three or four years at the firm. Most of their work during an audit involved hours of photocopying or sending out routine letters. The natural reaction of graduates placed in this situation was 'to lark about', especially when they were not being observed, to make the work tolerable. However, they would be 'severely rebuked directly and immediately if more senior staff saw them looking even tired or simply empty-handed, let alone obviously "messing about"' (1987, p. 3). Report cards were kept about the attitudes of trainees, and their progress was monitored at regular assessment interviews. The objective was to teach them to develop the right professional manner in front of clients.

After they completed their examinations, trainees became 'seniors' in the firm, and became responsible for managing the audit teams. Those who wanted to get on were required 'to adopt certain rather constraining ways, or strategies, of self-presentation' (1987, p. 4). Many of these had to do with presenting the right image:

> suits were, naturally, a necessary aspect of this as they had been since the first day of work, but not *any* old suits. They had to be discreet without being bland, well-cut without being extravagant (for seniors would be told by managers and partners that, if they wore extravagantly expensive suits, clients would think them overpaid). Individuals had to be well-groomed: if, in their first year as trainees, untidy mops of hair were accepted as a final echo of undergraduate sloppiness, by the time they became senior, neat (and, needless to say, more expensive) haircuts were treated as a token of burgeoning professionalism (again seniors would be told that clients would perhaps associate sloppy dress with sloppy auditing) . . . Concern for image went even so far as to include modes of transport – motorbikes were as unsuitable as

decrepit old cars. For it would be pointed out that motorbikes might give the impression of 'laddishness' and, therefore, possible inability to make calm and objective assessments; whilst clapped-out cars might suggest auditors were incapable of running their own affairs and, therefore, were unlikely to be able to assess those of another. (1987, p. 4)

However, the presentational demands on seniors extended well beyond having the right kind of car:

In personal manner, individuals had to train so-called abrasive edges: courtesy and patience had to replace abruptness; simplicity of expression had to supplant opacity; and an ease with clients that cultivated confidence had to supersede apprehension and self-consciousness. Above all, they had to learn to give the impression of mental acuity and intellectual finesse. (1987, p. 4)

Harper notes that as they progressed in their career, the accountants not only developed this professional image, but also came to believe in the part they were playing. Whereas trainees behaved and dressed differently when they left the office, partners were expected 'to portray the right image in all sorts of settings, even the most informal' (1987, p. 6). They were, for example, expected to entertain clients at home, so they no longer recognized a distinction between 'frontstage' and 'backstage'. Most trainees were unable to change in this way, so that only one in every seventy made it to partner.

Studying public settings

Goffman also published two books, *Relations in Public* (1971) and *Behavior in Public Places* (1963), which provide a set of concepts and ideas for researching behaviour in public places, such as the street or shopping malls, but which you could also use to conduct a study on a university campus based on observing interaction in corridors, the library or student bars.

Making interaction visible The difficulty in this kind of study lies in learning how to see things taking place in everyday social settings which we normally take for granted. As an example, it is worth reproducing Goffman's observations about what happens when pedestrians pass on the sidewalk or pavement (which is part of a longer analysis of this commonplace interactional event):

When a pedestrian in American society walks down the street, he seems to make an assumption that those to the front of a close circle around him are ones whose course he must check up on, and those who are a person or two away or moving behind his sightline can be tuned out. In brief, the individual, as he moves along, tends to maintain a scanning or check-out area . . . As newcomers enter the individual's scanning range – something like three or

four sidewalk squares away – they are commonly glanced at briefly and
thereafter disattended because their distance from him and their indicated rate
and direction of movement imply that collision is not likely and that no
perception by them of him is necessary for his easily avoiding collision. A
simple 'body-check' is involved, albeit one performed circumspectly (at
present) by women rather than by men . . . Once others have been checked out
satisfactorily, they can be allowed to come close without this being cause for
concern. Thus the individual can generally cease to concern himself with
others as soon as they have come close enough abreast of him so that any
interference from them would require an abrupt turn. And further, since he
apparently does not concern himself with oncomers who are separated from
him by others, he can, in dense traffic, be unconcerned about persons who are
actually very close to him. Therefore, the scanning area is not a circle, but an
elongated oval, narrow to either side of the individual and longest in front of
him, constantly changing in area depending on the traffic density around him.
Note that even as the individual is checking out those who are just coming into
range, so they will be checking him out, which means that oncomers will be
eyeing each other at something of the same moment and that this moment will
be similarly located in the course of both; yet this act is almost entirely out of
awareness. (1971, pp. 32–3)

There are equally detailed descriptions in the two books about 'greeting
behaviour', how people protect their personal space on tube trains, and
how they recognize and respond to potentially dangerous people or
events. Goffman also identifies a set of rules known as 'civil inattention'
which govern how we normally interact with adult members of society.
These make it rude either to completely ignore people, or 'to stare openly
or fixedly at others' (1963, p. 83). More generally, he challenges us to
develop our powers of observation in noticing the fine detail of interaction in public settings.

Doing research in public settings   This kind of close description is difficult
to do, since the phenomena of interest often have a fleeting character,
and cannot easily be captured using a video camera (Goffman 1971,
p. 18). Even in an age where most interaction in public places is recorded
on CCTV, you will probably still find that you cannot set up a camera for
very long without coming into contact with officialdom (although this
could, of course, form part of a project about public space).

Nevertheless, it is possible to achieve a great deal, especially if observations are supplemented with interviews about how people experience
and relate to public space. One topic you could look at in a student
project are the strategies used by beggars to attract the attention of
pedestrians, and the strategies used by pedestrians to resist this invasion
of their private space. Carol Brooks Gardner (1995) has also used ideas
and concepts from Goffman in examining how women experience
harassment in public places. These are political topics, which can be
contrasted with studies that describe what happens when people pass

each other in corridors, or how rules against talking are observed in libraries. Your main objective should, however, be to produce a piece of close description, informed by Goffman's ideas, which contributes to our understanding of how people interact in public places.

Some criticisms

After reading these chapters about symbolic interactionism, you should be in a better position to appreciate the distinction between method and methodology which I have argued is central to conducting theoretically informed qualitative research. Clearly, ethnographers like Howard Becker and Elliot Liebow, grounded theorists like Anselm Strauss and those employing dramaturgical analysis are all using similar methods: a combination of participant observation and interviewing. What makes them distinct forms of research are the methodological assumptions informing the way they collect and analyse data. To some extent this is simply because they each employ a particular technical vocabulary in talking about methods. However, becoming a competent researcher is not simply a matter of learning the right terminology: people in different traditions understand the process of doing research quite differently, and, as a consequence, produce very different kinds of qualitative studies. This should be evident from this introduction to different traditions in symbolic interactionism. It will become even more evident in later chapters when I review critical and postmodern approaches which have very different epistemological assumptions.

One interesting feature of grounded theory and dramaturgical analysis is that they both deviate significantly from the research conducted in the mainstream symbolic interactionist tradition. Here one has to be careful about over-simplifying debates, internal to traditions, which usually generate a range of methodological positions. Nevertheless, it would seem fair to say that many symbolic interactionists, especially on the anti-positivist wing of the tradition, are not well disposed towards grounded theory. Although Goffman is admired by everyone, it is also fair to say that many symbolic interactionists feel uncomfortable in using his ideas. This is because both these sub-traditions arguably lead away from the study of lived human experience in the way this was understood by George Herbert Mead and Herbert Blumer.

Blumer's (1969) paper on variable analysis, it will be remembered, was a principled critique of studies based on finding connections between variables, at the expense of addressing the nature of human lived experience. That being so, it seems likely that he would have disapproved of the accommodation Glaser and Strauss reached with the quantitative tradition at a theoretical level, and with the emphasis they placed on building theory rather than supplying rich descriptions of social settings. Here Glaser and Strauss would argue, as I have shown in this chapter, that it is important to advance beyond 'mere' general description. But one response might be that ethnographies like *The Taxi-Dance Hall* or *Tally's Corner* (which do organize their data into analytic themes) provide a greater insight into these social worlds than Strauss and his colleagues achieved for medical practice using a supposedly more scientific method.

Blumer is also one of the few people to have critiqued the work of Erving Goffman from a symbolic interactionist perspective, arguing that dramaturgical analysis results in a distorted or impoverished view of human beings. This is because people do not normally feel they are engaged in a theatrical performance, except in unusual situations such as a job interview or the position of the recovering mental patient (Blumer 1972; see also Messinger et al. 1962). This is not a criticism of the studies reviewed in this chapter, where staff in the abortion clinic and trainee accountants were conscious of the need to present the right image to particular audiences. However, there are clearly dangers in characterizing people as putting on an act when they are unaware they are doing this. Blumer also suggests that, even when dramaturgical analysis is relevant, this only addresses one aspect of what people are doing in that setting. The ethnographic studies reviewed in the previous chapter attempt to present a rounded picture of how people understand their problems and tasks in particular settings.

These have not been intended as serious criticisms, since one can hardly deny that grounded theory and dramaturgical analysis provide an impressive range of concepts and techniques for conducting qualitative research. It is possible to learn either relatively quickly, at undergraduate or postgraduate levels, and use them to collect and analyse research data, without thinking too deeply about epistemological issues, or debates internal to the symbolic interactionist tradition. However, it seems important that, if you are using any technique, you should also be aware of the alternatives and possible criticisms.

Further reading

Some introductions to grounded theory

Strauss, A. (1987) *Qualitative Analysis for Social Scientists*. Cambridge University Press, Cambridge.
Strauss, A. and Corbin, J. (eds) (1997) *Grounded Theory in Practice*. Sage, London.
Strauss, A. and Corbin, J. (1998) *Basics of Qualitative Research: Techniques and Procedures for Producing Grounded Theory*, 2nd edn. Sage, London.
Miles, M. and Huberman, A. (1994) *Qualitative Data Analysis: an Expanded Sourcebook*. Sage, London.

Some introductions to dramaturgical analysis

Manning, P. (1992) *Erving Goffman and Modern Sociology*. Polity, Cambridge.
Burns, T. (1992) *Erving Goffman*. Routledge, London.
Drew, P. and Wooton, A. (eds) (1988) *Erving Goffman: Exploring the Interaction Order*. Polity, Cambridge.
Smith, G. (ed.) (1999) *Goffman and Social Organization: Studies in a Sociological Legacy*. Routledge, London.
Messinger, S., Sampson, H. and Towne, R. (1962) 'Life as theater: some notes on the dramaturgic approach to social reality', *Sociometry*, 14 (2): 141–63.

EXERCISES

1   Re-examine the interviews that you collected in Exercise 1 of Chapter 2. Code these materials using the techniques described in Chapter 5 of Strauss's *Qualitative Sociology*. How useful did you find this approach?

2   Obtain access to the frontstage and backstage areas of any social setting. Write an account of the activities taking place in that setting using concepts from Goffman's *The Presentation of Self*. Examples could be a restaurant, shop or public house.

3   Conduct an observational study of one of the following, employing concepts from Goffman's *Relations in Public*:
   (a) greeting behaviour
   (b) strategies used by pedestrians to avoid contact with beggars
   (c) strategies used by beggars for making contact with pedestrians.

4

Investigating Practices: Ethnomethodological Ethnography

CONTENTS

Ethnomethodology offers a distinctive way of researching and conceptualizing social life, which goes further than symbolic interactionism in examining how people understand and interpret the world around them, and the practical content of their day-to-day activities. This chapter will supply some historical background about ethnomethodology as a research tradition, and introduce the main assumptions of the approach. It will then illustrate how ethnomethodological techniques can be used in describing work and organizational processes inside public and private sector institutions through looking at a number of case studies. These range from studies of how the police and medical personnel in casualty departments make decisions, to how technological change affects customer service inside banks.

Ethnomethodology as a research tradition

Ethnomethodology is the research tradition founded by Harold Garfinkel, an American sociologist who has spent most of his career at the University of California in Los Angeles. Garfinkel has developed a distinctive approach to conceptualizing meaning and action, and has also advanced a powerful and uncompromising critique of positivism in the social sciences (see my discussion about the importance of understanding this epistemological debate in Chapter 1). My focus in this chapter will be on how this way of thinking about social life can be used in researching a range of topics, rather than on the epistemological challenge it presents to sociology as a scientific discipline, although it is important to appreciate that there is often this additional dimension to empirical studies.

The term 'ethnomethodology' was invented by Garfinkel in the 1960s, when he was employed on a multi-disciplinary project studying how jurors make decisions. Garfinkel complained that the method used by psychologists on the project, which involved assessing which jurors had most influence on the deliberations, neglected what he viewed as the central issue: how jurors arrived at decisions, in real time, during the course of a deliberation. He noted that Bales's method tells us a lot about how the jury can be understood as a small group, but not 'what makes a jury a jury' (Heritage 1984, pp. 298–9). 'Ethno-methodology' was, therefore, to be a discipline concerned with the methods used by people, like jurors, in doing everyday things like reaching decisions. Garfinkel's own (1984a; first published 1967) study of the jurors focused on how they used common-sense knowledge and reasoning in deciding 'what was fact' from 'what was fiction', and the relationship between the legal rules they were meant to follow and what actually took place in the jury room.

A key feature of common-sense reasoning is what Garfinkel has termed 'the documentary method of interpretation' (1984b). This refers to the way in which we make sense of objects or events in the world in terms of an 'underlying pattern', which we use prospectively to interpret new events, and retrospectively to revise our understanding of past events. A simple example might be the way in which a student experiences and makes sense of a lecture course. If you experience the first lecture as a 'good' lecture, you will also expect future lectures to be good, since you are using the underlying pattern 'this is a good lecturer' prospectively to make sense of the course. If, however, at a later date, the quality of the lectures starts to deteriorate, you may revise the underlying pattern to 'this is a bad lecturer'. This not only means that you will expect future lectures to be 'bad', but that you retrospectively reinterpret the meaning of the first lecture as an aberration from this new underlying pattern. Garfinkel suggests that we are using the documentary method all the time. Jurors use it in reaching decisions (as they assess

TABLE 4.1   The 'ringing telephone' exercise

1	2	3
Lived *in vivo* activities	Method used in social scientific study	Social scientific reports
A ringing telephone	Method chosen to represent this on a whiteboard: ring = xx, pause = 0	How the call is represented using this method: 00000xx0xx0xx0xx'hello'

different pieces of evidence pointing to an underlying pattern of guilt or innocence), and it is relevant to all the studies reviewed in this chapter.

More recently, Garfinkel has introduced the approach to students by inviting them to see a distinction between how we experience and accomplish day-to-day activities in everyday life, and how these are transformed into the findings and arguments that one can read in academic studies. Students are asked to collect examples of a telephone ringing in various circumstances, and then experiment with different ways of representing the call. In the example in Table 4.1, the method used was to represent each ring with the symbol 'xx' and each pause between rings by the symbol '0'. The objective is to make them think about the distinctive character of each call (whether the phone was, for example, just ringing, or heard as summoning a particular person), which is not available from a tape-recording, or how the tape-recording is represented symbolically on a whiteboard.

Garfinkel asserts that all social scientific work, including studies of jury rooms based on using Bales's coding procedures, employs methods from column 2 in producing the reports listed in column 3. Ethno-methodology, by contrast, is concerned with what happens in column 1. It is concerned with the ordinary, day-to-day activities, in all their lived *in vivo* details, which are neglected or idealized by other approaches (for a more detailed discussion of the ringing telephone exercise, see Goode 1994, Chapter 5).

Ethnomethodology remains a relatively small research tradition when compared with symbolic interactionism, or even with conversation analysis, which I will be reviewing in the next chapter. It is worth noting at this stage that there are close family ties between conversation analysis and ethnomethodology (Harvey Sacks and Garfinkel worked closely together), but there has always been debate and disagreement inside this intellectual community over how to study the social world. Garfinkel has, for example, argued that one can only understand the content of occu-pational activities through becoming a competent practitioner (Lynch 1993, Chapter 7). Most conversation analysts, on the other hand, believe that one should concentrate on examining tape-recorded talk.

The best ethnomethodological ethnographies were arguably written during the 1960s by students of Garfinkel like Lawrence Wieder and Don Zimmerman, or by associates like Egon Bittner, Aaron Cicourel and

David Sudnow. Garfinkel also supervised a number of students in the 1970s who conducted ethnographic research in scientific and other occupational settings, including Michael Lynch and Eric Livingston. Today, there are not many ethnomethodologists in universities doing ethnographic as opposed to conversation analytic research, although ethnographies influenced by Garfinkel's ideas continue to be published about a range of topics including the experience of disability (Goode 1994; Robillard 1999), public policy (Gubrium 1992), entrepreneurship (Anderson et al. 1989) and police work (Meehan 1997). Larger numbers are, however, employed by IT companies like Rank Xerox to conduct research about how new technologies are used in the workplace. There is also an ethnomethodological community in Japan, and smaller research groups in France, Germany, Switzerland and Italy.

Viewing institutions as accomplishments

Ethnomethodology goes further than symbolic interactionism in examining how people are continually communicating information about themselves, and interpreting what is taking place in the world around them. The philosophical and sociological objective of the approach is to reveal how the ordinary world we know depends on this communicative and interpretive work; and how reality (in the sense of the objective character of the events and objects we encounter in everyday life) is produced and maintained through our own talk and actions.

The study most frequently discussed in introductions to ethnomethodology, and a particularly clear example of how ethnomethodology results in a distinctive way of conceptualizing ethnographic research, is Lawrence Wieder's (1974) book about the convict code in a half-way house for drugs offenders. I have only included a short summary in this text, since you can find it discussed at greater length elsewhere (see, for example, Gubrium and Holstein 1997, Chapter 3). I will also show how I came to use ideas from the approach in my own ethnography of a firm of criminal lawyers (Travers 1997).

The convict code

The convict code is a phenomenon that many sociologists and criminologists have written about when they have visited penal institutions. It is a set of rules that convicts know about and obey, and cause guards, welfare officers and other officials immense difficulties in managing prison populations. The rules tell prisoners not to co-operate with the authorities. Everyone in such places knows what happens if you break the rules: social ostracism, and sometimes injury or death.

Wieder encountered the code in an institution he was studying which had the official goal of rehabilitating drugs offenders after their prison sentence before returning them to society. The code offered a warrant, and explanation, for why inmates would not co-operate with the authorities, stop taking drugs, or even talk to Wieder when he tried to interview them as a sociologist. He was, however, told that the code consisted of a number of maxims, including 'Do not snitch' (do not inform on other residents), 'Do not cop out' (do not turn yourself in to the authorities if you have done something illegal), and 'Do not trust staff – staff is heat'. The difficulties faced by staff can be illustrated by Wieder's summary of another maxim, 'Show your loyalty to residents':

> Staff, in fact, is 'the enemy', and a resident's actions should show that he recognizes this. He should not 'kiss ass', do favors for staff, be friendly to staff, take their side in an argument, or accept the legitimacy of their rules. Any of these acts can be understood as a defection to their side, and makes a resident suspect of being the kind of 'guy' that would snitch. It is not that being friendly to staff or complying with staff's regulations is intrinsically illegitimate, but these matters indicate what kind of person one is and that one, thereby, may not be trustworthy in protecting residents and their interests. If a resident makes it clear in other ways (as, for example, in his private dealings with other residents) that he indeed is on the residents' side, these signalizing activities may then be understood in other ways by the other residents. They may be understood as efforts to manipulate staff in some concrete way, for example, a resident wants them to give him the best jobs they have, or wants to make the kind of impression on his parole agent that will lead the agent away from suspecting him when he otherwise might. (1974, p. 147)

Wieder, however, realized that what some sociologists might describe as difficulties in obtaining access, offered a means of investigating the code as an ethnomethodological topic. The second half of the study is an autobiographical account of how he learnt about the existence of the code, and how it was used, for a variety of purposes, in everyday situations. In this way, he shows how an objective feature of the half-way house (what Heritage 1984 calls an 'institutional reality') can be viewed as something that was produced or accomplished through the talk and actions of the members in the setting.

Whereas a symbolic interactionist ethnographer might have been content to supply illustrative instances of the code to convey 'lived experience', Wieder went further by attempting to make visible the interpretive and communicative methods used by people in the half-way house. He did this using the phenomenological method of reflecting carefully upon his own experiences: how he learnt about the code, and used it to interpret events taking place around him; and how he experienced it as a moral or constraining force.

Drawing on his fieldnotes, Wieder describes how he learnt to use the code to make sense of events and conversations. He gives the following example from his first week in the house:

I passed a resident who was wandering the halls after the committee meetings on Wednesday night. He said to staff and all others within hearing, 'Where can I find that meeting, where can I get an overnight pass?' On the basis of what I had already learnt, I understood him to be saying, 'I'm not going to that meeting because I'm interested in participating in the program of the halfway house. I'm going to that meeting just because I would like to collect the reward of an overnight pass and for no other reason. I'm not a kiss-ass. Everyone who is in hearing distance should realize that I'm not kissing up to staff. My behavior really is in conformity with the code, though without hearing this (reference to an overnight pass), you might think otherwise.' (1974, p. 160)

This passage is not simply about what the code meant to residents, but how Wieder built up a progressively developed understanding over time, through observing and interpreting day-to-day events in the half-way house. In ethnomethodological terms, it examines the taken-for-granted methods we use to constitute our experience of the everyday world. The most important of these is what Garfinkel (1984b) calls the 'documentary method of interpretation' which allowed him to make prospective and retrospective sense of day-to-day events.

Wieder was also interested in the moral, persuasive character of the code, and how it was used to frustrate the initiatives of staff. Again, he not only lists examples, but analyses these in considerable detail. Here is part of an extended discussion of how it felt to be on the receiving end of the code when a resident refused to answer his questions, by saying 'You know I won't snitch.' Wieder notes that this worked to 'reformulate' or 'recrystallize' the exchange at a number of levels:

1   It told what had just happened, for example, 'You just asked me to snitch.'
2   It formulated what the resident was doing in saying that phrase, for example, 'I am saying that this is my answer to your question. My answer is not to answer.'
3   It formulated the resident's motives for saying what he was saying and doing what he was doing, for example, 'I'm not answering in order to avoid snitching.' Since snitching was morally inappropriate for residents, the utterance therefore formulated the sensible and proper grounds of the refusal to answer the question.
4   It formulated (in the fashion of pointing to) the immediate relationship between the listener (staff or myself) and teller (resident) by relocating the conversation in the context of the persisting role relationships between the parties, for example, 'For you to ask me that, would be asking me to snitch.' Thus saying, 'You know I won't snitch', operated as a re-enunciation, or a reminder of the role relationships involved and the appropriate relations between members of those categories. It placed the ongoing occasion in the context of what both parties knew about their overriding transsituational relationships.
5   It was one more formulation of the features of the persisting role relationship between hearer and teller, for example, 'You are an agent [or state researcher] and I am a resident-parolee. Some things you might ask me

involve informing on my fellow residents. Residents do not inform on their fellows.' (1974, p. 153)

This kind of ethnography can be distinguished from the symbolic interactionist studies reviewed in earlier chapters because of the greater emphasis placed on studying language. This is understood as having a constitutive role in shaping our experience of social reality. In the case of the half-way house, newcomers learnt about the code by hearing people use it to interpret what was taking place around them. Wieder notes that this practice of 'telling the code' formed part of the same setting which it described: the two could not be separated (1974, p. 133). From this perspective, language use cannot be an incidental phenomenon one encounters as an ethnographer in social settings: the reality of the setting – what it means to the people there, and yourself as an ethnographer – is accomplished through hearing everyday talk.

A firm of 'radical' lawyers

My doctoral thesis in a department of sociology was based on four months of ethnographic fieldwork in a firm of solicitors called 'Gregsons', which was located in an inner-city district in the north of England (Travers 1997). This had become well known as a firm of 'radical' lawyers, in the sense that Jane Gregson, the charismatic owner, adopted a tough approach towards the police, and the lawyers working there were active members of the Haldane Society of Socialist Lawyers. This was one of the reasons that attracted me to study this firm. However, during the fieldwork, I tried to move beyond simply describing it as a 'radical' law firm, through examining how I and others came to see Gregsons in this way.

Once one adopts this approach to studying a social setting, the world becomes surprisingly complicated. What exactly was it that made Gregsons a 'radical' firm? On one level, this was evident from the fact that the lawyers working there sometimes described the police as 'pigs', and regularly antagonized the police and local magistrates. One of the assistant solicitors had been reprimanded for scowling in court to demonstrate her disapproval at the injustice of the proceedings. The firm was run from an office in a dilapidated building, which could be contrasted with the modern looking appearance of other solicitors' firms in the area.

These 'radical' characteristics could, however, be interpreted in different ways. The lawyers in Gregsons argued that they provided a better service than other solicitors because they cared about the welfare of their clients, and treated them like human beings. They were not 'just in it for the money' like other lawyers. The police regarded this as an act designed to win business. Other lawyers I spoke to felt that when Jane Gregson antagonized the police or magistrates, she was letting down her clients. Even the dilapidated premises were viewed in different ways. Admirers saw them as part of the firm's 'radical' credentials; critics dismissed them as further evidence that the firm was badly managed, and giving a poor service to clients.

The value of looking at Gregsons in this way is that it reveals not just that this was a 'radical' law firm, but how this was demonstrated in particular situations, and what this meant to different people. I was only able to do this from having read Wieder's study of the convict code, so this illustrates the importance of becoming familiar with the research literature in a particular tradition for doing theoretically informed qualitative research.

The study of work

Another productive area for ethnomethodological enquiry has been the routine activities of people at work. Here Garfinkel has criticized other sociological traditions, including symbolic interactionism, for failing to address what he calls the 'missing what': the practical content of routine occupational tasks. One example he used when developing these ideas was Howard Becker's symbolic interactionist research on jazz musicians. Becker played jazz for many years, to supplement his income while studying for his PhD and working on a series of research projects led by Everett Hughes, and he published some interesting articles about careers and occupational culture in the jazz world. These tell us almost nothing, however, about how one actually plays jazz. In a similar way, Anselm Strauss's research on hospitals concentrates on documenting the perspectives of doctors and patients, and the stages of medical work, but it does not address the work involved in performing a surgical procedure. Garfinkel wanted to address occupational activities in a way that explicated the technical and common-sense knowledge, or bodily skills in the case of jazz musicians, which competent practitioners took for granted.

Many of the best known studies influenced by this programme have examined work in scientific settings (for example, Garfinkel et al. 1981; Lynch 1985). However, ethnomethodologists have also examined the work of government employees like the police, doctors, social workers and school counsellors. More recently, a number of large private sector companies have funded ethnomethodologists to conduct research about technology and organizational processes. The rest of the chapter will review some public and private sector applications of the approach.

Public sector applications

Some of the best known ethnomethodological studies have made a contribution to political debate about the fairness of public sector organizations. A good example is Aaron Cicourel's (1968) study of police work, which in contemporary terms is a powerful and unusually well-documented ethnography about institutional racism. David Sudnow's (1967) ethnography about death and dying in two hospitals makes a political point about how doctors treat patients. My own study about the work of immigration appeals tribunals (Travers 1999) adopts a similar approach in examining how judicial officials make decisions about applications for refugee status in Britain.

Police decision-making

The best ethnomethodological studies about work supply a close and well-documented description of routine activities in the workplace, but also criticize the positivist assumptions which continue to inform how most researchers collect and analyse data in the social sciences. *The Social Organization of Juvenile Justice* is a good example, in that it tells us a lot about police work (at a level of detail which has not been matched by subsequent studies), but also makes us think critically about the value of official statistics.

This study was made possible by a grant from 'the U.S. Department of Health, Education and Welfare in cooperation with the President's Committee on Juvenile Delinquency and Youth Crime' which allowed Cicourel to spend four years observing the work of police officers who dealt with juvenile offenders in two American cities. He initially hoped 'to follow a cohort of juveniles in each jurisdiction from their first police contact through their disposition by probation officials or the juvenile court' (1968, p. 170). This proved to be difficult in practice, partly because officers refused to allow him to tape-record, but also because it was difficult to follow every stage of a case 'without being on call virtually twenty-four hours a day for many months'. However, Cicourel found that it was sufficient to document a range of cases at different levels of detail. In writing about how he conducted the study, he stresses the importance of spending a long time in the field:

> Considerable time was necessary to gain the confidence of officers (two years in City B and three years in City A) to learn about irregular activities, internal organizational problems, and political power struggles. I attribute my access to the fact that I participated socially with many officers in circumstances that had little or nothing to do with the study or the work of law enforcement; such situations always produced a more relaxed atmosphere when the study context was resumed. In City A, the informal social encounters did not occur until very late in the study, and it was not until that time I felt 'close' to the 'inside' details of day-to-day activities, jealousies, power conflicts, dissatisfactions with the job, the promotion system and the like.
>
> Without considerable social contact, 'friendly' exchanges, attempts to know the officers informally so that the researcher is on a first-name basis with all he works with closely, I doubt if the detailed operations of day-to-day police and

probation work could be observed in anything approaching what could be called their 'normal' working environment. The fact of being present in an office day-in, day-out, busy with 'paper work', but privy to every conceivable kind of case, interruption, annoyances, 'inside' discussions, being drawn into one's confidence, and the like, provides the researcher with an invaluable perspective on the everyday character of law enforcement. (1968, pp. 170–1)

Cicourel does not reveal much about the internal 'political struggles' he found in the police, which is perhaps unsurprising given that there is an unspoken rule among ethnographers not to hurt or embarrass the people or institutions they study (unless this is strictly necessary in the interests of politics or science). However, he does show how a 'moral panic' in the newspapers about juvenile crime in one city led, paradoxically, to an explosion in the recorded crime rate, since the new bureau of juvenile investigation, set up by the mayor's office, required officers to charge offenders who had previously only been cautioned.

The bulk of the study looks at how police officers conducted their work, drawing on his observation of interviews and court hearings, but also supplying anonymized extracts from the file cards compiled by the police, reports by probation officers and school teachers, and other official documents. These supply an unusually detailed insight into how officers reached decisions (for example, whether to charge or caution) in particular cases, through interpreting their previous dealings with a juvenile recorded on a file card. Cicourel describes the process of decision-making in the following terms:

a juvenile's fate is contingent upon how a particular officer (at a given here and now) interprets his past activities as revealed on the summary file card, whom he asks for advice or information about the youth from other officers, the kind of behavioral performance enacted by the juvenile during the interrogation procedures, and the parental responsiveness or lack of interest as evaluated by the officer. (1968, p. 202)

The study also found that most officers were prejudiced against black and working-class youths. Here, for example, are Cicourel's observations about the police report on a young black offender:

a police officer's interrogation of someone like Smithfield presumes that a male Negro is a basic source of trouble in the community, a generic source of trouble for all agencies of social control, an offender who cannot be trusted, and someone viewed as a prime suspect whenever there are crimes without suspects. Interviews I have observed between officers and lower-income Negro males typically involve direct accusations about the youth's dishonesty, his general style of life, and his defiance and disrespect of authority, as revealed by his posture, speech mannerisms, demeanor, dress patterns, lack of remorse, seemingly unconcerned view about the consequences of his acts, what could happen to him, and so on. (1968, pp. 215–16)

The charge that the police are 'institutionally racist' was regularly made by the black power movement in America during the 1960s, and it continues to be made in the United Kingdom by those campaigning for the Metropolitan Police to become more accountable following the death of the black teenager Stephen Lawrence. Cicourel's study is unusual in providing a well-documented analysis of police racism, rather than simply a political tract, but it should be noted that it offers no political solutions, and suggests that matters are unlikely to improve given the economic and social gulf between black and white Americans (1968, p. 216).

The Social Organization of Juvenile Justice remains important, not only as a critique of policing, but because it makes us question the value of statistics, which are still widely used in the media and by people in public life to support political arguments. A great deal of effort has been spent since the 1960s in eliminating possible sources of bias in official statistics, such as different recording practices, or the impact of prejudice on decision-making. Nevertheless, those collecting and using statistics, whether in government departments or academia, are still reluctant to accept that we need to understand how statistics are produced, by conducting ethnographic studies of work, in order to address the processes that matter inside institutions. To give a contemporary example, statistical indicators are becoming increasingly common in measuring the performance of public sector occupations. Very little research has, however, so far been conducted on how the figures are produced which become league tables or quality scores. Cicourel's study offers a model for conducting such a study, although clearly it would also depend upon obtaining access to the work of inspectors, and the various organizations which have an interest in producing statistics.

Death and social worth

David Sudnow's (1967) study about death and dying in two hospitals is worth reading as an example of how to look at one aspect of work in a large organization in some detail. There is a large literature in medical sociology, but still relatively little attention to the mundane practices involved in different types of medical work. This study is distinctive in examining the work of a range of people concerned with death, including hospital administrators, nurses and morgue attendants. There is a political message in the same way as in Cicourel's research on the police, and it arguably has more impact than other more explicitly critical studies because it is part of a careful and well-documented account of this aspect of medical work.

Sudnow spent about a year and a half doing ethnographic fieldwork, with permission from the hospital 'to investigate how staff members handled the treatment of "dying" patients' (1967, p. 7). He obtained most of his data by following people around and engaging in casual conversation about their work:

> Each day I accompanied members of the house staff on the morning rounds, engaged them in conversation, and attended their conferences. On special days during the week I attended various specialty conferences, e.g. vascular surgery, cancer clinic, obstetrics rounds, etc. During the rest of my day I spent most of my time standing about nurses' stations, overhearing conversations in corridors, following physicians as they treated their patients, witnessing surgical, obstetrics and autopsy procedures, sitting in waiting rooms and cafeterias, chatting with members of families, and the like. In both settings I was free to go where I pleased . . . I had, in each setting, persons who might be considered as 'informants', namely those with whom I had developed friendships and who, in conversation, supplied me with much information about their circumstances of work, technical matters, feelings about the institution, the practices of others, and information about happenings which took place when I was not present. (1967, p. 7)

Sudnow's study is politically controversial in that he shows how hospital staff made moral judgements as part of their work. He describes how doctors employed the procedures which will be familiar to viewers of television dramas such as 'ER' and 'Cardiac Arrest' to revive patients who were clinically dead on their arrival in hospital. Immense effort was expended on the young or the extremely wealthy. However, the elderly and the poor were often taken straight to the morgue.

What makes the study interesting, however, is not just this political point, but the detailed account of everyday activities, such as how dying patients were segregated on the wards, and the manner in which staff handled dead bodies. Sudnow contrasts the perspectives of those who had no direct contact with death, such as administrators, with those of doctors and nurses. He also describes the work of the morgue attendant, 'one of those people in the hospital whose mere presence at a scene indicates a certain event', in collecting dead bodies and conducting a post-mortem (1967, p. 53). Finally, there is an extended account of the procedures used to break the news that a patient had died to relatives, and the problems people faced in displaying grief appropriately in American culture. This last section was influenced by Erving Goffman who supervised the dissertation and, because of his own training as an anthropologist, required all his graduate students to spend at least a year in the field.

The work of immigration appeals tribunals

Most of my work to date, as a qualitative researcher, has been influenced by the ethnomethodological studies-of-work tradition in that I have tried to produce close descriptions of the work of practitioners in public sector institutions. My study of a firm of criminal lawyers (Travers 1997) contains a detailed account of a one hour episode in which a defendant was persuaded to plead guilty in the magistrates' courts. I have also published a study (Travers 1999) which looks at the work of practitioners in the system of administrative tribunals which hear appeals about immigration and asylum in Britain.

Immigration control will always be a contentious political and moral issue which forces us to confront the fact that people in many countries around the world do not enjoy the political freedoms or economic prosperity which are taken for granted in countries like Britain. A dramatic rise in the numbers claiming asylum under the 1951 United Nations Convention on Refugees has created major administrative and political problems for most Western governments. After doing very little about the issue for ten years, Britain has recently adopted a tougher policy by attempting to deter asylum-seekers from coming (for example, by removing social security benefits), and establishing a faster system for determining appeals. Very few people have so far been removed from Britain, so one development that seems likely is that more people will be placed in detention centres. The current objective is to hear appeals within a period of six months, and return unsuccessful applicants to their countries of origin. In recent years, only a small percentage of people have been recognized as refugees, although a larger number have received what is known as 'exceptional leave to remain'.

My main objective in researching immigration control was to understand the decision-making process which resulted in so few people being recognized as refugees. I achieved this by gaining access to the work of three occupational groups working in tribunals. I began by looking at day-to-day work in the Immigration Advisory Service, a government-funded agency which provides advice and representation to people appealing against decisions made by the Home Office. I then obtained permission from the Immigration Appellate Authority who operate these tribunals, and the Lord Chancellor's Department, to study the work of the adjudicators who hear immigration and asylum appeals. Finally, I obtained permission from the Home Office to look at appeals from the perspective of the presenting officers who represent the government.

Whereas Cicourel in the generously funded conditions of 1960s America had three years to collect his data, and an unspecified time to write up the study, I have had the misfortune to have become interested in sociology at a time when the subject is no longer fashionable, and it has become difficult to obtain funding to pursue lengthy periods of ethnographic research. My doctorate was based on only four months of fieldwork, which just about gave me enough time to analyse the data, and write a thesis, in the remainder of a two year studentship. In this project, I had to work within even tighter constraints. I collected most of the data in forty-three days of fieldwork. I spent thirty days with the Immigration Advisory Service, ten days with the Immigration Appellate Authority, and three days with a unit of Home Office presenting officers.

These tribunals are open to the public, so it is possible to learn a lot simply by sitting at the back of a hearing room. I wanted to go further, however, in understanding how practitioners understood the legal and evidential issues in appeals. To do this, I adopted Cicourel's strategy of spending time with practitioners, and observing their day-to-day activities. I also attended meetings and training sessions in the Immigration Advisory Service and the Immigration Appellate Authority, and got to know a variety of people working in the three organizations. Finally, I used my access to obtain documentary records relating to the appeals I observed, including the determinations which were sent to appellants after the hearing.

To obtain asylum, an appellant has to show that he or she has 'a well-founded fear of being persecuted for reasons of race, religion, nationality, membership of a particular social group or political opinion'. Many appeals are refused on legal grounds, since the circumstances described by appellants are not considered to amount to persecution 'for a Convention reason'. Others fail because the adjudicator decides, after reviewing documentary evidence, that the appellant does not have a well-founded fear, since it would be safe to return to a particular country. Many are refused simply because the adjudicator does not believe the appellant.

My objective in writing up the study was to present enough detail, in the form of extracts from determinations and the evidence given in hearings, as well as a summary of the relevant law, so that the reader would be able to form his or her own judgement about a small number of cases. These illustrate how some appeals can be decided very quickly, but that it is often difficult to tell whether an appellant is telling the truth, or making up a plausible story in order to gain admission to Britain.

The political significance of my study is that most appeals are refused, despite a low burden of proof. The British government has always argued that this conclusively proves that most asylum-seekers are really economic migrants and should be treated harshly. An alternative explanation, which does not require having to suggest that adjudicators are influenced by negative stories about asylum-seekers in the media, is that they become case-hardened over time, through listening to large numbers of appeals. The study tries to demonstrate that reality is considerably more complex than the one sided politicized versions that appear in liberal and right-wing newspapers. In common with other ethnomethodological studies about public sector institutions, it makes a political point through presenting a detailed account of how decisions are made by these administrative tribunals, without suggesting that there are any easy solutions. The problem for politicians in a liberal democracy is that they need to show they are taking tough action to deter people from claiming asylum, out of a fear of losing votes, but can only do this effectively if they take draconian measures which cost a great deal of money.

Private sector applications

An unexpected development in the history of ethnomethodology as a research tradition is the way it is now being used to study the social effects of technology. Governments anxious to find ways of promoting technological development in case they are left behind by competitors have channelled money away from humanistic or purely scientific research to projects geared to increasing economic output. The biggest source of funding has come from large technology companies like Rank Xerox, which employs ethnographers trained in ethnomethodology, as well as cognitive psychologists and computer scientists, in its research laboratories at Palo Alto, California in America and Cambridge in the United Kingdom. Ethnomethodologists in Britain and America have played a leading role in developing new fields such as the study of human–computer interaction, and computer-supported co-operative work (CSCW). There are a number of specialist journals in this field which publish ethnographic research.

Technology companies employ ethnomethodologists because they are interested in obtaining detailed accounts of everyday working practices, which can help computer scientists design better products. Studies have also focused on the difficulties that arise when new technology is introduced into the workplace. Researchers usually have permission not only to interview people extensively, and observe working practices, but also to tape-record conversations, make video-recordings, and copy the content of files and other documents. Two examples are a project conducted by John Bowers, Graham Button and Wes Sharrock (1995) for Rank Xerox about the introduction of a new device to co-ordinate work in the printing industry, and a study by Richard Harper, Dave Randall and Mark Rouncefield (2000) about technological change inside banks.

Co-ordinating work in the printing industry

This study was based on several months of fieldwork in a large printing company in the United Kingdom. A team of researchers were commissioned to assess the effectiveness of a new management information system which was introduced into the company after it won a number of contracts to provide printing services to the British government. In order to bid for a contract, the company had to demonstrate a 'commitment to install and use a Management Information System (MIS) with "real shopfloor data-capture" to monitor workflow' (Bowers et al. 1995, p. 53).

This new system involved recording information about each job (for example, time taken and materials used), which was then used to organize work more effectively in the company. Managers hoped that it would enable them to improve workflow, by 'ensuring, for example, that no one operator is conspicuously occupied while others are idle, that no one job needlessly ties up the shopfloor while other jobs are waiting, and that machines are appropriately used to their best capabilities' (1995, p. 54).

The first task of the ethnographers was to discover how workflow was managed on the shopfloor before the introduction of this new system. They describe, for example, how it was common practice for operators to juggle jobs, so that some work was always done in advance before an order was received. They would also continually reschedule work to deal with contingencies such as emergency jobs, machines breaking down, and staff availability. Bowers et al. describe these practices as 'workflow from within':

> Workflow from within accomplishes the smooth flow of work through methods which are internal to the work. To do printwork competently requires that, on receipt of a job, an operator is able to orient to such matters as: Is this job properly for me? Should it be done next? How urgent is it? To whom should I pass it when I am done? And so forth. By resolving these questions in working on the job, not only is the job done, so is the organization of the shopfloor in part accomplished. Workflow from within characterizes the methods used on the shopfloor which emphasize the local and internal accomplishment of the ordering of work. Workers juggle their in-trays, jump the gun, glance across the shopfloor, listen to the sounds coming from machines, re-distribute work in the here and now so that what to do next can be resolved. In the here and now, in real time, workers encounter multiple jobs of a varied nature, requiring artful scheduling and completion. (1995, p. 63)

The objective of the new system was to improve workflow by giving managers information about how long jobs were taking and which machines were being utilized, so that they could use resources more efficiently. Unfortunately, it not only failed to do this, but actually prevented people from working effectively. The researchers found that the new management information system created a series of problems for workers since it took up a lot of time entering data, and the categories used by the system did not relate to the actual procedures used in scheduling work. The way in which the system envisaged the organization of work (what they call 'workflow from without') conflicted with the adhocing practices used on the shopfloor. Using the new system actually disrupted the smooth flow of work. Workers solved this problem by entering data retrospectively at the end of the day, rather than in the course of the work, but this created additional demands on their time, rather than improving productivity in the printing firm.

This study illustrates how it is possible to study the complex practices which underpin a division of labour, by spending time as an observer in an occupational setting. It also has practical implications for companies planning to introduce these systems, and the computer scientists who design these tools. These researchers concluded that companies need to be more realistic about the costs and benefits of introducing new technologies. In this case, the printing firm did obtain more detailed information about work processes (which was required for 'good organizational reasons'), but this was only obtained through disrupting the smooth flow of work.

Technological change inside banks

The driving force in capitalist economies has always been the need to increase profits, and the productivity of labour. This has intensified in recent years, as companies have invested in computer technology, which has made it possible to reduce the size of the workforce. Ethnomethodologists, and other social scientists, have been employed to describe and monitor these changes by companies which are interested in managing technological change.

A good example is a series of projects, conducted by a team of ethnomethodologists based at the University of Lancaster, about change in the banking industry. Until relatively recently, customers obtained most advice and financial services from their local branch. Today, however, the management of accounts and decision-making on loans has been transferred to 'virtual call centres'. Hundreds of local branches have closed, and the rest have become either shopfronts for organizations whose real activities are based many miles away, or geared to selling new financial products.

Funding to support these research projects was obtained from a variety of sources. One of the earliest was co-funded by a bank and a company which supplies technology and 'business solutions' to banks (and initially developed because a member of the research team happened to know someone who worked in a bank). Harper et al. describe the objectives of this project in the following terms:

> Our task . . . was specified by both sides and that was to provide an insight into the culture, working patterns and problems of the bank during a period when it was undergoing radical change – and indeed the pace of such change was expected to increase in the future. The goal was to share ethnographic insights with the supplier and use these as a basis for deepening relations between the two organizations. It was understood that the findings would be of a research nature, intended to act as reminders of features of bank practice to bank staff themselves, and understanding of the inner world of banks that the supplier would not ordinarily have access to. It was recognized also that a considerable added value for the ethnography would be to provide richer, more comprehensive understandings of bank processes than would be generated by the supplier's own analysis techniques. (2000, p. 72)

Later projects were jointly funded by the bank and the 'Virtual Society?' programme of the Economic and Social Research Council. The result was that one fieldworker was able to spend five years of almost continuous fieldwork, documenting the effects of technological and organizational change in a large high street bank.

The findings made by this research team are similar to Bowers et al.'s study of the printing industry in that they demonstrate the difficulties that arise in organizational and technological change, and the longitudinal nature of the study reveals how managers and workers worked through a whole range of minor and major problems over time. One issue the bank had to contend with is that knowledge about customers had previously been of an informal character, shared by teams of cashiers and local managers who knew their customers well. When work was transferred to the call centre, each worker had to develop a knowledge of the account, often in the course of a telephone enquiry, through interpreting the information available on a screen. This created interactional difficulties and a reduction of levels of service for some customers, although in other cases the fact that full information about the history of an account was immediately to hand meant that workers were able to handle some queries more effectively than cashiers drawing on their local knowledge in a branch.

A related issue which greatly concerned managers was how to ensure a standardized way of assessing risk. The new technology made it possible, at least in theory, for computer software programs to make decisions on loans, or take action when accounts went into the red. Harper et al. (2000), however, suggest that, although these provided a useful tool, in the end discretionary judgement was always necessary in managing accounts. Computers were not always able to recognize risky situations, or to know when customers should be given some leeway in, for example, rectifying an under-payment. Moreover, accessing and interpreting this information required teamwork, not least in working out how to access the right information from the computer system. Although it has been suggested that a lot of routine clerical work can be replaced by computers, this study suggests that human judgement, and local knowledge, will always be required in dealing with customers, whether the service is provided by tellers, virtual call centres or over the internet.

Another theme which is developed in this study, which is worth mentioning since it could form the basis of an undergraduate project in a different setting, are the difficulties experienced by banks in using new technology. These arose because companies usually 'bolt on' additional pieces of software to existing systems, rather than investing in new packages. The result was that the systems developed all kinds of minor faults, and users had to learn how to work around problems created by programs which had become outdated due to organizational changes in the bank. The most spectacular example of this, which was probably an apocryphal story told by managers to dramatize the difficulties they experienced on a regular basis, was a 'phantom branch', which had been closed some years ago, but remained open as far as the computer was concerned, because no one had found a way of removing it without damaging other records (2000, p. 146).

Some practical issues

Ethnomethodological research usually involves making a greater demand on the people you wish to study than the other qualitative traditions reviewed in this book. One cannot, for example, learn very much about the content of everyday work activities simply by interviewing practitioners. Nor is it possible to learn very much by observing someone, for example, spending a day inputting data into a computer. To understand what people do at work requires being able both to observe their activities, and to interview them at length and repeatedly about how they understand their day-to-day tasks. Garfinkel goes further than this by calling on researchers to become practitioners in the areas of work they wish to address as sociologists (what he calls the 'unique adequacy requirement of methods'). From this perspective, you can only adequately describe work in a particular occupational setting if you are already a competent member.

This makes it difficult for an undergraduate to pursue this kind of qualitative research, although there may be opportunities to use your own experience of serving in a bar, or doing other kinds of part-time work. Students on placements may have access to more technical activities – for example, how social workers or probation officers make decisions. In either case, a lot will depend upon whether you can obtain permission from relevant gatekeepers, and co-operation from practitioners, in recording details of the work. You may need, for example, permission to tape-record talk at work, or to video activities like serving behind a bar, or the co-ordination of activities in a fast-food restaurant. In my experience, however, most professionals are interested in research that attempts to describe and understand their everyday tasks and problems. You can also achieve a great deal with very little data – for example, examining what takes place in one or two episodes.

One criteria of adequacy in this kind of research is the extent to which you are able to describe everyday activities, in a way that preserves what is involved in doing a particular task in real time in a particular occupational setting. One thing you may notice is that it is harder than it might first appear to describe the world around you. You can, however, develop your own abilities as an ethnographer by reading previous studies. These also illustrate how it is possible to describe occupational activities in a way that addresses questions of interest to public and private sector institutions.

Although I have focused on studies which have practical applications in public and private sector institutions, there is also a wider range of topics that you can address that are just as interesting, and could form the basis of a sociology project. Anyone who is musical could, for example, take up Garfinkel's complaint that Howard Becker's study of jazz musicians tells us nothing about the playing of jazz, by investigating what is involved in making music. A good source here would be David Sudnow's (1978) *Ways of the Hand*, which is a phenomenological account of how he learnt to play improvised jazz piano, drawing on the writings of Garfinkel and the phenomenological philosopher Maurice Merleau-Ponty. You could adopt a similar approach in investigating a sport or hobby. Students supervised by Garfinkel in the 1970s have attempted to describe what is involved in becoming competent at basketball, or in obtaining insight from studying with a Zen Buddhist master. You could also conduct an observational study of something as apparently simple as how people wait in line (Livingston 1987, Chapter 2), negotiate their way through traffic (Lynch 1993, pp. 154–8) or walk along a street (Ryove and Schenkein 1974).

You can treat any of these topics as a means of developing your observational skills, without becoming too concerned about theoretical and methodological issues. However, a good undergraduate project should always include a review of relevant literature, a discussion of ethnomethodology as a research tradition, and the problems experienced in collecting data. There should also be some discussion of the implications of your findings for other studies about the same phenomenon. The whole point of ethnomethodology is to appreciate mundane phenomena which are taken for granted or ignored by other sociological approaches: this is the central theoretical argument. Although undergraduates (and not just undergraduates) often find it difficult to produce a theoretically informed piece of analysis, a good way to begin is simply by building a strong argument in support of the theory you are using into the way you introduce the topic, and present your research findings.

Further reading

For general introductions to ethnomethodology

Cuff, E.C., Sharrock, W.W. and Francis, D. (1998) *Perspectives in Sociology*, 4th edn. Routledge, London, Chapter 7.
Heritage, J. (1984) *Garfinkel and Ethnomethodology*. Polity, Cambridge.
Livingston, E. (1987) *Making Sense of Ethnomethodology*. Routledge, London.

For discussion of work as a topic

Sharrock, W.W. and Anderson, R.J. (1986) *The Ethnomethodologists*. Ellis Horwood, Chichester, Chapter 6.
Travers, M. (1997) *The Reality of Law*. Ashgate, Aldershot, Chapters 2 and 3.

For more studies of public sector institutions

Cicourel, A. and Kitsuse, J. (1963) *The Educational Decision-Makers*. Bobbs-Merrill, Indianapolis.
Meehan, A.J. (1997) 'Record-keeping practices in the policing of juveniles', in M. Travers and J. Manzo (eds), *Law in Action: Ethnomethodological and Conversation Analytic Approaches to Law*. Ashgate, Aldershot, pp. 183–208.

For more studies of private sector institutions

Engestrom, Y. and Middleton, D. (1996) *Cognition at Work*. Cambridge University Press, Cambridge.
Harper, R. (1998) *Inside the IMF*. Academic Press, London.

EXERCISES

1 Write a proposal for conducting an ethnomethodological study about occupational practice in any setting that interests you.
2 Write an ethnomethodological analysis about the practice of either
   (a) researching and writing an essay; or
   (b) any technical activity in which you are recognized as a 'competent member' (for example, serving in a bar or restaurant, performing in a play, participating in a sport).

You should be trying to preserve technical details of the activity, and how it is done in 'real time'. How is 'competence' displayed and recognized in the activity?

5

Researching Language: Conversation Analysis

Easily the most important development in the history of qualitative research in the last thirty years has been the invention of cheap, portable devices that make it possible to make audio- and video-recordings of interaction in everyday and institutional settings. Ethnographers in the first and second Chicago Schools had to rely on memory or notes made in the field when writing about different social worlds (see Chapter 2). Today, the tape-recorder not only makes it possible to record interviews, but opens up a whole new way of collecting data and representing social life on the printed page. It has also made it possible for a new inter-disciplinary field to develop, known as discourse analysis, which is one of the big growth areas in the contemporary academy.

One of the most successful and influential traditions which has capitalized on the opportunities made possible by the tape-recorder is conversation analysis (often abbreviated to CA), a subfield of ethno-methodology which has developed into a discipline in its own right. This chapter will introduce some of the work pursued in this tradition, and the related field of membership categorization analysis. It also suggests some ways in which you could conduct a student project based on collecting and analysing talk, or documents such as newspaper articles.

Conversation analysis as a research tradition

The source and continuing inspiration for conversation analysis are the lectures given by Harvey Sacks while he was teaching at the University of California at Irvine between 1963 and 1975. Sacks died at the age of forty when he lost control of his car, possibly due to the influence of marijuana, although the most likely explanation is that he was simply a careless driver. The lectures were tape-recorded and transcribed by Gail Jefferson, a student at Irvine, and mailed in a kind of correspondence course to sociologists and sociolinguists who had become interested in Sacks's ideas. They were only published in 1992, which partly reflects the fact that it has taken some time for conversation analysis to become recognized as a useful and 'respectable' research method. In sociology, where many still have a Durkheimian preference for dealing with macro-phenomena, studying fragments of talk is still sometimes considered to be rather a trivial pursuit.

Harvey Sacks's interest in language

Language is something we largely take for granted as a feature of the social world, and it is not usually treated as a topic or a problem in disciplines like sociology and psychology, or applied disciplines like education, medicine and criminology. Sacks had an ethnomethodological interest in language: he viewed it as a central part of the common-sense methods we use in making sense of the world around us and displaying the meaning of our actions. Sacks, however, went further than Garfinkel in explicating how language worked. He did this by focusing on the methods and procedures used to accomplish everyday conversation. He also identified a set of methods which members employed in producing descriptions about the world. These have subsequently developed into the traditions of conversation analysis and membership categorization analysis.

Sacks believed that one can only develop a truly scientific approach to studying society (in the sense of making observations which can be checked out, and replicated, by other researchers) through studying tape-recordings of conversations. He was critical of the way in which sociologists usually employ 'hypotheticalized, proposedly typicalized versions of the world as a basis for theorizing about it':

> Often enough in sociological reports, somebody will say, 'Let us suppose that such and such happened,' or, 'Typical things that happen are . . .'. Now a reader finds himself perfectly willing to grant that such things happen. On the basis of assertions, suppositions, proposals about what is typical, some explanation about the world is built. (1984, p. 25)

Sacks felt that it was necessary to go beyond what 'an audience of professionals can accept as reasonable', by addressing 'the kind of things that actually occur'. He believed that one could make most progress in establishing sociology as a science by making observations about tape-recorded conversations:

> I figured that sociology could not be an actual science unless it was able to handle the details of actual events, handle them formally, and in the first instance be informative about them in the direct ways in which the primitive sciences tend to be informative – that is, that anyone else can go and see whether what was said is so. And that is a tremendous control on seeing whether one is learning anything. (1984, p. 26)

This commitment to building a scientific discipline, which can make cumulative discoveries about language, explains why some conversation analysts have been critical of ethnography as a research method. Sacks admired the carefully documented studies produced by Chicago School ethnographers about different social worlds. There is, however, usually no way of checking out or verifying the account supplied about a particular setting or social group in these studies. By contrast, tape-recordings could be made available to other researchers, and the transcripts published as part of research reports.

The development of a scientific discipline

Over the last twenty years conversation analysis has grown from a subfield of ethnomethodology, on the margins of social science, to a large and growing inter-disciplinary field. In a similar way to grounded theory, one can argue that it has been successful in attaining credibility, and obtaining research funding, because it is viewed as a scientific means of collecting and analysing data. If one compares each of these traditions with the ethnographic tradition in symbolic interactionism discussed in Chapter 2, it will be apparent that they each offer a systematic way of collecting data through procedures like the 'constant comparative method' and analytic induction. This is not entirely the whole story, since there is still a tension within conversation analysis between positivists and interpretivists, because it has grown out of the decidedly anti-positivist tradition of ethnomethodology (for an interpretivist critique, see Lynch and Bogen 1994). Most practitioners, however, are comfortable with the idea that it should be viewed as an emerging science.

The best known conversation analyst today is Emanuel Schegloff, who is also Sacks's literary executor, and has developed and applied his ideas at the University of California in Los Angeles. Schegloff is, however, only one member of a large and growing international group of scholars practicising and teaching this research method in different academic disciplines. These include Anita Pomerantz, George Psathas, Don Zimmerman, Doug Maynard, Deirdre Boden, John Heritage, Jorg Bergman, Paul Drew, David Silverman, Rod Watson and Anssi Perakyla. During the 1970s, a large number of studies were published investigating everyday conversation building on Sacks's observations in the lectures, mainly in language journals such as *Language* or in edited collections. Since then there has been a shift towards studying talk in institutional settings, such as the interaction between doctors and patients, or teachers and pupils, or in specialized forms of communication such as human–computer interaction. Some of these studies have been funded by organizations and companies which have a practical interest in improving professional practice, or designing better software. This kind of research has been published in a wider range of journals including *The International Journal of Pragmatics, Discourse Processes, Text, Discourse and Society* and *Research on Language and Social Interaction* (which is worth consulting for specialist debates about methodological issues).

Studies of everyday conversation

The basic methodological procedure in conversation analysis is to identify structural regularities or patterns in conversation (what Atkinson and Heritage 1984 call 'structures of interaction') and then to identify the methods used by conversationalists to produce these regularities. Through using this method, analysts have built up a progressively detailed, cumulative understanding of ordinary conversation. In this section, I will talk about some general findings conversation analysts have made about everyday conversation (as opposed to talk in institutional or occupational settings), and illustrate some methodological issues with reference to two case studies: Anita Pomerantz's (1988) study of 'candidate answers'; and Candace West and Don Zimmerman's (1997) work on gender differences in conversation.

Explaining 'structures of interaction'

The best known studies by conversation analysts have been concerned with explaining 'structures of interaction' in everyday conversation. A good example is the paper co-authored by Sacks, Schegloff and Jefferson (1974) which identifies a 'mechanism' or set of rules which explains why people talk in orderly turns, with very few occasions of overlapping speech. This is an obvious feature of conversation, that we take for granted. The paper demonstrates, however, that it only happens because we are continually monitoring what other people are saying, and employing a shared set of rules as a cultural resource that allows us to engage in conversation. The paper shows, for example, that there are certain points when one can legitimately start talking, such as when a speaker finishes a sentence, and leaves an opening for someone else to have the next turn in the conversation. When overlapping speech does occur, one party quickly drops out.

Although turn-taking might seem obvious or trivial, it is very much at the heart of conversation analysis as a discipline. People do take turns to talk, and in doing so they respond to what was said in the previous turn. This makes it possible to identify sequences of conversational actions, such as the fact that answers usually follow questions. A whole body of conversation analytic work has identified 'adjacency pairs' of conversational actions (for example, 'question'–'answer', 'invitation'–'response', 'greeting'–'return greeting') in which the first action produces an obligation to reply with the appropriate second part of the pair. This usually happens in the next turn of talk, but it is also possible to delay the response. However, in the end, the second part of the pair has to be produced, or a negative inference may be drawn about a failure to answer a question.

There are a number of other structural regularities one can find in any short piece of conversation, which have been extensively documented in conversation analytic studies, along with the methods used by conversationalists to produce these structures. These include the procedures which people use to 'repair' or correct mistakes and misunderstandings (for example, Schegloff 1987a), demonstrate a 'preference for agreement' (Sacks 1987), respond to compliments (Pomerantz 1978), and obtain permission to tell stories (Sacks 1972).

The standard procedure in these studies is to identify a structural regularity by looking at a few examples of conversation, and then to develop the analysis by collecting a larger corpus of materials about the same phenomenon. The best example of this is Emanuel Schegloff's (1968) work on the opening of telephone calls. Schegloff developed an initial understanding of a structure that explained how people answered calls in terms of the rule 'answerer speaks first'. He later came across a telephone call (the 500th call) where the caller spoke first, after there was a short pause by the person answering the phone. Rather than simply explaining this as a deviant case, he came to see the exchange in terms of a 'summons'–'answer' adjacency pair. The ringing telephone acted as a summons which imposes an obligation to supply an answer. In this case, a delay in answering produced a repeat summons, just as a failure to respond to a question can have similar consequences.

It will be apparent that there are some similarities between conversation analysis and grounded theory, since each employs the same method of analytic induction in building an analysis. There are, however, important differences between the two traditions. Conversation analysts work with transcripts produced from tape-recordings, rather than field-work reports, which results in a harder, more scientific form of analysis. On the other hand, notwithstanding Schegloff's study, it could be argued that elaborate techniques of sampling and analytic induction are not usually required in conducting this kind of research. This is because, as Sacks suggests, there 'is order at all points': if you tape-record any conversation, anywhere, you will find the same structures and regularities. Sacks himself made most of the discoveries that have been made about conversation during his lectures through discussing a small collection of transcripts.

Offering a candidate answer

This study by Anita Pomerantz (1988) is a good example of how conversation analysts identify and then explain a 'structure of interaction'. It examines a common device 'used pervasively in our culture' to obtain information, which Pomerantz calls 'offering a candidate answer'.

Pomerantz became interested in this device through 'close and repeated examination of the tapes and transcripts' of six telephone calls made by a 'clerk in a high school attendance office' who was checking up on absent students. She noticed that the clerk often asked questions which incorporated a possible answer: for example, in one call the clerk asked 'Was Arthur home from school ill to:day?' Having identified a possible topic to investigate, she then collected more examples. She obtained some of these by reviewing her own 'collections of tapes of natural interaction' (1988, p. 362). These included tapes of police–suspect interrogations. She also asked her students 'to record instances in their homes', and 'made field-notes of ones that I encountered or overheard' in or around the university campus. She draws on ten illustrations in the paper, of which some are transcripts of tape-recordings and others are extracts from fieldnotes.

The analysis 'explores the shared knowledge and reasoning that participants rely on in using and understanding this method of seeking information' through a careful discussion of this collection of data. Pomerantz begins by noting that when people receive requests for information, they make inferences about the purpose behind the question. She illustrates this with a number of examples, including this short piece of data obtained from her own fieldnotes:

I parked the car and was walking to my office at Temple University. A block away from the building, a truck pulled over and the passenger pointed up the street and asked, 'Is that Temple?' I confirmed that it was. (1988, p. 368)

Pomerantz reports that she assumed that this was a request to get to Temple University, from the fact that 'he was in a car going somewhere' and 'as a member of this culture I know that drivers typically have destinations and that drivers sometimes go to unfamiliar destinations'. The point of discussing this simple exchange in a street is to make us think about the interpretive work involved in responding to a request for information. This is the purpose of the paper: to make us appreciate the range of ways in which people can request information which, in Sacks's words, cannot easily be imagined without repeated examination and comparison of conversational data.

In the next part of the paper, Pomerantz identifies a method which conversationalists can use to 'imply expectations regarding the recipient's knowledge'. Through asking an 'unmarked question', such as 'What time is it?', a speaker implies that the person being addressed should know the answer. On the other hand, marking the question, for example by saying 'Would you know . . .', indicates that the recipient is not expected to know the answer. Moreover, you can also display what you know, and want to hear, through offering a candidate answer. Pomerantz shows how these devices were used in combination in the following extract from the recordings made of the school attendance office:

[Med. 6]
(The high school attendance clerk called to speak with the mother but the absent student answered. When the clerk was told that the mother was not home, she sought some information regarding the absence from the student.)

Clerk: Well how- have you been home from school i:ll Renee,
        (0.5)
Stud: Yeah
        (2.0)
Clerk: Okay, when was the first day that you were out ill
        (2.2)
Stud: I don't know
Clerk: Well you know how long it's been, couple weeks? or what.
Stud: Yeh

(1988, p. 368)

Pomerantz notes that the clerk starts by asking an unmarked question ('when was the first day that you were out ill'), but when the student failed to respond, she followed with a marked question ('[do] you know') which also incorporates a candidate answer. Pomerantz suggests that the vagueness of the candidate answer, when she had originally asked for a specific date, indicated to the student that she now only had to supply 'an approximation'. She suggests that 'information seekers have [a range of] ways of displaying more or less knowledge and/or uncertainty', which can be studied in everyday or institutional settings.

Gender differences in conversation

One interesting feature of conversation analysis is how findings about conversation have a cumulative character. Pomerantz's analysis of how people design questions depends on a prior body of research about turn-taking and adjacency pairs. This point can also be made about a rather more controversial series of studies which have sought to demonstrate that men dominate or control women, or less contentiously that there are structural differences in the way men and women participate in conversation.

The possibility for overlapping speech was recognized in Sacks et al.'s (1974) paper on turn-taking, but they suggested that there was pressure on each party to drop out in order to maintain an orderly exchange of turns. West and Zimmerman (1997) have built on these findings by suggesting that there are two types of overlapping speech. The first occurs when a speaker adds a 'tag question' or a conjunction after reaching the completion of a sentence or phrase which allows another person to speak:

(T14: 59–60)

B1:   I don't like it at all [but –]
B2:   [You]d on't

(1997, p. 523)

West and Zimmerman contrast this to the following example of overlapping speech:

(T1: 114–115)

A1:   It really sur[prised me becuz-]
A2:   [It's jus' so smo:g]gy . . .

(1997, p. 523)

Here A2 starts speaking before A1 has reached the end of a sentence or phrase that would permit someone else to start speaking. They characterize this as a 'deep interruption' which is a 'violation' of the turn-taking rules, and is a means by which one can maintain control over what is being talked about, and display dominance over others 'in face-to-face interaction'. They also argue that men engage in this second type of interruption far more than women. It is suggested that this reflects, and also helps to maintain, male power over women in a patriarchal society.

To evaluate this argument, you would need to read West and Zimmerman's study, and Sacks et al.'s paper on turn-taking, but you might also want to consult your own experience. You might already feel that men talk more than women, or control the topics covered in a conversation. You might also agree with West (1995) that women make better listeners, and are more skilful at dealing with people than men. This might encourage you to check out and perhaps build on their argument, by collecting and analysing your own corpus of tape-recordings.

The main argument against West and Zimmerman's analysis is that the 'deep interruptions' they identify cannot be distinguished in a strong way from other examples of overlapping talk. Critics have suggested that one can only make strong claims about 'interruptions' if there is evidence in the conversation that people resent being interrupted. This raises an interesting set of issues since one can imagine people who resent the fact that they are continually being interrupted but never complain during a conversation. On the other hand, fierce competition for a turn at talk (here I only have to think of dinner table conversation among my own family) may not always indicate a struggle for interactional dominance. These are empirical questions, and to answer them within this tradition you would have to collect a set of tape-recordings, and develop an argument or analysis through examining the detail of turns at talk.

Studies of institutional interaction

One issue raised by Sacks et al. (1974) was the relationship between everyday conversation and interaction in institutional settings, such as legal hearings, church services or professional–client interviews. They suggested that these could be understood as a range of more restrictive 'turn-taking systems', which resulted from modifications to the relatively open or informal character of turn-taking in everyday conversation. Since then, conversation analysts have adopted two approaches towards the study of institutional talk. Some have pursued this programme by conducting comparative studies of different turn-taking systems. Others have focused on how devices or procedures from everyday conversation (such as offering a candidate answer) are employed for particular purposes in occupational and institutional settings.

The structure of news interviews

This study by John Heritage and David Greatbach (1991) is a good example of the first approach, in that it describes the particular turn-taking arrangements in news interviews. This is among the easier forms of institutional interaction to study, along with radio programmes (see, for example, Hutchby 1992), or publicly televised courtroom hearings in America, because one simply has to record a number of television news programmes. Their data is taken from British television programmes, although they also consider the infamous Bush–Rather interview (which developed into an argument, rather than an interview) as a deviant case.

The basic argument, which is illustrated and refined through discussing a number of extracts, is that turn-taking in interviews differs from ordinary conversation in a number of ways. The main finding (which might lead to the complaint that conversation analysts simply state the obvious) is that the interviewer asks the questions, and the interviewee answers them. The analysis is, however, considerably more subtle and insightful than this. To begin with the authors show how this is a 'normative' feature of interviews, which is particularly evident in multi-party interviews in which interviewees sometimes ask permission to ask a question to another interviewee. They also show the kind of difficulties created, and the strenuous efforts of the interviewer to restore the normal turn-taking system when an interviewee tries to ask a question (which is usually an attempt to criticize the journalist or the television programme).

The question–answer sequences in interviews are produced by the fact that interviewees allow the interviewer to construct a 'compound' question, and interviewers allow interviewees to talk at length, whereas in everyday conversation questions and answers are usually shorter. Heritage and Greatbach give an example of how 'an initial "prefatory" statement (arrow a) establishes a context for a subsequent question (arrow b)':

(W.A.O.: 25.1.79)

IE: a → .hhh *The* (.) price being asked for these
letters is (.) three thousand *pou*::nds.
IE: b → Are you going to be able to *r*aise it,
(0.5)
IR: At the moment it . . .((continues))

(1991, p. 99)

Difficulties arise for interviewers when interviewees object to the 'prefatory' statements before questions. These create interactional difficulties, in that the interviewee has either to retreat, or persist with the question. They also threaten the perceived neutrality of news interviews, which interviewers accomplish by not expressing personal opinions or engaging in 'affiliative work' (for example, by indicating approval or disapproval during the answer given by an interviewee, which is a

feature of ordinary conversation). The following extract from the Bush–
Rather interview illustrates the kind of difficulties that can arise:

(Bush/Rather: 3.00)

Rather:		You have said that y- i f you had know:n:
		you sed th't'f hed known: this was an
		a:rms for hosta ⎡ges swap, .hh that you
Bush:	a →	⎣Yes
Rather:		would have opposed it.=[ ]hhh You've a:lso=
		= ⎡said that- that you did not ⎤ =
Bush:	b →	⎣Exactly. (Many-) May I-⎦
Rather:		= ⎡know:: that you: ⎤
Bush:	c →	⎣May I May I⎦ *answer that.*
Rather:	d →	Tha⎡t wasn't a ques⎤tion.
Bush:	e →	⎣(Th- right ⎦
Rather:	d →	It was ⎡a statement.⎤
Bush:	e →	⎣Yes it was ⎦ a statement, =
		= ⎡an' I'll a:nswer it.= T h e President=⎤
Rather:		⎣Let me ask the question if I may first.⎦
Bush:		=cre*a*ted this progra:m, [ ]hh has testifie-
		er: stated publicly, [ ]hh he di:d no:t think
		it was arms fer hostages.

(1991, p. 128)

Heritage and Greatbach suggest that Bush's interjections at a and b are
unusual features of interviews in themselves, since the talk is produced
for an overhearing audience. In this case, Bush does not allow Rather to
ask a question, but responds to the prefatory statement. They also show
how some interviewers pre-empt this problem by designing potentially
contentious questions as reported speech by a third party (for example,
'Your political opponents say that . . .'). Interviewees are less likely to
create interactional problems in responding to these questions, and the
neutrality of the interview is maintained.

The perspective-display sequence in medical interviews

This study by Doug Maynard (1991) is based on examining tape-
recordings collected at 'clinics specializing in developmental disorders'
in young children, such as 'mental retardation, autism [and] attention
deficit disorder'. A symbolic interactionist approach to this topic might
be to interview doctors about the problems they encounter, and how
they categorize different types of illnesses or patients. Maynard, however, looks at the different interactional strategies used in delivering this
kind of diagnosis to parents. He identifies a general conversational
method or procedure, which he calls 'the perspective-display sequence',
and then examines how it is used in this particular occupational setting.

The 'perspective-display sequence' is something you can find in everyday conversation, and involves getting somebody 'to display an attitude or perspective' (1991, p. 167) about some topic, before you give your own opinion. You might, for example, have observed this occur, or used it yourself in sounding out someone's opinion before expressing your own views about a film or political event. Maynard supplies the following example from his own collection of conversational materials:

15.092

A: So what do you thi::nk about the bicycles on campus?
B: I think they're terrible
A: Sure is about a mil:lion of 'em

(1991, p. 167)

Maynard found that doctors employed the same device in delivering diagnoses to parents. They would often invite parents to give their views on their child's condition, before offering a medical diagnosis. This, in itself, may not sound particularly insightful or interesting, but Maynard again goes further by describing in some detail how two different types of 'perspective-display sequence' were regularly used in the clinic. In the first type, doctors 'marked' the invitation for parents to display a perspective by specifically referring to 'a problem as a possession of the queried about child' (1991, p. 169). An example would be asking a parent, 'What do you see as his problem?' In the second type, doctors asked an open or 'unmarked' question, such as 'Now since you've been here, how do you see R now Mrs C?' (these are both simplified examples).

The following is an example of where a doctor began by asking an 'unmarked' invitation (line 1), and then followed this by a 'marked' question (line 17) once this parent had started to talk about the difficulties her child was having at school:

47.001 (Simplified)

1	Dr E →	How's B doing.
2	Mrs M:	Well he's doing uh pretty good you know especially
3		in the school. I explained the teacher what you
4		told me that he might be sent into a special class
5		maybe, that I wasn't sure. And *he* says you know I
6		asks his opinion, an' he says that he was doing
7		pretty good in the school, that he was responding
8		you know in uhm everything that he tells them. Now
9		he thinks that he's not gonna need to be sent to
10		another
11	Dr E:	He doesn't think that he's gonna need to be sent
12	Mrs M:	Yeah that he was catching on a little bit uh more
13		you know like I said I- I- I *know* that he needs a-

14		you know I was 'splaining to her that I'm you know
15		that I know for sure that he needs some special class or
16		something
17	Dr E: →	Wu' whatta you think his problem is
18	Mrs M:	Speech
19	Dr E:	Yeah. yeah his main problem is a- you know a
20		*lang*uage problem
21	Mrs M:	Yeah language

(1991, pp. 174–5)

Maynard notes that the 'marked invitations seem most fitted to convergent views', where the parent already accepted that there was a problem. This was because the doctor could then almost immediately go on to deliver the diagnosis. Unmarked invitations were used when doctors were unsure how parents would react. They did not prevent disagreement, but allowed the diagnosis to be delivered in a gentler way, by allowing the parent to formulate the problem. He also found some cases where doctors delivered their diagnoses in a 'straightforward' way, without employing either version of the perspective-display sequence. He suggests that these may be cases where the doctor knows that the parents will not agree with a diagnosis, and wants to avoid 'any public disagreement' (1991, p. 189).

Some practical applications

It should already be apparent that all the qualitative research traditions reviewed in the first part of this book have practical applications, in the sense of addressing questions of interest to public and private sector organizations as well as academic audiences. This is certainly true of conversation analysis, which has been highly successful in obtaining funding for applied projects. One can see, for example, even from the studies I have summarized, that a careful description of how journalists interview politicians or doctors interview patients could have some value to these occupations, even if only as a means of encouraging practitioners to reflect on their own practices. Similar research has been conducted in law courts, police stations, school classrooms, doctors' surgeries and HIV advice centres. There have even been studies about the interactional difficulties that arise in administering social scientific surveys (Suchman and Jordan 1990).

Few of these studies have been taken up in the public sector, or used systematically in training professionals (probably because organizations like the police or hospitals simply do not have the resources to engage in major initiatives to improve 'customer service'). There have, however, been some interesting recent developments, in which occupational groups as varied as speech therapists, computer scientists and museum designers have become interested in conversation analysis as a means of obtaining detailed descriptions of interactional phenomena. There is already too much literature to summarize here, but two examples of this applied research which will give some idea of what is happening at the 'cutting edge' of these fields are Lucy Suchman's (1987) work on human–computer interaction, and a preliminary study by Dirk vom Lehn, Christian Heath and Jon Hindmarsh (2000) about interaction in museums.

Improving human–computer interaction

The revolution in information technology that has transformed many aspects of social life in the last thirty years has also resulted in some unexpected opportunities for ethnographers who are interested in describing organizational processes and the uses of technology. The two ethnomethodological studies I reviewed in the last chapter used ethnographic methods to study technological change in a printing company and a large bank. Conversation analysts have conducted similar studies about the introduction of new technology in control rooms on the London Underground, although with more emphasis on the close analysis of audio- and video-recordings of interaction in these settings (Heath and Luff 1996).

The most interesting and distinctive studies by conversation analysts have investigated human–computer interaction as a speech-exchange system. One project has examined the effectiveness of an experimental system which was intended to simulate ordinary conversation in answering queries made by telephone to an airport (Wooffitt et al. 1997). The best known study is by Lucy Suchman (1987) who examined the difficulties users experienced with an 'intelligent' photocopier. This persuaded many computer scientists to adopt an ethnomethodological conception of action as a 'situated' response to current circumstances, rather than viewing it as guided by a rational plan (the model of action in cognitive science).

The machine Suchman studied was a prototype of the copiers one finds in many offices today which display screens instructing people how to proceed (which included pictures of the copier with arrows pointing to relevant parts of the machine). Unlike today's copiers, there was a complicated system for making double-sided copies which required making a master copy in one device, and then putting loose copies in a different part of the machine. The copier was tested by asking pairs of users to talk through the steps they were taking in making copies. Users were often confused by these and other features, mainly because they did not read the initial instructions carefully, and the machine had no way of knowing that they had made a mistake.

Suchman provides a close analysis of these difficulties using a transcription system which was designed to capture not only the talk that took place around the copier, but the manner in which the machine and the user understood what was happening at any point in time. She represented this by the following four columns:

	The user		The machine
Actions not available to the machine	Actions available to the machine	Effects available to the user	Design rationale

(1987, p. 116)

The first column recorded the talk and actions of users (for example, in working out how to open the lid of one device on the machine). The second column recorded what the machine knew the user was doing (for example, by pressing the start button, or opening the lid). The third column recorded what the machine was telling the user through the display (and Suchman reproduces all the displays as part of the study). Finally, the fourth column indicates how the machine understood what was taking place when, for example, someone pressed a button, which was built into its programming.

The analysis itself is difficult to reproduce without providing a lot more data (including the displays), but what Suchman effectively shows is that the computer was unable to remedy or 'repair' errors made by users, since it could only see the user's behaviour and reasoning procedures through the 'keyhole' provided by its limited sensory equipment. She argues, provocatively, that computer designers need to develop machines that incorporate more 'diagnostic and interactional abilities' (1987, p. 184). This has yet to occur, which will be evident to anyone who has tried to use the 'help' facilities on word-processing packages, or operate a video-recorder, either because this is technically impossible or, one suspects, because there is too little commercial incentive for large corporations to produce perfect products.

Interaction in galleries and museums

Another technical discipline which has become interested in conversation analysis is the new field of visitor studies, which examines the behaviour of people in art galleries and museums. This has developed, particularly in North America, as more emphasis has been placed on improving the quality of exhibits and the experience of visitors. Most of the studies in this literature employ quantitative techniques in, for example, counting the length of time people spend looking at particular exhibits. However, one team of conversation analysts at King's College, London have also made a contribution by examining how people interact through analysing video-recordings made in museums (vom Lehn et al. 2000).

Although most conversation analytic research is concerned with the analysis of audio-recordings, there have also been some attempts to develop transcription systems that can deal with visual features of interaction (Heath 1997). These have so far been limited to representing the direction of gaze alongside a transcript, and showing how it is co-ordinated with talk. There have also been studies which capture how people working in police stations or other service industries respond to telephone queries, through tape-recording the talk and analysing this alongside a video-recording of the information they called up on a computer screen.

Relatively few studies have looked at visual phenomena that are unrelated to talk (although, see the pioneering work of Ray Birdwhistell 1970). One reason for this may be that, notwithstanding the possibilities offered by the world wide web, it is considerably more difficult to record such phenomena as gaze, body language, facial expressions and the like, and publish this data for academic purposes, than everyday or institutional conversation. For one thing, it is more difficult to anonymize data, which is often the first assurance a researcher gives when seeking permission to tape-record conversations. Heath and his colleagues solved this problem in the case of museums by setting up their equipment next to posters describing their objectives, and offering anyone viewing exhibits the opportunity to have the videotape wiped if anything embarrassing occurred, which presumably could include a family argument, or the exposure of an extra-marital affair. A member of the research team was present at all times by the cameras to field queries.

The study itself was designed to record interactional activities taking place near exhibits in order to develop some preliminary research questions or themes that might be relevant to the practical concerns of the people who design galleries and museums. They discovered, for example, that when people stop by a particular painting in a gallery, they do not immediately look at that item, but their eyes glance to the paintings on either side. This is an interesting finding because some behavioural psychologists have conceptualized the effectiveness of an exhibit in terms of its 'stopping power' (which has implications for how one might wish to arrange a set of paintings in a gallery). Although I have not reproduced the three video stills here, the following passage illustrates the kind of observations one can make from looking at something as apparently simple as someone stopping to look at an exhibit:

'Stopping', in this example, is characterized through the position of the man's body in regard to the wall – he turns his lower limbs towards the wall so that his upper body faces the prints. This is the stage at which one might conventionally begin to measure the 'stopping power' or 'holding power' of the exhibit. However, it is apparent from Images 1.4–1.6 that the print directly before him does not solely hold his attention, as we might imagine. Although Image 1.4 shows the man gazing directly at the image opposite him, a moment later he turns from the print, and looks towards the prints on his right (Image 1.5). He once again turns to the left to once again glance at the prints he has passed (Image 1.6). (vom Lehn et al. 2000, p. 113)

How this visitor 'assembles a context' for viewing this particular exhibit is not available from the video-recording (and might also be difficult to obtain by interviewing people on how they choose which items to look at in art galleries). One can, however, see from this study how close observation of what people do in galleries, including how they interact with other visitors, can generate interesting findings. There is no indication, from this particular paper, that what they discovered led to any changes in the way exhibits were displayed in these galleries and museums. The authors do suggest, however, that the 'detailed analysis of sequences of video' afford 'deeper insights into how visitors manage their experiences of exhibits' than relying solely on quantitative measures, such as the length of time people stand by a painting. This is something you might be able to pursue, even without using video-recordings, through observing the length of time people spend in front of different exhibits, and what they appear to be doing.

Membership categorization analysis

Sacks's interest in language was not confined to the methods and procedures used in conversation. Many of his lectures also develop a set of intriguing observations about how people use language in describing the world. Relatively few people have tried to develop and apply these ideas, which can be compared with the large programme of research conducted about the structure and organization of conversation. There is, however, a growing recognition that this second approach can be used in combination with conversation analysis, and offers a powerful means of studying any social setting in its own right.

Language as a cultural resource

Language is something we take for granted much of the time as the medium through which we communicate, in the same way as fish are unaware of water. Sacks, as an ethnomethodologist, wanted us to become aware of how language works. He did so, in characteristic fashion, by spending a long time analysing an inconsequential piece of text, the opening of a children's story which read, 'The baby cried. The Mommy picked it up' (Sacks 1992). The question that interested Sacks was how any reader could immediately hear that the baby was the baby of this mother.

The mechanism that allows us to do this, according to Sacks, is that we understand people, events and objects in the world as belonging to collections of categories, which he calls membership categorization devices: so a baby belongs to the collection 'family' ('baby', 'mother', 'father', etc.). Once a category is introduced from a collection, then we expect subsequent categories to belong to the same collection. We know how to assign categories to collections (in this case, we know that the baby is a young child) because we associate them with certain actions or characteristics (babies cry, and mommies pick them up). Moreover, we can also make sense of the two sentences, because a set of moral rights and obligations is built into the two categories. They form what Sacks terms a 'standardized relational pair' in the same way as other pairs in the same collection such as 'husband' and 'wife'. We *expect* mothers to pick up crying babies.

The cultural knowledge we employ in reading the opening of this children's story represents only a tiny portion of the cultural knowledge we are using all the time. Membership categorization analysis invites you to look at the world ethnomethodologically by reflecting on your own cultural knowledge, and the interpretive procedures through which it is applied, as you encounter different events or objects in the world. It can also be used to study how social actors employ membership categories in written and spoken discourse. Two examples, each of which focus on the moral rights and obligations built into membership categories, are John Lee's (1984) analysis of a newspaper headline about a gang rape, and Rod Watson's (1997b) work on murder interrogations.

Reading a newspaper headline

This study by John Lee (1984) adopts a similar approach to Sacks in examining the interpretive work involved in reading the following nine word headline which attracted his attention when reading a newspaper:

Girl Guide Aged 14 Raped at Hell's Angels Convention

Lee begins by noting that when he saw this headline, he expected that the story would be about a horrific rape perpetrated by a Hell's Angel. This was, of course, exactly what the story was about, but what interested him about the headline as an ethnomethodologist was how he understood it immediately and 'unproblematically' in this way.

Employing membership categorization analysis, he notes that the collection 'parties to a rape' is formed by 'two morally contrastive categories – innocent victims and evil-doers'. The evil-doer in this story belongs to a membership category that is 'conventionally' associated with evil acts. The headline does not need to say that the rape was committed by a Hells' Angel, because we can use this cultural knowledge to work out what has happened. Lee, however, suggests that it allows us to infer more than this:

Had the story read – raped at Labour Party Convention – then I would not necessarily have concluded that the rape had been committed by a member of the Labour Party or a delegate to the convention, and I would certainly not have concluded that it even might have been a rape which the delegates gave official support to. I would have been more inclined to think of dirty work done in hotel bedrooms, possibly by interlopers. Strangely, I do not think this way with respect to a Hell's Angels Convention. My knowledge of Hell's Angels and my knowledge of conventional beliefs about Hell's Angels suggests to me that they are not simply evil-doers but officially evil-doers and that they are self-proclaimed as such, so that a Hell's Angels Convention unlike a Labour Party Convention might have evil as its official business. This knowledge armed me with the possibility that this might not be just a Hell's Angel rape but a particularly loathsome and degrading public occasion which might have the most severe consequences for the girl. (1984, p. 71)

The other side of the pair 'parties to a rape' requires an innocent victim, and Lee suggests that journalists need to characterize 'the victim as properly both innocent and a victim', in writing a story about the 'harrowing or nightmare-like experience of being raped'. In this case, the victim was a 'Girl Guide', a category associated with 'such notions as innocence and helpfulness' (1984, p. 72). However, just in case the reader might be cynical about the attributes conventionally associated with Girl Guides, the journalist also added the description 'aged 14'. Since the category 'youth' is also bound to qualities like 'innocence and naivety', this makes it even more likely that the reader will view her as an innocent victim.

Membership categories in murder interrogations

The same techniques used by Lee in examining a newspaper headline can be used to investigate language use in newspaper articles and government reports. They can also be used, in combination with analytic resources from conversation analysis and ethnomethodology, in studying spoken discourse. A good example is Rod Watson's (1997b) work on how categories are employed in murder interrogations.

Watson examines extracts from interviews with murder suspects in America. He begins by noting that the use of a single category by suspects, such as 'nigger' or 'faggot', in describing the victim is enough to provide any member of our society with an understanding of the motive behind the offence. An example can be found in this extract from an interview with a white male accused of killing a black male:

```
1    P:    Why did you shoot at this G. . .
2    S:    He's a nigger
3    P:    Did you eh were you alone when you er shot him?
```

(1997b, p. 92)

Watson's interest as an ethnomethodologist lies in explicating the cultural knowledge that allows us to infer immediately that the motive for the offence was racial prejudice even when one 'is not explicitly provided' (1997b, p. 80). The term 'nigger' belongs to the category 'black people in America' but it is not the only way of describing the members of that group. Watson notes that there can be many 'labels' for a particular membership category:

> The racial category that the suspect labels 'nigger' can also be labelled 'Afro-American', 'Black', 'Coloured person', 'Negro' and so on. Society members have a choice between these various category labels . . . However, it is clear that these labels are not all equivalent; on the contrary they may be seen as ranked on a hierarchy . . . such that 'nigger' might ordinarily count as a downranking or downgrading label and 'Afro-American' an upranking or upgrading label for the category. (1997b, p. 80)

Here we read 'nigger' as a downgrading label, and this makes it possible to see racial prejudice as a motive for the offence. Watson also notes, however, that how we hear the term depends on our understanding of the context, in this case the interrogation of a white suspect accused of killing a black man. In other situations, the term 'nigger' can have a very different meaning:

> if the speaker is not white but is *also* categorized as a black person, and he calls some other black person a 'nigger', then the term may not necessarily be a 'put-down'. In some local ghetto cultures in the USA, young male blacks may call each other 'nigger' as an upranking rather than a downgrading label, connoting solidarity, shared category-incumbency and the like. (1997b, p. 82)

A more subtle practice which Watson identifies involves suspects describing the victim's actions in a way which suggests that they were partly to blame for the offence. The newspaper headline analysed by John Lee indicates that a journalist reporting a story about a horrific rape needs to have an innocent victim (in this case a fourteen year old Girl Guide) in order to justify focusing on the experience of the victim. If the person who had been raped had been, for example, a prostitute, or a member of the Hell's Angels herself, then this would have weakened the story, and made it more difficult to obtain a criminal conviction. One example from Watson's data illustrates how suspects also try to shift the blame onto the victim, not by explicitly assigning them to particular categories, but suggesting this in the way they describe their actions. This is an extract from an interview with a male suspect accused of killing a female and then dismembering her:

```
107  P:    all right continue
108  S:    hhhhn I kept walkin:g (.3) and::d (.8) I̲ to̲t to the
109        intersection (.2) orf:B      an      (1.0) when this
```

```
110           girl walked up to me ? (.6) an propositioned me.
111           (1.0)
112    P:     what did she say: exactly te yer L. . .
113    S:     you look like ch tough: guy:: (1.2) y. look like the member
114           of a gan:g:
115           (1.2)
116    S:     I told'er: I'm: not a member of the gan:g:? (.) I'm an
117           independent (.3) °hhh (.4) an: she propositioned me again
118           (1.2)
119    S:     I asked her:: ? (.3) if she'd: like to go to a par:ty, (.5)
120           she said yers: (.) °hh⌈hh
120a   P:                          ⌊What did she as:k actually say to y.ou:
121    S:     °hh⌈hh
122    P:        ⌊ye you can word it(.) use:rr, .(.3)
123           (0.3)
124    S:     she asked me if I would like to get lai:d::
125    P:          (some of the the) words:
126           (1.0)
127    P:     allright
```

(1997b, p. 95)

There are two points of interest about how membership categories are used in this exchange. The first is at lines 113–17 where the suspect describes himself as an 'independent' rather than a 'member of a gang'. Watson suggests that both these are understood by the speakers (and by ourselves as analysts) as belonging to the collection 'types of tough guy' (1997b, p. 83). This is an illustration of Sacks's 'consistency rule' which states that, once a category is introduced, we hear subsequent categories or actions as belonging to the same category (the same principle that allows us to hear that the mommy is the mother of the baby). The category 'gang' has what Sacks calls a 'team-like' quality, so that we expect members of gangs, like families, to stick together, and possibly work together. Watson, therefore, suggests that what is happening here is that the suspect is sensitive towards this possibility, and may be trying to 'avoid implicating others, even if only in the minimal sense of not detracting from the plausibility of the theme of his confession, namely that he committed the offence himself' (1997b, p. 89).

A second interesting feature of this extract is the way in which the suspect describes the victim (see also Wowk 1984). I have already suggested that one way to discredit someone, which happens in murder interrogations, and perhaps more widely in social life, is not to describe them directly as, for example, a 'liar', 'alcoholic' or 'person of low morals' (to give some examples), but to describe their actions so that the listener places them in the category. In this extract, we see at lines 117 and 124 that the victim is described as 'propositioning' the suspect, and 'asking him to get laid', and later in the interview he describes her as 'getting pricky' and throwing beer over him, before he killed her with a punch. Watson notes that these are actions one might associate with the category 'tramp'. Defence lawyers would find it easy to portray the victim in this way (and possibly mitigate the offence) since we normally expect that a woman should 'wait to be asked' rather than 'walking up to a man and propositioning him' (1997b, p. 87).

Doing conversation analytic research

The volume by Paul ten Have (1999) in this series offers a good practical introduction to doing conversation analytic research, and includes sections on the legal and ethical issues involved in tape-recording conversations in everyday and institutional settings, different methods of transcribing, and exercises that will get you started in doing analysis. There is even a helpful section on the practical issues involved in giving conference presentations based on transcripts. He notes, for example, that it is important to give your audience time to read the data before making observations!

Ten Have suggests that the best way of learning conversation analysis is if you join a group of experienced practitioners (which would limit you to studying in a small number of universities in America and Europe). It could be argued that this is the only way of learning how to do conversation analysis at an advanced level, and that it is not sufficient simply to learn about the approach from books, or in a summer school. You can, however, also address a wide range of topics in an undergraduate project in an interesting way by developing a sensitivity towards language. The following comments are intended to supplement specialist texts by addressing some of the practical issues that might arise in an undergraduate project.

Collecting, transcribing and analysing data

It is often easier to conduct a conversation analytic study than to do a fieldwork study, since all that is required is to obtain a small corpus of tape-recordings. If you are fortunate enough to know someone working in an institutional setting, and they are willing to support this kind of research, all you might require is one or two tape-recordings of an interview or a meeting. You can also build up a corpus of data by tape-recording friends (for example, if you are interested in studying interruptions).

You should, however, expect to spend a lot of time in transcribing your data, and reading previous studies which will allow you to develop an appreciation for what is happening in your own data. The quickest way of teaching beginners how to transcribe, when they do not have access to a research group, is play a tape-recording of data which has already been transcribed, so that it is possible to relate the symbols and notation used by conversation analysts to what one hears on the tape.

There is, however, no short way of learning how to do an analysis. Ten Have proposes a systematic method for exploring any conversational materials, by making students describe features like turn-taking and adjacency pairs. The objective of this kind of exercise is, however, simply to make you think about the data: what analysis you develop will depend on your skills in applying concepts and resources from the literature to your own materials. A 'single case analysis' involves examining one transcript in detail (for example, Schegloff 1987b). You can also develop an observation into a research question that could be explored if you collected more data, using the constant comparative method employed by grounded theory researchers and conversation analysts.

Doing a membership categorization study

There is now a growing literature that employs ideas derived from Harvey Sacks's lectures on membership categorization (Hester and Eglin 1996). You could also use the same approach in designing an undergraduate project. Here the data does not necessarily need to be conversational materials, but could also be from ethnographic observation (every social setting is, after all, organized in terms of different categories of people), or the analysis of texts such as newspaper articles, or even TV commercials. You could, for example, take an episode of a television soap opera, and analyse how the writers are exploiting our shared cultural knowledge about different types of people in order to produce a believable plot. To do this kind of analysis well would involve reading and summarizing (and perhaps also critiquing) existing studies, and attempting to apply the basic concepts to a small corpus of data.

Mixing methods: ethnography and discourse analysis

Perhaps the most contentious issue which features in methodological debates between conversation analysts and other research traditions is whether the analysis of tape-recorded conversations should be supplemented by data obtained from ethnographic fieldwork. I will be contrasting the way in which conversation analysts and critical discourse analysts understand the issue of 'context' in the next chapter. For now, however, I want to remain inside the interpretive tradition, and consider the arguments for and against mixing methods.

If you conduct a small ethnography, for example, by spending a few weeks observing and interviewing people in a workplace, it may also be possible to tape-record people talking at work, or at some work-related meeting. In this kind of project, it might seem natural to combine some kind of ethnographic account, perhaps modelled on the symbolic interactionist or ethnomethodological ethnographies reviewed in previous chapters, with a conversation analytic study of language use in that work setting.

This mixing of methods is emphatically rejected by Emanuel Schegloff (1991), and by most conversation analysts (see Nelson 1994; and Ten Have 1999, pp. 53–60). As should be clear from my summary of Sacks's views on conversation analysis as a science, the whole point of this method of analysis lies in confining observations to what can be heard on a tape-recording (or viewed on a videotape). There is a great, and understandable, reluctance to bring into the analysis additional information that has been obtained from ethnographic fieldwork, or from subsequent interviews with the participants in a conversation. This is partly on scientific grounds, since there is no longer a means of checking the analysis against publicly available data, but also because the analytic questions that interest conversation analysts (for example, how turn-taking works) can only be addressed through the close inspection of transcripts.

There are, however, other analysts who believe that knowing something about the cultural or institutional context is either necessary, or helpful, in supplementing the analysis of what can be heard on a tape. The most forceful argument has been made by Michael Moerman (1988) who has conducted anthropological research which combines ethnography and conversational analysis. My own research in the ethnomethodological studies-of-work tradition (Travers 1997) is based on using transcripts to explicate the practical reasoning used in work (which, in my view, can only be understood by conducting ethnographic fieldwork in addition to recording conversations). Finally, Doug Maynard (1984) and Marjorie Goodwin (1990) have demonstrated how it is possible to combine the two approaches in the same study, while respecting their analytic distinctiveness. These debates are, of course, what makes qualitative research interesting at an advanced level, but you could also discuss the relative merits of ethnography and discourse analysis, and the extent to which they can be combined, in an undergraduate dissertation.

Further reading

For general introductions to conversation analysis

Ten Have, P. (1999) *Doing Conversation Analysis: a Practical Guide*. Sage, London.
Hutchby, I. and Wooffitt, R. (1998) *Conversation Analysis: Principles, Practices and Applications*. Polity, Cambridge.
Psathas, G. (1995) *Conversation Analysis: the Study of Talk-in-Interaction*. Sage, London.

For some useful collections

Atkinson, J.M. and Heritage, J. (eds) (1984) *Structures of Social Action: Studies in Conversation Analysis*. Cambridge University Press, Cambridge.

Boden, D. and Zimmerman, D.H. (1991) *Talk and Social Structure: Studies in Ethnomethodology and Conversation Analysis*. Polity, Cambridge.
Drew, P. and Heritage, J. (1992) *Talk at Work: Interaction in Institutional Settings*. Cambridge University Press, Cambridge.

For introductions to membership categorization analysis

Silverman, D. (1998) *Harvey Sacks: Social Science and Conversation Analysis*. Polity, Cambridge, Chapters 5 and 7.
Hester, S. and Eglin, P. (eds) (1996) *Membership Categorization*. University Press of America, Lanham, MD.

EXERCISES

1 This is designed as an exercise for a group of four students. Each should tape-record a ten minute, two party conversation between a man and a woman, and transcribe this using Gail Jefferson's transcription conventions. Pay special attention to cases of overlapping speech.
Identify any instances of interruptions. Does this support or weaken West's (1995) arguments about how men exercise control over women in conversation?

2 The same groups should make and transcribe a tape- or video-recording of ten minute extracts from four news interviews. How do these support or differ from the analysis of turn-taking by Heritage and Greatbach (1991)?

3 Analyse any newspaper story about a crime using membership categorization analysis.

Part II

CRITICAL PERSPECTIVES

One feature of academic life, which we often take for granted, is the way students are required to talk about political and moral issues, and are encouraged to develop their own values as part of their degrees. Many of the young people who obtained posts in the expansion of higher education during the 1960s had progressive political views, or identified with movements pressing for social and political change. The most influential intellectual movement during this period was Marxism, a political philosophy based on the idea that there should be a more equitable distribution of economic resources. Another important movement was feminism, which advocates greater economic and political rights for women.

Since the collapse of communism in the Soviet Union and Eastern Europe in the late 1980s, and the shift to the right by political parties in America and Western Europe, Marxism no longer has much influence in universities. However, the last four decades have also seen the rise of a number of new social movements seeking to change the way our societies are organized, or representing the interests of minority groups. These include the green movement, the gay liberation movement, and groups representing disabled people and ethnic and racial minorities. New developments in social theory, in the form of postmodern and poststructuralist theory, have replaced Marxism as a way of thinking critically about the world, which has had radical implications for qualitative research.

Given this general intellectual climate, it is perhaps unsurprising that ethnography and discourse analysis have also taken a 'critical' turn. There are, for example, Marxist and feminist traditions in ethnography, which draw on techniques from the interpretive traditions reviewed in the first part of this book, but give them a political slant. There have also been a number of traditions in sociolinguistics which have adopted a critical approach towards language use in a variety of social settings.

In conducting or evaluating research in these traditions, it is important to understand how they relate to more general developments and debates in structural-conflict theory. Chapters 6 and 7 will review a range of qualitative studies by Marxist and feminist sociologists and discourse analysts. Chapter 8 will examine the significance of postmodernism and poststructuralism for ethnography and qualitative research.

6

From Description to Critique

CONTENTS

According to Karl Marx, the object of intellectual inquiry was not simply to understand the world, but also to change it. This became the rallying call, and central philosophy, for many radicals who obtained posts in universities during the 1960s. Marxism has, of course, informed and generated all kinds of intellectual activity, ranging from abstract theorizing to quantitative studies about economic inequality. It has also, however, influenced many qualitative researchers in the disciplines of sociology, anthropology and sociolinguistics. This chapter introduces the political and epistemological assumptions of this critical tradition, through discussing a number of well-known studies.

The critical tradition

Although researchers committed to one form or another of radical politics often like to present themselves as battling minorities in a conservative academy, there can be no argument that they have become a powerful force in higher education, and have transformed conceptions of scholarship and the curriculum throughout the social sciences and humanities. Certainly, a good deal of qualitative research is now conducted from a 'critical' perspective. This is published in specialist journals, such as *Critique of Anthropology*, *Discourse and Society* and the new journal *Ethnography*, but has also become part of mainstream work in disciplines like sociology and sociolinguistics. The new inter-disciplinary field of cultural studies, which applies different varieties of critical theory to cultural objects and texts, can also be viewed as a variety of qualitative research, and has, to some extent, transcended the boundary between ethnography and cultural analysis (see, for example, Willis 2000). To understand this body of work it is necessary to know something about the history of radical politics in the academy, and the epistemological assumptions informing empirical research in this tradition.

The academy and dissent

Although most people today would accept the idea that university academics should be involved in promoting political views through their research and teaching, it is worth remembering that this is only a relatively recent development. Universities were generally rather conservative places for much of the twentieth century, and it was only during the 1960s, when there was a large-scale expansion of higher education in America and Western Europe, that large numbers of young people with radical political views obtained academic posts.

The most influential theorist during this period was the nineteenth century thinker and political activist, Karl Marx, who believed that the industrial working class would eventually establish a fairer and more equal society through obtaining political power in a socialist revolution. His ideas had become deeply unfashionable during the 1940s and 1950s but obtained a new lease of life as young people became politically radicalized by the Vietnam War, and by campaigns about a whole range of issues including the arms race, the growing economic divide between the First and Third Worlds, and discrimination against women, homosexuals and racial and ethnic minorities. Marxism had a wide appeal during this period not only because the organized working class was politically important, but also because it is a highly optimistic theory which predicts, as a matter of scientific fact, that there will eventually be a transformation to a better society, in which people will be far happier and more fulfilled than today, and poverty will be eliminated.

Marx believed that there would be a mass uprising of workers in the nineteenth century, protesting against growing unemployment and inequality created by technological change. This has not so far happened in Europe or America, and the socialist revolutions in underdeveloped countries during the twentieth century have been either defeated or tamed by the 'free world', but most thinkers in the Marxist tradition have remained optimistic about the prospects for change, at least in the long run. The most pessimistic variety of Marxism in the 1960s was the 'critical theory' developed by members of the Frankfurt School, a group of left-wing scholars who had fled to America in the 1930s as refugees from Nazi Germany. They believed that a revolution was no longer possible since the working class had become affluent under capitalism. Nevertheless, leading figures such as Herbert Marcuse attracted a huge following among students and critical intellectuals in America, through arguing that most people lived a shallow, one dimensional form of existence, and would be much happier in a different economic and social system. The most influential theorist in the 1970s, Louis Althusser, acknowledged the present stability of capitalism, but believed that it would eventually self-destruct because of systemic internal contradictions. Althusser viewed Marxism as a science (albeit one without much predictive force), whereas the critical theory tradition saw it as an emancipatory movement of a similar nature to psychoanalysis: revolution was not inevitable, but would only happen once people came to the realization that they would be happier living in a different social and economic system.

Marxism has almost disappeared from academic life, following the collapse of the Soviet Union in 1989, in the sense that it is now again deeply unfashionable to be a Marxist, although it lives on in a variety of guises. Two developments have contributed to the death of Marxism, but have also filled the vacuum left as it has declined. The first has been bodies of theory generated by academics committed to new social movements which are based around a single oppressed group or political issue (and which, it has been argued, Marxism cannot adequately address). The largest and most influential of these has been feminism, which like Marxism had been around a long time, but only succeeded in becoming a mass movement during the 1960s. There are now also vocal social movements committed to ending discrimination against homosexuals, disabled people and ethnic and racial minorities. The largest campaigns in the United Kingdom, at least in recent years, have been organized by the green movement, protesting against road-building schemes and genetically modified crop trials.

The second development, which has posed an even greater challenge to Marxism, has been the growth of postmodernism and poststructuralist theory as an alternative way of being critical in the academy, although the extent to which they allow you to be 'critical' is a contentious issue. Poststructuralism is an intellectual movement which has been around for a long time but only took off in universities during the 1980s, when Marxism was in steep decline. The most influential poststructuralist theorist today is arguably Michel Foucault who is often interpreted to be advocating a theory of history not dissimilar to Marxism, in which oppressed groups like prisoners, homosexuals and mental patients are viewed as engaged in acts of resistance against economically dominant groups and state bureaucracies. However, others have argued that this is a fundamentally mistaken view of Foucault, who is a much darker and more pessimistic thinker than Marx, and offers few resources for engaging in progressive or left-wing politics.

Foucault, and other postmodern theorists like Jean Baudrillard, Jacques Derrida and Jean-Jacques Lyotard, arguably pose some serious epistemological problems for critical theory, since they challenge the view that a better way of life (the utopian end of history envisaged by Marx) is even possible. They also question why we have to believe what Marx, rather than anyone else, has to say about social and political issues. Postmodernism and poststructuralism also challenge the idea that one can represent the world unproblematically, and I will be discussing their implications for the practice of ethnography in Chapter 8. It is worth noting, for now, that none of the studies reviewed in this chapter and the next, some of which were written quite recently, are at all troubled by poststructuralism as an intellectual movement (and most of them do not even acknowledge that it exists). The epistemological assumptions that inform most ethnographies and discourse analytic studies published by critical researchers today have not changed substantially since the 1960s.

Critical theory as an epistemology

The key epistemological assumption informing empirical and theoretical work in the critical tradition is that the analyst has a superior insight into the nature of human happiness and well-being, and how to achieve this, than most ordinary members of society. Marx, for example, argued that the bourgeoisie in the nineteenth century not only owned the factories that exploited working people, but also owned or controlled the institutions through which ideas are communicated, such as schools and the mass media. Workers might have been content with their lot, but this was because they had come to believe that inequality was normal and natural, and there was no alternative to capitalism. In reality, they were being exploited economically, and had no control over their own lives. The objective of the critical theorist is to challenge this 'dominant ideology' by suggesting that things can be different, but also by explaining why it is that they come to hold false beliefs. Raymond Geuss explains how this is meant to occur in the following terms:

> A critical theory brings to the agents' awareness unconscious determinants of their own consciousness and behavior in that it points out to them that their own coercive social institutions are 'determining' them (by distorting the communication structure in society) to cling to their ideological world-picture. In the initial state the agents falsely think that they are acting freely in accepting the world-picture and acting on it: the critical theory shows them

that this is not the case by pointing out the social determinants of their consciousness and action of which they were not aware. (1981, p. 70)

Another way of putting this is that a critical theory is meant to free people
from the grip of false ideas by making them aware of the social institutions that have caused them to think in this way. If successful, it will
lead to what Geuss calls 'emancipatory action' (1981, p. 89). Not only will
people become emancipated from false ideas, but they will also act on
those ideas in producing a better world. This will not necessarily be an
uphill task for the critical theorist, since circumstances will arise in which
people become aware that they are being exploited. Marx, for example,
believed that workers would develop class consciousness during periods
of mass unemployment. They can only, however, develop into an effective political force once they understand the reasons why they are
exploited (which is only available from the critical theory) and the action
that must be taken to produce a better world.

This epistemological position is also known as realism (Bhaskar 1978)
and can be contrasted with the other epistemological positions of positivism, interpretivism and poststructuralism which I summarized in
Chapter 1. Realists share Durkheim's belief that sociology should be
concerned with the study of large-scale macro-phenomena, and that it is
possible to obtain a scientific understanding of society and history that is
superior to common-sense knowledge. They are usually highly critical of
interpretive approaches, such as symbolic interactionism and ethnomethodology, for only being concerned with the surface features of
society, and for either serving the interests of economically dominant
groups or not engaging with political or moral issues.

Whereas many interpretivists have been fierce opponents of quantitative methods owing to their opposing epistemological assumptions
(see, for example, Blumer's critique of variable analysis in Chapter 2),
critical theorists have no principled reason to favour quantitative or
qualitative methods. Matters are, in fact, slightly more complicated than
this since many feminists regard surveys and statistical analysis as
instruments of oppression, and I will explain why this is so in the next
chapter. Most commentators influenced by the Marxist tradition have
argued that quantitative and qualitative methods are complementary
(see, for example, Devine and Heath 1999), and can be combined or used
separately in doing critical research.

Ethnography and critique

Although many of those who obtained university posts in the 1960s were
interested in different varieties of critical theory, rather fewer have
conducted studies based on interviews or long periods of ethnographic

fieldwork. The best qualitative studies have been produced by individuals or groups of researchers in the critical tradition who have chosen to specialize in ethnography as a method, such as the Centre for Contemporary Cultural Studies directed by Stuart Hall in Birmingham during the 1970s, or by researchers who have been trained in particular traditions in ethnography and discourse analysis, but have later adapted the methods and techniques used in these fields for political purposes. That said, in Britain, one can think of a number of ethnographic studies, written mainly in the 1970s, in fields like the sociology of education, law and industrial relations, by Marxist sociologists (see, for example, Beynon 1973; Carlen 1976; Hall et al. 1978; Pryce 1979).

The three books I have chosen to discuss in this section employ different methods and techniques in collecting qualitative data, but each is clearly informed by the epistemological assumptions of critical realism. Paul Willis's (1977) *Learning to Labour*, which is still the best known and most widely cited example of critical qualitative research, was written by a British sociologist at the Centre for Contemporary Cultural Studies during the 1970s, when Marxism was still a vigorous and effective political movement. Pierre Bourdieu et al.'s (2000) *The Weight of the World* is a wide-ranging study of how people experience social inequality in France based on ethnographic research and unstructured interviews. The third book, edited by Michael Burawoy and called *Ethnography Unbound* (1991), is a collection of short ethnographies written by post-graduate students who took a seminar with him on participant observation in the late 1980s at the University of California, Berkeley. In each case, I will be focusing on the epistemological assumptions that inform the analysis, and how the ethnography is used to advance a political argument.

Learning to Labour

This British ethnography by Paul Willis (1977) reports the findings of a three year research project funded by the Social Science Research Council during the 1970s. Willis conducted the study by getting to know a group of twelve male youths, whom he calls 'the lads', who were in the same year of a single-sex school located in a working-class estate in the Midlands. He followed them around during their last two years in the school, and when they later entered the workplace, and conducted regular tape-recorded group and individual interviews, as well as getting them to keep diaries. He also interviewed their parents, who were doing manual jobs, about their attitudes towards work and education. The 'lads' all had a dismissive attitude towards school: they saw it as irrelevant to their own lives, and the kind of jobs they would be doing in the future. Willis also got to know two other groups of 'academic' or 'conformist' working-class students in the same year at this school, and three other groups of 'non-conformist' pupils at other schools.

Structurally, this study is distinctive in that it is organized into two parts: an ethnography about schooling, which mainly sides with the lads' view of education; and a theoretical discussion which draws out the implications for 'working class culture in general . . . and the maintenance and reproduction of the social order' (1977, p. vii). Willis notes in a methodological appendix that he has an ambivalent attitude towards ethnography, which 'records a crucial level of experience . . . and insists upon a level of human agency which is persistently overlooked', but at the same time cannot tell the whole truth about the settings it describes. He complains that 'the method is also patronizing and condescending – is it possible to imagine the ethnographic account upwards in a class society?' (1977, p. 194). This point has also been made by other critical sociologists, and it is difficult to dispute that most ethnographic studies have been conducted by middle-class academics for professional audiences about the 'problems' of disadvantaged or deviant groups (see Gouldner 1962).

The ethnography forms the bulk of the study, and is organized into three chapters which start with the lads, but broaden in focus to address the nature of manual work and the role of the careers service in schools. The first chapter conveys a vivid account of the lads' attitude towards schooling, through descriptions of their behaviour, cleverly juxtaposed with extracts from group interviews, and interviews with their teachers and 'conformist' students. Here, for example, is how Willis describes the problems they created in the classroom:

> The lads specialize in a caged resentment which always stops just short of outright confrontation. Settled in a class, as near a group as they can manage, there is a continuous scraping of chairs, a bad-tempered 'tut-tutting' at the simplest request, and a continuous fidgeting about which explores every permutation of sitting or lying on a chair. During private study, some openly show disdain by apparently trying to go to sleep with their head sideways down on the desk, some have their backs to the desk gazing out of the window, or even vacantly at the wall. There is an aimless air of insubordination ready with spurious justification and impossible to nail down. (1977, pp. 12–13)

The anti-school attitude of the lads is also evident from their school reports ('a most uncooperative member of the school . . . hindered by negative attitudes', '[he] could have done well at most subjects, but decided that he did not want to develop this talent to the full'), and from extracts from transcripts of group interviews. The following extract gives a taste of how Willis lets the lads speak in their own words:

PW: What's the last time you've done some writing?
Will: When we done some writing?

Fuzz: Oh are, last time was in careers, 'cos I writ 'yes' on a piece of paper, that broke me heart.
PW: Why did it break your heart?
Fuzz: I mean to write, 'cos I was going to try and go through the term without writing anything. 'Cos since we've cum back, I ain't dun nothing [It was half way through the term].

(1977, p. 27)

In the theoretical discussion that follows the ethnography, Willis develops a Marxist analysis of why the lads did not value schooling. In part, he views their contempt for academic work as a form of resistance against the exploitation of the working class, since they are refusing to go along with the fiction that they will get good jobs by working hard at school. However, he also suggests that in not achieving their full potential, they are allowing themselves to be exploited, which serves the interest of capitalism. One reason for this, according to Willis, is that they value manual work because it has a masculine character which allows them to look down on women (so that sexism is created by, and serves the needs of, capitalism).

My interest, here, is not in the specifics of this argument (which would be harder to make today, when there are far fewer manual jobs), but in how the ethnography as a whole is informed by the epistemological assumptions which underpin any piece of research by a critical theorist. Although Willis argues that the lads are unconsciously resisting capitalism when they do things like play truant or make trouble for 'conforming' pupils, it seems clear that he believes that they have only an imperfect understanding of the structure and history of the class system in British society, and what needs to be done to produce a fairer and more equal society.

A number of critical ethnographies about education in Britain have adopted a similar approach to Willis in conducting group interviews with pupils, and contrasting the perspectives of different official and anti-establishment perspectives inside the school. This has continued to be a lively and vital tradition into the 1990s in that Mairtin Mac an Ghaill (1988; 1994) has recently published two powerful critical ethnographies about the treatment of black and homosexual pupils inside the school (see Devine and Heath 1999 for a discussion of his most recent book). One interesting feature of Mac an Ghaill's work is that he was a teacher in the schools where he conducted the research, and became friendly with small groups of students who had become politicized through being on the receiving end of racism and homophobia. They met regularly at his house, and one gets the impression that he became their mentor (in the manner of the inspirational teachers portrayed in films like *Dead Poets Society* or *The Prime of Miss Jean Brodie*), but also had his own political consciousness raised by the students.

The Weight of the World

One objection that might be made about Willis's study is that it only focuses on a group of pupils in one school, and uses this to make unwarranted generalizations about the experience of the working class. This criticism cannot, however, be made so easily about *The Weight of the World*, a study recently published by Pierre Bourdieu et al. (2000), working with a team of sociologists in France, which is based on thirty-eight interviews over a three year period with people affected by social change across a whole society.

The objective of this study, according to the book jacket, was to examine 'new forms of social suffering that characterize contemporary societies – the suffering of those who are denied the means of acquiring a socially dignified existence, as well as the suffering of those who are poorly adjusted to the rapidly changing condition of their lives'. The interviewees included workers who had recently been made redundant or were coping with technological change, people living in deprived housing estates, and teachers, social workers and police officers coping with the strain of doing public sector jobs. Extracts from the interviews are presented, with introductory commentaries by the sociologists who conducted them, in sections with headings like 'The Shop Steward's World in Disarray' or 'Broken Careers', which can be sampled like short stories or read together as a political statement about inequality and injustice.

Although not everyone might wish to read a 650 page text, you can learn a lot from reading a few of the sections. Each contains an introduction by the sociologist who conducted the interview, and then a lengthy extract from the interview itself, which preserves it as a conversation, and sometimes as an exchange of views and a sharing of common experiences between interviewer and interviewee. What is particularly impressive about this book as a piece of qualitative research is the way it allows the interviewees to speak in their own words through the interviews, so we get a sense of the complexity of their social surroundings, their understanding of social change and politics, their aspirations, their regrets and their fears. In the case of the interviews with professionals we also get a lot of detail about their day-to-day practical concerns. My particular favourites are the interview with a 'building superintendent' in a problem housing project who is thinking of voting for the anti-immigration party of Jean Le Pen (a theme in many left-wing studies is that racism is a by-product of the economic divisions produced by capitalism); and the interview with a teacher who has sacrificed a great deal materially, and personally, by investing everything in her work, only to find that the job now requires her to become a 'social worker' rather than an 'educator', and that her students are only interested in material advancement rather than improving their minds ('The Difference' and 'A Double Life').

What makes this a critical study is not, however, simply the selection of interviews with people adversely affected by social change, but the way it communicates a particular way of thinking critically about the world. The introductions to each section do not simply set the scene, but tell readers how to interpret the interviews, and often challenge the imperfect understandings of the interviewee, contrasting these to the more complete knowledge possessed by the critical theorist. The underlying political argument seems to be that people could be happier in a more equal society, even though they are only half-aware of this in their everyday lives.

Bourdieu's epistemological assumptions are made most explicit in the introduction and conclusion to the book. In the introduction, he expresses the hope that the reader 'will adopt the comprehensive view that the scientific method both requires of and grants to us' by reading the interviews together with the 'theoretical analyses' rather than simply reading 'at random' (Bourdieu et al. 2000, p. 1). In his methodological discussion in the conclusion (which is significantly titled 'Understanding'), he also argues that the objective of the analysis should be to challenge common-sense assumptions that may be shared by both the interviewer and interviewee:

> Social agents do not innately possess a science of what they are and what they do. More precisely, they do not necessarily have access to the core principles of their discontent or their malaise, and, without aiming to mislead, their most spontaneous declarations may express something quite different from what they seem to say. Sociology (and this is what distinguishes it from the science of little learning that opinion polls are) knows it has to find the means to challenge, beginning with the very questions it poses, all the preconstructions, all the pre-suppositions belonging to both the researcher-interviewer and the respondent. (2000, p. 620)

According to Bourdieu, the goal of the critical sociologist should be to see through the 'representations in the press, and above all in television, which are everywhere imposed on the most disadvantaged', and bring interviewees closer to an awareness of the truth, like a psychoanalyst or a 'midwife', in the course of talking to them about their lives (2000, pp. 620–1).

Ethnography Unbound

There have been fewer radical intellectuals in America than in Europe, in the sense of people who have engaged in class politics through academic writing, although sociologists like C. Wright Mills in the 1950s and Alvin Gouldner in the 1960s have made important and vigorous contributions to the critical tradition. Only a few American sociologists with left-wing political views have specialized in conducting qualitative research or ethnography, although there is a vigorous tradition of critical anthropology (see, for example, Nash 1979; Rosaldo 1980; Taussig 1980). One recent exception is a collection published by a group working with Michael Burawoy (1991) over a two year period at the University of California at Berkeley, which contains ethnographies based on fieldwork in a number of settings, including a collective bakery, a government agency helping people infected with the AIDS virus, and a co-operative of Latina domestic workers.

This text is particularly worth reading because it contains a thoughtful and informed essay contrasting symbolic interactionist and ethnomethodological approaches to ethnography with those in the critical tradition of the kind one would never find in a British study, where there is very little dialogue or discussion between these traditions. It also contains some useful discussion about what is practically involved in doing critical research, which I will summarize later in this chapter. None of the contributions necessarily match up to the standard of some of the ethnographies I have discussed elsewhere in this book, either in terms of penetrating the social worlds of the people studied in great depth (as one would expect in symbolic interactionist work), or employing critical theory in a sophisticated way to interpret qualitative data. However, they do again illustrate how it is possible to use an ethnographic report to advance a political message by framing an account of what was observed in the field around a discussion of how critical theorists understand the same issues (the main theorist used in this text is Jürgen Habermas). This can be compared to the similar techniques used in *Learning to Labour* and *The Weight of the World*.

Critical discourse analysis

Relatively few ethnographies (critical or otherwise) are now published, which partly reflects the fact that it has become difficult for sociologists to obtain funding, even in graduate school, to spend long periods of time doing fieldwork. There have, however, been a large number of studies published in the inter-disciplinary field of discourse analysis, which has become one of the fastest growing areas of work in the human sciences. A significant amount of this is by researchers working in the discipline of linguistics, such as Robert Hodge (Murdoch University, Australia), Gunther Kress (University of Technology, Sydney, Australia), Norman Fairclough (University of Lancaster, UK), and Teun A. van Dijk (University of Amsterdam, The Netherlands), although important contributions have also been made by social psychologists such as Michael Billig, Jonathan Potter and Margaret Wetherell (University of Loughborough, UK). Van Dijk edits the journal *Discourse and Society* which mainly publishes critical research.

To understand work in critical discourse analysis (CDA) it is necessary to appreciate how researchers working in different traditions in linguistics are interested in language, and then how they combine these resources with ideas and concepts from critical theory in addressing a range of topics. After discussing some general principles, I will illustrate what the approach involves by discussing two case studies: Norman Fairclough's (1989) analysis of an interview with Margaret Thatcher, and Michael Billig's (1992) study of everyday talk about the British royal family.

Principles of critical discourse analysis

There is no shortage of texts which introduce critical discourse analysis as a subfield of linguistics (see, for example, Cameron et al. 1992; Chouliaraki and Fairclough 1989, 1999; Hodge and Kress 1993; van Dijk 1996). These writers mainly draw upon the Marxist tradition in social theory, and are particularly interested in the relationship between language and ideology (ideas which benefit economically dominant groups in society). The central argument is that language has to be studied from a political perspective, and that researchers working in linguistics can help to emancipate people from false ideas through revealing how language serves the needs of the economically powerful. This message has also been communicated through various editorial statements which have appeared in *Discourse and Society*, including the following 'call to arms' by Norman Fairclough:

> This is a call for co-ordinated action against neo-liberalism on the part of critical language researchers.
>
> What's happening in the contemporary world is that a restructured ('global') form of capitalism is gaining ascendancy. There are winners and there are losers. Amongst the losses: an increasing gap between rich and poor, less security for most people, less democracy, major environmental damage. If markets are not constrained, the results will be disastrous. The political priority is to challenge this new order (which frames other issues, e.g. racism and sexism), and especially the claim that it is inevitable. Language is an important part of the new order. First, because imposing the new order centrally involves the reflexive process of imposing new representations of the world, new discourses; second, because new ways of using language – new genres – are an important part of the new order. So the project of the new order is partly a language project. Correspondingly, the struggle against the new order is partly a struggle over language. (2000a, p. 147)

Left-wing writers like Fairclough are now rather circumspect in citing Marx, and no longer use phrases such as 'class struggle', 'means of production' and 'contradiction between base and superstructure' (one way of using language that certainly has changed in the last twenty years). However, one can still see, even from this short extract, how the basic substance of this nineteenth century political argument remains much the same in the twenty-first century. From a Marxist perspective, the world has always been viewed in terms of a growing gulf between rich and poor, where the mass of workers have little security in times of ceaseless technological change, and there is no real democracy because all the main political parties accept that there is no alternative to free-market economics. This is simply an updated version of the same message, with 'globalization' and 'neo-liberalism' the latest stage of capitalism.

One can see, therefore, that critical discourse analysts have a very different understanding of 'context' to conversation analysts, and the other interpretive traditions I reviewed in the first part of this book. For the critical researcher, context is conceptualized as the workings of society as a whole, and the aim of the analysis is to show how the actions and beliefs of people in particular situations are shaped by wider Durkheimian social structures, which exist separately from individuals. This is often conceptualized in terms of making a distinction between 'micro' and 'macro' levels of society (and some researchers have also argued that particular institutions, such as schools or business organizations, should be viewed as part of an intermediate 'meso' level bridging the two). The interpretive researcher, on the other hand, is only interested in how people understand what they are doing in any social setting, and does not accept that there is a 'macro' level of analysis, or that the analyst knows more about society than the people he or she is studying. These two ways of conceptualizing context cannot be reconciled, so interpretive and critical researchers will always disagree over how they understand language.

As one might expect, critical discourse analysts usually choose texts which communicate an overt or concealed political message, such as the speeches of politicians, or advertisements (which, in this tradition, are viewed as having a key role in reproducing racial and sexual stereotypes, and persuading us to buy products we do not really need or want). Fairclough has become particularly interested in the language of management consultants, which is employed to justify lay-offs and the 'dismantling of "state bureaucracy" and "unaffordable" welfare programmes' (2000a, p. 148). Hodge and Kress (1993) have conducted a similar study about the language used in news reports during the 1991 Gulf War, which in their view secured an ideological as well as an actual military victory for the British–American alliance. More generally, introductions to CDA recommend that any piece of text or talk can be used to advance a political argument. A good example is Chouliaraki and Fairclough's (1999, pp. 38–9) analysis of a short piece of family talk in which a worker complains about the actions of his employers.

The method used to analyse discourse varies, but it usually involves drawing on ideas and resources from linguistic theory, and then linking this to an analysis of the ideological role of the text. In *Language and*

Power, Fairclough (1989, pp. 118–19) recommends a six stage method which involves first describing how language is used, for example by considering evaluative terms or what metaphors are used, and then moving on to what he calls the stages of 'interpretation' and 'explanation'. Interpretation involves moving beyond a surface description and examining the 'discourse type(s)' used by the participants, such as the 'rules, systems or principles of phonology, grammar, sentence construction, vocabulary, semantics and pragmatics', and also the 'schemata, frames and scripts' (1989, p. 162). The most important part of the analysis is, however, the sixth stage of explanation. The objective here is to 'explicate the relations of power and domination, and the ideologies which are built into these assumptions', by developing a sociological analysis of the wider structural context using theoretical resources from the critical tradition.

The discourse of Thatcherism

Fairclough's recent work has included a book (Fairclough 2000b) aimed at a general audience which looks critically at the language of New Labour, a political movement which he believes has won power by making promises through 'empty rhetoric' which it can never realize so long as it accepts economic neo-liberalism (effectively by acknowledging that the state should not intervene to protect people from 'the negative effects of the market'). His best known work was, however, conducted during the 1980s, when he examined the language used by Margaret Thatcher, the Conservative Prime Minister who has done most to promote neo-liberal policies in Britain.

Fairclough took as his data a 127 line extract from a radio interview between Michael Charlton and Margaret Thatcher which was broadcast on BBC Radio 3 on 17 December 1985. Although I do not have the space to include the whole transcript, which also makes it difficult to summarize the analysis, it is worth including a short extract to give the flavour of this encounter. The interview opened with Mrs Thatcher, in characteristically forthright and populist language, responding to a mildly critical question about Britain's economic performance during the 1980s:

```
(1)   MC:   Prime Minister you were at Oxford in the nineteen
            forties and after the war Britain would embark on a
            period of relative prosperity for all the like of which it
            had hardly known but today there are three and a
(5)         quarter million unemployed and e:m
            Britain's economic performance by one measurement
            has fallen to the rank of that of Italy now can you
            imagine yourself back at the University today what
            must seem to be the chances in Britain and the
```

(10)   prospects for all now
    MT: they are very different worlds you're talking about
              because the first thing that struck me very forcibly as
              you were speaking of those days was that now we do
              enjoy a standard of living which was undreamed of
(15)   then and I can remember Rab Butler saying after we
              returned to power in about 1951–52 that if we played
              our cards right the standard of living within twenty-
              five years would be twice as high as it was then and
              em he was just about right and it was remarkable
(20)   because it was something that we had never thought
              of now I don't think now one would necessarily think
              wholly in material terms because really the kind of
              country you want is made up by the strength of its
(25)   people and I think we're returning to my vision of
              Britain as a younger person and I was always brought
              up with the idea look Britain is a country whose
              people think for themselves act for themselves can act
              on their own initiative they don't have to be told
(30)   don't like to be pushed around are self-reliant and
              then over and above that they're always responsible
              for their families.

(Fairclough 1989, pp. 172–3)

Fairclough begins his analysis by examining some of the distinctive
linguistic features of the interview. He notes, for example, that Mrs
Thatcher almost always uses the pronoun 'we' inclusively, in a way
which incorporates those she is addressing (for example, lines 13–14,
'now we do enjoy a standard of living which was undreamed of then').
There is only one example where she uses it exclusively so that it refers
only to the Conservative Party (as it happens it is in this extract at lines
15–17, 'I can remember Rab Butler saying after we returned to power in
about 1951–52 that if we played our cards right'). Fairclough suggests
that this is an effective rhetorical, and ideological, device used by Mrs
Thatcher. It represents everyone 'as being in the same boat' and
'assimilates "the people" to the leader' (1989, p. 182). It is also, in his
view, 'somewhat mystificatory' since the claim that the British people are
better off (the 'we' in lines 13–14) conceals the fact that there are 'gross
disparities' between the standard of living of different groups and
regions in Britain.

In the interpretation stage of the analysis, Fairclough discusses how
Mrs Thatcher employs linguistic resources to address a problem faced by
all political leaders – how to sustain their authority while also 'claiming
solidarity' with the people – and argues that she was uniquely able to do
this as a woman by talking tough but modifying this by including some
features from 'feminine' discourse, such as phrases which give the
impression of 'self-effacement'. An example he gives is where she says at

one point, 'I wonder if perhaps I can answer', rather than interrupting the interviewer more directly (1989, p. 184). In this extract, one could make a similar claim for the way in which she uses the phrase 'I think' in lines 21 and 25, rather than expressing her view of Britain in a more authoritative or masculine manner.

Finally, in the explanation stage, Fairclough examines how Mrs Thatcher's discourse contributes to relations of power in wider society. Here he draws upon the analysis of Thatcherism put forward by neo-Marxist sociologists like Stuart Hall, who characterized it as a form of 'authoritarian populism' which combined an emphasis on law and order with a commitment to the free market, and was highly effective in moving 'the limits of acceptable political action decisively to the right' during the 1980s. Fairclough is particularly interested in the way the language used by Mrs Thatcher maintains the 'economic and political domination' of a 'capitalist class' over 'the working class and other intermediate strata of society' by emphasizing 'solidarity with the people' rather than the authority of the governing class. He argues that this is a concession at the level of discourse because of 'the increase in the capacity of the working class . . . to determine the course of events within capitalism – through the growth of the trade unions, through political representation in Parliament and government via the Labour Party, and so forth' (1989, p. 194). Similarly, he argues that Mrs Thatcher exploited the fact that she was a powerful woman in giving interviews; but her masculine language also demonstrates the way in which women are contained within a society run to serve the economic interests of men.

Talking of the Royal Family

This book by the social psychologist Michael Billig (1992) represents a different way of doing critical discourse analysis in that it examines a large corpus of data, rather than one text in great detail. It is also based on examining sixty-three tape-recorded interviews with families in the East Midlands of England, rather than the language used in newspaper reports or political speeches. The central argument is, however, similar to that of other analysts in the critical tradition in that Billig believes that economically subordinate groups are unwitting victims of ideology which leads them to accept the 'incalculable wealth' enjoyed by the British royal family. He defines ideology as 'ways of talking and thinking that render ordinary people unrebellious and accepting of their lot in life' (1992, pp. 12–13).

Michael Billig is one of those fortunate left-wing academics in Britain who has received generous funding from the Economic and Social Research Council (which must have been persuaded that this study of 'family discourse' would contribute to strengthening British public institutions, despite the fact that Billig is presumably committed to abolishing the royal family). The interviews themselves were conducted by Marie

Kennedy, who was employed as a research assistant, along with three other women who 'performed the difficult, painstaking task of transcribing the tapes' (1992, p. ix). It is interesting to note, in passing, how this has become a standard way of conducting qualitative research in Britain, since the ESRC prefers to support institutions by providing funds to hire research assistants, rather than replacement teaching costs for academics who wish to collect and analyse their own data.

The central problem which interested Billig is why the monarchy continues to receive popular support in Britain, when many other European countries have become republics. Rather than being satisfied with opinion poll findings, or with attitude surveys conducted by some social psychologists, he decided to explore what people thought about the monarchy in more detail, by interviewing a cross-section of families. There was no attempt to obtain a representative sample in the sense of including people with strongly monarchist or republican views (one suspects that there are rather more of the former in Britain). Instead, the research team gained access to a cross-section of ordinary middle-class and working-class families, through approaching people suggested by friends or other interviewees, or by knocking on doors. The interviewer 'sought to spark off discussion amongst the participants, and then, if possible . . . fade into the background' (1992, p. 17).

In analysing the data, Billig starts by critically assessing the arguments used by people when asked to justify why there should be a monarchy. Many interviewees suggested that the monarchy made Britain 'the envy of the world', and had an economic value in promoting tourism. Billig is interested in the fact that people appear to believe this, even though there is little evidential basis for either belief. He is critical of what appears to them as common sense and believes that it conceals the real reason why they support the monarchy, which is 'not being openly admitted' (1992, p. 44): it allows us to feel superior to other nations, and especially America, at a time when Britain is in economic and political decline.

This analysis is developed using concepts from Freud (which again illustrates the attractions of psychoanalysis for critical theorists) who believed that the mutual hostility between neighbouring countries could be explained 'as a means of maintaining the separate identity of each group' (1992, p. 54). Billig characterizes the manner in which the British view America in the following terms:

Monarchy has become a topic in which the ambivalence of the relationship with America can be expressed . . . The Americans are richer and more powerful than 'us'. They can buy anything they want ten times over. But they cannot buy that which they are imagined to desire above all else. They cannot buy 'our' monarchy, 'our' history, 'our' nation. They cannot buy 'us'. In this argumentative turn, the tourist theme has transcended its own rationality. Money is no longer the rational justification, but tourism provides a rational justification beyond rationality. 'We' need the imagined admiration and 'we' need the threat of envy, for these confirm what is 'priceless' beyond the reach of dollars. (1992, p. 53)

Billig also suggests that monarchist ideology helps people to accept the privileges enjoyed by the royal family, through allowing them to reverse their actual social positions. He notes, for example, that members of both 'the poor and modestly middle-class imagine that they are employing the wealthiest family in the land' (1992, p. 115). Another theme in the interviews is that no ordinary person would wish to swop with the royals, because of their lack of freedom from press intrusion. The following passage is a good example of how he contrasts his own superior understanding of society as a critical theorist with the belief of one family that the royals would be envious of their life on a council estate where women were afraid to go out at night because of youths congregating on the street:

> As the mother and her daughter talked about the desirability of their own life, the lines of common-sense were leading towards a thought which was so ideologically pointed, that it could only be uttered innocently as common-sense. Would 'they' – royalty – like to be able to walk along the road, eating chips?, asked the interviewer. 'I bet they would', replied the mother quickly. The daughter agreed. Immediately, and without prompting, she widened the particular into the general: 'I bet they'd love to live the way we live'. 'Ours' was the enviable life, the one which 'they' would desire to live. 'Our' imprisonments were momentarily forgotten, as the mother and her daughter, confined within the safety of their home, imagined the envy of the royals. Outside the house, the gangs of the evening were gathering on the path to the chip shop. (1992, p. 143)

The reason why this works as a piece of critical writing is that we are directed to contrast the imperfect understanding of the people on this council estate, with the reality that the royal family would probably not want to swop the burden of attending ceremonial dinners, and being constantly on display, for the freedom of eating a bag of chips walking along the street, especially since there was no freedom to do this anyway, at least in the evening. This text only hints, rather than explains, how it is that people come to hold these false beliefs, but the implication is that they are communicated through the mass media, and serve the interests of economically dominant groups in British society.

Being critical

The research methods used by critical ethnographers and discourse analysts are identical to those employed by the interpretive traditions reviewed in the first part of this book. Critical ethnographers will experience the same problems in negotiating access, and the same emotional and practical difficulties in the field, as ethnographers in the symbolic interactionist tradition which I discussed towards the end of Chapter 2. There is, however, much less emphasis in these studies on discussing the methodological issues that interest researchers in the interpretive tradition. This is because the main objective is to put forward a progressive political viewpoint through the analysis of quali-tative data.

Critical research is not for everyone in that it can arguably only be done effectively if you feel a sense of injustice about the way particular groups are treated in society, in which case it is likely that you may already be involved in a pressure group or political organization. From my experience, only a small minority of undergraduates are even remotely interested in politics, and some of these have quite right-wing views. There is, however, usually a high level of support for progressive causes (be it the legalization of cannabis or opposition to genetically modified foods) among students taking degrees in sociology or social policy.

Having progressive political views is the first step towards doing qualitative research from a critical perspective as an undergraduate, but it involves rather more than simply attaching a political statement to an ethnographic account or the analysis of a few interviews. Although it seems likely that Norman Fairclough loathes Margaret Thatcher, and everything she stands for, and Michael Billig probably has similar feelings about the royal family, it is significant that such feelings are never expressed in their studies. Instead they express their political views using a rather more measured academic language, in which theoretical resources from critical theory are applied to particular topics.

The key epistemological assumption informing work in critical theory, which should be clear from this chapter, is that it involves claiming that your own understanding of the world, as a researcher, is superior, because more complete and scientific, than the people you are studying, whether these are royalist members of the British working class, or racist shopkeepers responding to social change in rural France. To write critically about the world, from this perspective, involves bringing this epistemological position to the data, and showing the ability to relate what is happening in any given situation to a wider structural context which may be hidden from people in that local setting.

The usual way of doing this is to find a way of relating the 'micro' events one observes in the field to a 'macro' level of analysis, and interpretive approaches like symbolic interactionism, ethnomethodology and conversation analysis are often dismissed or criticized by critical theorists for their refusal to acknowledge the existence of this 'macro' level. Making the step from describing the world to engaging in critique can, however, also be difficult for researchers who want to apply ideas from critical theory to their data. Once one takes this step, the perspectives and understandings of people on the ground are necessarily subordinated to the needs of the theory. One postgraduate student in Michael Burawoy's seminar became conscious of this as a problem when he was pressed to start thinking critically about the data he had collected through doing fieldwork in a pressure group representing people infected with the AIDS virus:

> How then to get on with it? Apparently, I needed a distance from my 'subjects' that I wasn't likely to find or able to create in the field. At Michael Burawoy's suggestion, I turned to the literature on new social movements as a way of pulling back from the field site. It did provide distance, but also led to what I would call the problem of theory worship. Riding my bicycle to campus after a day of reading, I pulled over suddenly to scribble a theoretical framework that would bridge the theory and the interest I had started with: I could ask how the balance between strategic and identity-oriented actions (which the new social movements were reputed to involve) affects the production and power of representations that challenge the dominant discourse (my original interest). From here, I went into a period of wild abstractions; the problem for me – and I was still in search of something that felt like a genuine problem to be worked through – was how to use the theory to shed light on ACT UP. More accurately, I was trying to squish my data into a somewhat prefabricated theoretical framework, to make them fit. (Burawoy 1991, p. 56)

All theoretically informed qualitative research involves interpreting data using ideas and concepts from a body of theory, and so you will probably experience similar feelings when you start to think about your own data using any of the theoretical traditions reviewed in this book. The easiest way to ensure that you are doing a theoretically informed piece of research is to employ what is sometimes known as the 'sand-wich' method. The dissertation or project should start by introducing a theoretical framework and questions suggested by the previous litera-ture, follow this with three or four chapters analysing the data, and end with a conclusion that returns to issues raised by the theory. There are, however, more interesting and imaginative ways of combining ethno-graphic reportage with critical analysis, and the studies I have reviewed in this chapter demonstrate a wide range of techniques which you can employ in your own work.

Further reading

General reading on critical theory

To do critical research, you need to become familiar with the Marxist and post-Marxist tradition in sociology, and employ ideas and concepts from this literature in making sense of contemporary events and social institutions. If you are a complete beginner, I would recommend reading some of the following:

Marx, K. and Engels, F. (1967) *The Communist Manifesto*. Penguin, Harmondsworth.
Marcuse, H. (1964) *One Dimensional Man*. Routledge, London.
Breitman, G. (1965) *Malcolm X Speaks*. Grove Weidenfeld, New York.
Fanon, F. (1963) *The Wretched of the Earth*. Grove, New York.

Critical research

Harvey, L. (1990) *Critical Social Research*. Unwin Hyman, London.
Mills, C.W. (1959) *The Sociological Imagination*. Oxford University Press, New York.
Kincheloe, J. and McLaren, P. (2000) 'Rethinking critical theory and qualitative research', in N. Denzin and Y. Lincoln (eds), *The Handbook of Qualitative Research*, 2nd edn. Sage, London, pp. 138–57.

Critical discourse analysis

Fairclough, N. (1989) *Language and Power*. Longman, London.
Chouliaraki, L. and Fairclough, N. (1999) *Discourse in Late Modernity: Rethinking Critical Discourse Analysis*. Edinburgh University Press, Edinburgh.
Hodge, R. and Kress, G. (1993) *Language and Ideology*, 2nd edn. Routledge, London.

EXERCISES

These are intended as possible group projects for students who already feel that there is something wrong with the way society is currently organized. If you do not feel this way, there is little point in conducting critical research!

1 Focus on a group or issue in your area that concerns you. It could, for example, be homelessness, the relationship between ethnic communities and the police, or social deprivation. Using qualitative research methods, collect a corpus of data about the problem. Attempt to convey a political viewpoint when writing up your materials, showing how they illuminate wider social issues and problems.

2 Obtain the text of a political speech from *Hansard*, or record and transcribe a television interview with a politician. Analyse the data using ideas and theoretical resources from critical discourse analysis.

7

Feminism and Qualitative Research

Feminism has been one of the most influential political and intellectual movements in the last thirty years. It has had a tremendous impact on sociology, and feminist ideas and approaches are becoming increasingly important across the whole of the social sciences and humanities. The broad-based nature of feminism as an intellectual movement means that it is compatible with many types of sociological work, and it is possible to conduct feminist research using a range of research methods. It is, however, true to say that feminists have a preference for employing qualitative research methods. They are also usually more self-conscious than most qualitative research traditions about the political and epistemological assumptions informing the research process.

This chapter begins by providing some background on feminism as a political movement, and the distinctive way in which feminists conceptualize and conduct qualitative research. It then reviews a number of case studies which illustrate how feminist researchers have employed a range of methods, including unstructured interviewing, ethnographic fieldwork and autobiographical research. Finally, it suggests some ways in which you could design and research an undergraduate dissertation or project. This has partly to do with choosing a suitable topic, but the most important step is to start to think about your own life from a feminist perspective by 'making the personal political'.

Feminism as a political movement

Feminism has a lot in common with Marxism as a political movement in that it is based on the assumption that women are an economically exploited group who nevertheless view their exploitation as being natural and normal because men control the media and the educational system. Feminists are not committed to a political revolution in the same way as Marxists, although some have argued that a working-class revolution, along the lines Marx predicted, would be an essential pre-condition for female emancipation. They have, however, been extremely active during the nineteenth and twentieth centuries in improving the position of women, through the legislative and political process, and through public information campaigns (and this has many parallels with the gains secured for the working class through the labour movement and social democratic political parties in Europe and America).

In recent times, political successes have included obtaining the right for women to vote and have abortions, securing legal protection against discrimination and sexual harassment at work, and getting rape taken more seriously as a criminal offence (although the conviction rate remains extremely low). Partly because of feminist political campaigns and lobbying activities, but also because of structural changes in the economy, women have made huge economic advances as a group, especially after the Second World War, so they are now represented in most occupations. However, because women still choose or are made responsible for child-care, they continue to earn less than men collectively, and to be concentrated in lower-paid occupations doing part-time work, or at lower levels in the hierarchy in higher-paid jobs. A good example is academic life, where a lot of the people teaching subjects like sociology or cultural studies are women (many of whom are on part-time contracts), but there are very few female professors.

In the cultural sphere, feminists have waged a sustained, and generally successful, campaign to raise awareness of feminist political concerns, and to combat the sexist treatment of women in the mass media. Although it is still common to see women represented, for example, in advertisements or television soaps, as primarily or exclusively housewives and mothers, one is just as likely to see portrayals of the difficulties faced by career women in balancing home and work. Similarly, young children are less likely to be taught reading skills from books which portray society as primarily a man's world.

The universities are also in the cultural sphere, and many academic disciplines have been transformed by feminism. This has happened because large numbers of women who were politically active in the feminist movement obtained lecturing posts during the expansion of higher education in the 1960s. All the qualitative studies I have reviewed in previous chapters are mainly concerned with the experiences and perspectives of men. They also all use sexist language, in the sense of referring to the people they are describing, and the reader, as if these are all male.

Although many textbooks still get published which barely acknowledge the existence of feminism as a theoretical perspective, this is much less likely to be the case today. There is now a large body of feminist scholarship in almost all areas of the social sciences and humanities, and feminists have become a powerful pressure group inside professional organizations such as the American Sociological Association. Feminist work is regularly published in mainstream journals and edited collections, as well as in specialist publications such as *Signs* or *Women's Studies International Forum*.

These goals have been achieved through conventional forms of political activity, such as trying to build support inside political parties, and organizing mass rallies and demonstrations. The feminist movement has also, however, developed a distinctive form of grass-roots activism based on groups of women meeting to discuss and share their problems, which is known as 'consciousness-raising' (Spender 1980, pp. 129–33). Other movements representing low-status and subordinate groups have employed similar techniques to build support (a good example is how the slogan 'black is beautiful' was used by black power activists during the 1960s to raise the self-esteem of American blacks). However, feminists have taken this a step further by encouraging women to talk about their personal troubles, such as their experience of emotional and physical abuse at home, or discrimination at work, and to view these in political terms.

Epistemology and method in feminist research

Feminism also has a lot in common with Marxism as a critical theory, in that the feminist researcher believes that she has a superior and more complete understanding of society than the people she is researching. The objective is to liberate women from 'false consciousness' by showing that they could lead more fulfilling lives if society was organized differently, and exposing the institutions and social processes that have caused them to accept the economic dominance of men. The 'feminist standpoint' epistemology advocated by theorists such as Sandra Harding and Dorothy Smith contains similar ideas to those put forward by Marxist philosophers like Georg Lukacs. Each tradition believes that oppressed groups have a better understanding of the world, and how human beings can create a society in which everyone will be happier, and enjoy more freedom, than their oppressors. This should, however, more accurately be understood as an epistemological claim on behalf of the theoretical tradition, since actual members of the subordinate group are often unable to perceive that they are oppressed.

Although there is nothing distinctive in epistemological terms about feminism (so the term 'feminist epistemology' is, in my view, mis-leading), some varieties of feminism have made distinctive ontological claims about the difference between men and women which have important practical, as well as theoretical, implications for the way feminists conduct research. This explains why many (but by no means all) feminists have a preference for qualitative research. It also explains the emphasis placed on reflexivity (the requirement that the researcher should be highly self-conscious and reflective at all stages of the research process).

Why do (some) feminists favour qualitative methods?

It is hard to imagine women obtaining full economic equality with men without there also being an even more fundamental shift in cultural attitudes, not least so that men will want to take an equal part in bringing up children. Here there has always been a debate within feminism on the extent to which women have innately different values and capacities. Liberal feminists have argued that the two sexes are basically the same, and that the way for them to progress, in a world without discrimination, is to act and think more like men. This is how successful women like Margaret Thatcher have viewed the issue of feminism. Marxist and socialist feminists similarly place an emphasis on changing the structures that produce gender differences through socialization.

By contrast, some radical feminists have argued that women and men belong to two different species. Women have positive qualities such as the ability to nurture the young, work co-operatively, express their emotions and respect the environment. Men, on the other hand, are naturally aggressive, individualistic and coldly rationalistic; and, if they are left unchecked, will destroy the planet. Proponents of this view accept what opponents of the movement have long argued (that women are naturally suited to child-rearing), but turn the argument back against men. Radicals such as Mary Daly (1978) and Andrea Dworkin (1981) have argued that women should not campaign for economic equality, since this means accepting the world on male terms. Instead, they should construct utopian communities in which women live separately from men, or attempt to secure dominance for female cultural values.

Whatever the implications for feminist politics, one can begin to see how many feminists might have an aversion to positivism as an epistemological position on principled grounds, since it involves accepting male values, such as the fact that 'objectivity' should be a research goal. It will be remembered, from my discussion of different epistemological positions in Chapter 1, that Durkheim believed that the goal of social science should be to improve on the imperfect and subjective knowledge we have about the world in our everyday lives. Feminists, however, regard this as a spurious objectivity which serves the interests of men.

The Canadian sociologist Dorothy Smith (1987) has put forward a particularly forceful version of this argument in an essay entitled 'A sociology for women'. Smith wrote this at a time when relatively few women were working in academia, and when the majority of studies published employed an objective style or vantage point in writing about the world. She gives the example of one woman who found that displays of anger and emotional involvement were viewed as illegitimate in a conference about battered wives where participants were expected to discuss the issues in a 'calm' and 'detached' manner (1987, pp. 71–2). On the first day, she reported feeling 'antagonistic' and 'uncomfortable' towards a feminist who made an angry speech criticizing the organizers of the conference. However, she soon changed her views:

> The next day I started to realize how I had been affected by the norms of the majority. And in the process had been denying others the expression of their feelings and had been valuing people's contributions predominantly on the basis of intellectual consistency, articulation and coolness.
>
> In the first workshop, one woman – in an emotional and somewhat rambling statement – expressed her feeling of being battered by the conference itself. The expression of her feelings was only briefly responded to by the workshop speaker. However, she had spoken for a lot of people at that workshop, in that there was a lot of frustration being experienced – and not spoken of – at the tone of the conference. Her speaking led other women to speak from their feelings.
>
> And that's when I really started feeling angry. I recognized that my acceptance of the professionals' norms had been a critical factor in my discounting and criticizing [the speaker from the previous day] and others during the course of the symposium, and consequently in my feeling separated from people. These norms value intellectual perception so highly and emotions so lowly; they are a basic cause of violence in our culture. And that was not being dealt with. (1987, pp. 71–2)

Smith suggests that the 'scientific attitude' underpinning the papers presented at this conference, and the assumption that objectivity derives from 'a point external to any particular position in society', is widespread in social science. The challenge facing feminists is not simply to ensure that more sociologists study topics like battered wives, but also to change the way in which they conduct and conceptualize research. Here she seems to parallel the arguments of radical feminists by suggesting that women need a distinctive method which draws upon interpretive approaches such as symbolic interactionism and ethnomethodology, and addresses the world of 'lived experience'. Similarly, Liz Stanley and Sue Wise (1983) have argued that these theoretical traditions have often been dismissed by quantitative sociologists precisely because they threaten the male idea that one can describe the world objectively in the same way as natural science.

Although not everyone would agree with this negative assessment of positivism (see, for example, Oakley 2000, and my discussion of Liz Kelly's 1988 study *Surviving Sexual Violence* below), most feminist researchers do seem to have a preference for using qualitative research methods, such as interviewing and ethnography. There are, however, important differences between the way they conceptualize qualitative research, and how this is understood by the interpretive traditions which I reviewed in the first part of this book. Dorothy Smith, for example, recommends that the researcher should begin by interviewing women about their everyday experience, but then show how this is shaped by wider structural forces (what she calls the 'relations of ruling'). This way of doing research is informed by similar epistemological assumptions to the critical tradition which I discussed in the previous chapter, in that it seems clear that Smith expects to find that the average housewife will only have an incomplete and imperfect understanding of society. Her goal as a critical theorist is to free women from what she views as the false beliefs that benefit men as the economically dominant group. By contrast, symbolic interactionists and ethnomethodologists are only interested in describing and explicating how people understand their own actions.

Reflexivity and the research process

The most distinctive feature of feminist qualitative research is the emphasis placed on reflexivity or engaging in reflection about the research process. Studies are usually written in the first person, and often include a lengthy autobiographical account of how the researcher came to a particular topic, and the emotional and other difficulties she experienced conducting interviews or doing fieldwork. There is usually a lot more discussion and acknowledgement of the difference in perspective and awareness between the researcher and the people being studied, than one finds in Marxist ethnographies, and the ethical dilemmas that arise in conducting research. These include the extent to which one can use intimate details about people's lives, and how one should respond to negative reactions from interviewees (Fonow and Cook 1991b). Some commentators have even argued that it is impossible for feminists to conduct ethnography, since this is a profoundly unethical pursuit (Stacey 1988; see also Richardson 1997, p. 117).

There are two reasons why feminists place so much emphasis on reflexivity. In the first place, it is understood politically as a means of promoting female cultural values in an academy which is still dominated by 'objective' or positivist styles of analysis. Liz Stanley and Sue Wise have noted that most research studies, whether these employ quantitative or ethnographic methods, present their findings so that the role of the researcher disappears from the analysis:

> Although many people working in the social sciences privately discuss the idiosyncracies, quirks, and problems of doing research, public discussions and written accounts remain rare. The personal tends to be carefully removed from public statements: these are full of rational argument and careful discussion of academic points of dispute and are frequently empty of any feeling of what the research process was actually like. (1991, p. 226)

It will be remembered that the symbolic interactionist ethnographies reviewed in Chapter 2 are also often reflective about the research process, and often contain autobiographical accounts which describe how the researchers obtained access to particular institutions or social worlds, and the emotional difficulties they experienced in the field. Feminists, however, arguably have a distinctive understanding of reflexivity which arises from their commitment to consciousness-raising, as a means of raising political awareness among women.

According to Margaret Fonow and Judith Cook, the objective of doing a feminist research project should be not only to raise the consciousness of the people you are studying (which may not always be possible, or desirable on ethical grounds), but also to reflect politically on your own life:

> Under ideal circumstances, transformation occurs, during which something hidden is revealed about the formerly taken-for-granted aspects of sexual asymmetry. Thus, in this model, previously hidden phenomena which are apprehended as a contradiction can lead to one or more of the following: an emotional catharsis . . .; an academic insight and resulting intellectual product; and increased politicization and corresponding activism. (1991b, p. 3)

This emphasis on the researcher as well as the researched gives feminism a distinctive character as a critical research tradition. The researcher is expected not simply to produce emancipatory knowledge, but to demonstrate that she has come to view her own life differently through conducting empirical research.

Feminist ethnography

Any research method can be used to address political questions, and the conversation analytic study by West and Zimmerman I reviewed in Chapter 5 is a good example of how one can study language use from a feminist perspective (see also Cameron 1995, Spender 1980 and Todd and Fisher 1988 for other studies by feminists working in the discipline of linguistics). There is also a large and diverse body of feminist work in oral history, and a smaller but growing literature in biography and autobiography (see Stanley 1993). I will not be discussing these research methods in this chapter, but will instead concentrate on feminism as a qualitative tradition in sociology.

Feminist researchers have employed a variety of ethnographic methods to address women's lives (Reinharz 1992). In the rest of this chapter I will discuss five case studies, all of which are informed by epistemological assumptions similar to those of the critical ethnographies reviewed in the previous chapter, although they go further in acknowledging the difference in perspective between the researcher and researched. They also illustrate the distinctive feminist understanding of reflexivity, in the sense of a requirement that the researcher should become politicized through the research process.

Surviving Sexual Violence by Liz Kelly is based on unstructured interviews with British women who have been sexually assaulted or raped. *Formations of Class and Gender* by Beverley Skeggs examines the experiences of a group of working-class women in Britain through conducting a series of interviews over a twelve year period. *Gender Trials* by Jennifer Pierce is a participant observation study of the difficulties faced by women working in two large law firms. 'Experiences of sexism' is an autobiographical account by Liz Stanley and Sue Wise, about their experience of receiving obscene telephone calls. Finally, *Making Grey Gold* is a participant observation study about the lives of people working in, and affected by, private organizations caring for the elderly, which draws on ideas and concepts from the work of Dorothy Smith. Interestingly, the researcher in this case, Tim Diamond, is male, so this study illustrates how men can also conduct feminist research.

Surviving Sexual Violence

Perhaps the easiest way to address the experience of an oppressed group, and the one which is most likely to have an impact on politicians and get taken up by the press, is to conduct a series of unstructured interviews. This study by Liz Kelly (1988) is a good example in that it is based on interviews with sixty women who had experienced different kinds of sexual violence. Kelly was an activist in one of the first British groups to set up a refuge for battered women during the 1970s, and the sample was mainly drawn from people she met through giving talks at women's groups, although she also got some response from writing letters to newspapers and magazines, and from leaving tear-off strips in a community bookshop. The objective was to document their experiences, and to raise awareness about violence against women as a political issue.

Kelly begins by introducing her own political perspective, and also discusses how she was affected emotionally by the research process. She notes, for example, that she came to redefine some experiences in her own childhood as examples of sexual violence:

> While interviewing and transcribing, buried memories of my own emerged: I remembered five separate episodes of assault or harassment from my childhood or adolescence. The fact that this also happened to a woman who transcribed several interviews, and to many women when they read their own transcripts, resulted in my paying attention to how common the forgetting of painful or confusing experiences is. (1988, p. 17)

Some commentators believe that feminists employ more egalitarian methods in conducting interviews, because their objective is to establish a dialogue with respondents rather than simply to treat them instrumentally as sources of data. Kelly's study is a good example in that she spent a lot of time sharing her own experiences and opinions with respondents, and also supplied them with transcripts and gave them some control over the data that was used in the final study. The important point to note, however, is not that feminists conduct interviews in a strikingly different way to, for example, symbolic interactionists, but that each tradition understands the process of research in the light of its own methodological assumptions. To put this another way, one would expect a feminist researcher to write about, and perhaps agonize over, the issue of whether or not she had established an equal relationship with interviewees, more than a symbolic interactionist. The way in which Kelly writes about methods (which includes talking about her own life and emotions, and her concerns about letting interviewees read the transcripts) makes this a feminist piece of research.

Another interesting point to note about this study is that it contains a chapter which employs quantitative methods in analysing the interview data. We learn, for example, that only seventeen of the women in the sample 'did not experience some kind of sexual violence before the age of 16' and only ten women 'had never experienced violence in a heterosexual relationship' (1988, p. 95). This illustrates the fact that not all feminists have an anti-positivist bias, and it is significant that Kelly employed a systematic method of coding in organizing the data into analytic themes that is very similar to the techniques used by grounded theorists in the symbolic interactionist tradition. As I suggested in Chapter 3, grounded theorists are on the positivist wing of the interpretive tradition and their research is explicitly informed by a commitment to the idea that research findings should be 'objective'. Kelly also notes that, although feminists have questioned the 'usefulness and, indeed, possibility of objectivity', this does not mean that they should 'reject any principles for ensuring that their work contains honest and accurate accounts' (1988, p. 5).

Perhaps the most important difference between this and a grounded theory study, which is also worth noting, is that Kelly starts out with a theoretical understanding of society which enables her to assess and explain the accounts supplied by her interviewees. This is particularly evident in Chapter 9 where she suggests some reasons why 'feminism was not perceived by the majority of the women interviewed as providing . . . a framework which validated their understanding of sexual violence' (1988, p. 231). Although she does not directly challenge or question the accounts supplied by the interviewees (compare this to the approach adopted by some analysts in the previous chapter), Kelly still claims to know more about the causes of male violence, as a feminist, than the people she was studying. A grounded theory study, by contrast, would attempt to build up a picture inductively of how these women understood their own lives, without contrasting this to the superior understanding of the analyst.

Formations of Class and Gender

In addition to conducting interview studies, feminists have also conducted fieldwork studies as participant and non-participant observers. This British study by Beverley Skeggs (1997) grew out of her friendship with a group of eighty-three working-class women whom she got to know while teaching a further education course in which they were learning how to be carers for elderly people. It is based on interviewing the women and staying in touch for a period of twelve years, and develops a theoretical analysis of their lives using resources from critical theory (in particular the work of Pierre Bourdieu). It is, however, a distinctively feminist study which contains a lot of reflexive discussion about her own working-class background, and the difference between her perspective as a feminist and the women she was studying.

Despite the fact that she collected data from a large number of women over a long period, it is perhaps worth noting that only a small number of extracts from the interviews appear in the book, and we learn relatively little about her relationship with particular individuals. Skeggs herself admits that 'they are so much more insightful and interesting than this book can convey in words', and that 'sadly, the affectivity of the research has nearly disappeared in the academic analytical filtering process' (1997, p. 15). She states, somewhat regretfully, in the conclusion that the book is about 'issues in feminist and cultural theory', rather than 'a description of the lives of the women' (1997, p. 160). This illustrates how even in the feminist tradition a commitment to describing women's lives is often subordinated to the need to develop a theoretically informed understanding of everyday experience.

Much of the study is written using the forbiddingly dense, theoretical language used by British academics in the field of cultural studies, and it is worth noting in passing that, if you want to obtain professional recognition in this field, you have to write at length about feminist theory and epistemology, and establish your own position in relation to the literature. Skeggs's general argument is, however, relatively simple. She suggests that these women experienced the world in ways which were shaped by their structural position in society. They invested a lot of energy in trying to pass as middle class by buying clothes and cosmetics, because they were made to feel ashamed of their class background. They also invested a lot of time in caring work, and in cultivating femininity, because of the pressures exerted on them to conform by their families and wider society.

Although Skeggs continually describes them as working-class women, and believes that class was 'completely central' to their lives, it is significant that the women themselves did not accept that they were working class, and they also took their work as carers for granted, rather than seeing it in academic terms as a way in which one 'constructs' femininity. The following comments also illustrate how many of the women had a low opinion of feminism:

> You know what really disturbs me about feminism and I guess the real reason why I wouldn't want to be a feminist, is the way it's so anti-men. It just doesn't make sense all this stuff about evil oppressors and that. I look at Kevin, and I think, well, my dad too and his brother, it's like what have they got going for them. They've no future. They've no job, they're miserable, they don't know what to do with themselves. I worry if Kevin can keep going you know he keeps saying he's got nothing to live for and no hope. And he's meant to be strong and in control and all that. All I see is a desperately unhappy, sad, pathetic little boy. It's rubbish, they just don't know what they're talking about. (1997, p. 152)

This is a particularly poignant extract in that Skeggs tells us that Kevin, this interviewee's ex-boyfriend, subsequently committed suicide after being unemployed for five years. Feminism is portrayed as a 'man-hating', middle-class movement of little relevance to the difficulties these women experienced in their everyday lives. Skeggs responds sympathetically to these views in her analysis of the interviews, and also notes that she had similar conversations when she taught them on the caring course. The whole study is, therefore, to some extent, a dialogue between someone from a working-class background who has become a university lecturer, and people from her own class background who understand the world in a very different way. Although the academic necessarily gets the last word, this is arguably a distinctively feminist text in the way it acknowledges the difference in perspective between the critical researcher and the researched.

Gender Trials

This study by Jennifer Pierce (1995) is based on spending fifteen months working as a paralegal in the litigation departments of two large law firms in San Francisco. Her main concern was to document two occupational cultures in these firms. The lawyers were predominantly male, and saw themselves as being 'Rambo litigators'. The paralegals (a job which involves giving administrative support to the lawyers) were predominantly female. They often described their work in gendered terms, as providing 'mothering' support for the lawyers.

Pierce was initially refused permission to conduct a fieldwork study on the grounds of 'the risks that my research might pose to client confidentiality', and also the fact that it 'would be potentially disruptive to an already busy and over-worked department' (1995, p. 18). Because of this, she decided to conduct the research covertly, through obtaining a position as an assistant litigator in the two firms. While she was in the firm, she revealed that she was also 'a graduate student in sociology doing a dissertation on occupational stress among legal workers' (1995, p. 19), and obtained permission to interview a cross-section of staff. She did not, however, reveal that her real purpose was to write about legal work from a feminist perspective. Her best data was obtained when women in the office 'confided in me about their personal troubles', without knowing that she was a sociologist.

Pierce's study demonstrates what can be achieved through spending a long time in a particular setting focusing on a specific research question. It reveals how the work of women in these offices has an emotional component, in that it involves giving reassurance and boosting the egos of bad-tempered men, in the same way as wives. They get little thanks for their work, and men regard them as intellectually inferior, and incapable of understanding legal arguments, because they are women. Women coped psychologically with these pressures by treating the men like children, or by pretending that they enjoyed a personal relationship. One example she gives is an 'experienced paralegal' called Debbie who put up with her 'intimidating' boss:

> Her repeated justifications of what Michael was really like often sounded unconvincing. In making these statements, she spoke with resignation and sighed frequently. Even her body language – with her shoulders slumped forward, her forehead creased in a frown, and her eyes carrying dark circles below them – conveyed the opposite of what she asserted. Moreover, her frequent complaints of fatigue suggested that she was over-worked and unhappy. (1995, pp. 165–6)

Pierce later 'naively' showed this lawyer a 'literature review' when he expressed an interest in her dissertation. She includes the following extract from her fieldnotes in the study which describes his negative response:

> He was really hurt because my prospectus, in his words, 'portrays all these wonderful secretaries and paralegals who support these asshole attorneys'.

And how did I think he would respond, but to take it personally because [he raises his voice] 'wasn't this really about me and Jane [his secretary] and Debbie [a paralegal]?' He added sneeringly, 'And it's so well-written and polished. All these footnotes and references. You must have spent a lot of time working on this.' (1995, p. 209)

It will be evident from these two extracts that this is an unashamedly partisan ethnography which sets out to portray men (and the macho culture of litigation in general) in a bad light. She is also highly dismissive of women who act in a 'nicey-nicey' way towards their employers (a version of the traditional feminist distaste towards 'submissive' wives). From a symbolic interactionist or ethnomethodological perspective one might want to complain that it only provides a partial and one sided view of law firms, in that we do not learn much about how the men understood their relationship with paralegals and secretaries. One could also complain that Pierce offers her own interpretation of what people 'really' feel about their work, rather than letting them speak in their own words.

These criticisms, however, to some extent miss the point since this style of ethnography does not pretend to be objective, and indeed denies that objectivity is either desirable or possible. To appreciate the ethnography in its own terms, you have to admire the way it uses ethnographic data to advance a persuasive (but at the same time thoroughly contentious) case about the experience of women in law firms. Pierce's study illustrates that, if you want to challenge relations of power, it may be necessary to employ covert methods, and you should expect to offend powerful groups in society. This is because, as she observes, 'sociology as public philosophy is not intended to please the people we study but rather to address the social and political conditions of their lives' (1995, p. 214).

Experiences of sexism

Although all the studies I have so far examined contain some autobiographical detail about the authors, there is also a certain reticence in the way they share sensitive and personal experiences from their own lives. Skeggs, for example, does not tell us that much in *Formations of Class and Gender* about her experience as a working-class woman in academic life (although see Mahony and Zmroczek 1997 for some accounts) or how becoming an academic affected her relationship with particular informants. This may partly result from the fact she mainly draws on theoretical resources from structural sociology, whereas feminist researchers who have engaged to a greater extent with the interpretive tradition are often more successful in writing about their own lives and experiences.

This study by Liz Stanley and Sue Wise (1991) is a good example of how you can use your own life as sociological data, although most readers would probably not want to employ this particular strategy in collecting research data, if they were in the same circumstances. Stanley and Wise are lesbians, and their home telephone number was used in small newspaper advertisements and posters offering help to gay women during the mid 1970s. As a result of this they received large numbers of obscene calls, and they decided that, rather than immediately hanging up, they would keep the callers talking and tape-record the calls.

They present transcripts which illustrate the different purposes of callers, for example, to ask for sex, or to obtain sexual stimulation from the experience of talking to a lesbian. A large number of men also threatened sexual or non-sexual violence against lesbians. The following call is a good example (although most callers used more sexually explicit language):

R: Hello, it's Liz.
C: Liz, the les is it?
R: I beg your pardon?
C: So you should . . . You need whipping and then stringing up in public as an example.
R: An example of what?
C: Of what happens to degenerates in a decent society.
R: Do decent societies publicly hang people then?
C: They do where there are people like you . . . you're too sick to know what decent means . . . you need making an example of, flaunting yourself, and perverting normal women with your sexual practices.

(1991, p. 270)

In discussing the significance of this data, Stanley and Wise focus on their emotional response to the calls, and their need to make sense of this from a feminist perspective:

The most immediate impact the calls had on us was to dominate our lives. The calls could and did occur at any time of the day or night and thus, in a physical sense, intruded in our lives to a very marked degree. We have already pointed out that we usually received one such call a day. But during the period of time before, during, and immediately after the 'research period' we were receiving many of them each day. The calls dominated our lives in another sense: to be subject to a constant barrage of obscenity and sexually-objectifying threats is to experience oppression in a very direct way; and we therefore experienced a need to make some kind of sense of what was occurring in terms of feminist theory and analysis. (1991, p. 274)

Eventually they were forced to end the project, which required them to remain 'unemotional' and 'cool' in order to keep the callers talking. They experienced feelings of 'anger' and 'outrage', but also fear of being attacked physically, in addition to suffering verbal abuse, in case a caller managed to discover their address. Matters were made worse, however, by the negative reactions when they presented their findings to different audiences. Many gay and heterosexual men found the tape-recordings sexually stimulating, and even most heterosexual women advised them to 'ignore the calls' or 'to laugh them off'. They were also accused of being 'extreme' or 'paranoid' in their reaction to the calls. This made them feel even more pessimistic about the prospects for challenging this kind of oppression which is only an extreme case of the routine violence and sexist abuse experienced by women. The paper is not, therefore, simply an objective report about their data, but a phenomenological investigation into what it means to be a feminist: how they came to see reality differently through conducting research on obscene phone calls.

Making Grey Gold

Perhaps the theorist who has most influenced qualitative work by feminists in North America (and to a lesser extent in Britain) is the Canadian sociologist Dorothy Smith. I have already mentioned the fact that she has combined ethnomethodology and Marxism in interesting ways in developing a feminist methodology that starts with the lived experiences of women, and shows how these are shaped by what she calls the 'relations of ruling' in capitalist society. Although Smith has advocated what she calls a 'sociology for women', she has also supervised and advised a number of male students. This study by Tim Diamond (1992) is arguably the best example one could recommend to anyone interested in doing empirical research informed by her ideas. It is based on spending three years working as a care assistant in a number of nursing homes, and contrasts the experience of residents, and the people caring for them, with the bureaucratic and profit-driven concerns of the managers running this industry.

Although Diamond collected the data in three years, he spent several more years reading and analysing the fieldnotes, reading relevant literature, and writing the book (1992, p. 5). There were probably many reasons why it took him so long to publish the study, but it seems worth repeating the point, which I made in an earlier chapter, that the best work often results from spending a lot of time thinking about the data, and experimenting with different ways of representing the world on the printed page. Diamond wanted to follow Smith in 'exploring the disjunctions between everyday life and administrative accounts of it' (1992, p. 6). The method he employed to do this was, however, quite unusual, in that he chose to write the whole study in a similar way to a novel, so there is very little discussion of theory or politics in the main text:

> While I was getting to know nursing assistants and residents and experiencing aspects of their daily routines, I would surreptitiously take notes on scraps of paper, in the bathroom or otherwise out of sight, jotting down what someone

had said or done. The basic data are these observations and conversations, the actual words of people reproduced to the best of my ability from the field notes. In trying to preserve the context in which things were said and done, I employ a novel-like format so that the reading might move along as a story. Increasingly, as the chapters proceed, I intersperse sociological commentary with the conversation. The literature and theory that inform these reflections are cited as endnotes rather than as part of the discussion, so as not to interrupt the flow of the narrative. In pursuit of the same objective, I often choose not to pause to indicate which nursing home each speaker was in, but rather to organize comments made in different settings around the key themes they illuminate. (1992, p. 7)

Diamond's sociological novel is organized around a metaphor of old people and their carers being like 'gold', which is mined and then shaped for profit by the American health care industry. The first part describes his experience on a training course, and the view of the low-paid workers in the industry, who are mainly African-American or Hispanic women who have to do three part-time jobs in order to survive. The second part looks at the day-to-day experience of the people living in these homes, who are also mainly women, and their carers. It contains some vivid accounts of elderly people going hungry, even though they are receiving their allotted caloric intake according to the regulations, and the way in which residents are forced to rise very early in the morning, since it saves costs if care homes are run like hospitals to a bureaucratic schedule rather than in response to their actual needs. Another theme is the way in which the physical and emotional skills involved in caring (remember here that Smith, and feminists in general, are interested in critiquing 'male', abstract knowledge) are not recog-nized or adequately renumerated by the nursing homes. The following passage is a description of the expert work of changing a bed which a resident has 'messed' during the night:

'Good morning, Monica,' Mrs Johnson began with an uplifting chuckle. 'C'mon, let's get you up and rolling!' Without hesitation, continuing her talking, she folded the blankets down to the bottom of the bed and with her right hand rolled Monica over on her left side, deftly wrapping the soiled bottom sheet toward the center of the bed, then turned to me with, 'Here, hand me that Kleenex box. Quick! You got to be quick about this!' and turned to Monica, talking and cleaning, 'Okay, up once, okay, now over,' and lifted her lower half completely with just one hand, folded the clean part of the old bottom sheets under her to help finish the cleaning, unwrapped a new bottom sheet and another for protection and slid them down the side of the bed where Monica was not lying, simultaneously turning to me, 'Now that washcloth and towel, quick! You've got to have these right at your side before you start,' and to Monica, 'There you go,' rolling her over onto the new bottom sheets and folding a new top sheet and blankets over her. I gasped in amazement. Mrs Johnson had executed the entire operation, turning it into one continuous fluid motion, in little more than two minutes. (1992, p. 133)

The final part of the ethnography contrasts the bodily needs and experience of the residents with the way in which they become accounting entries for the purposes of the people who manage the homes, and it is implied that there is pressure from government and shareholders to rationalize and save costs, even if this creates more work for people on the ground. It concludes with some 'fanciful' suggestions, which report comments made by staff and residents about how nursing homes could be made more humane. Although Diamond does not expand on why they are 'fanciful', the reader is meant to draw the conclusion that the lives of these women will not improve until there are profound changes in society as a whole.

Making the personal political

In the previous chapter, I suggested some ways in which you could make your own work political by applying some body of critical theory to a collection of interviews or your observations in a short ethnographic project. A key part of the analysis would be to use materials from the study to show how the people you are studying are oppressed, but also to explain from a theoretical perspective how this oppression has arisen, and why people do not understand the conditions of their own lives in the same way as the theory. The main example in the previous chapter was class-based forms of oppression involving economic exploitation, but you could just as easily use the same approach in investigating the experience of groups which face other forms of social discrimination, such as ethnic minorities, homosexuals or disabled people, or on a wider scale the millions still suffering from poverty and hunger in the Third World.

Although feminism can be understood as another variety of critical theory, I have also suggested that it is distinctive in placing a considerable emphasis on the personal experience of the researcher, who is expected to develop politically and to write about this as part of the research process. The people most interested in conducting research from this perspective will be women who are already conscious of sexism in their own lives, and may already be politically active in the women's movement. Doing feminist research at graduate school level often has a similar character to participating in a 'consciousness-raising group', although the aim is to publish work which promotes feminist cultural and political values in academic life. Some of the studies reviewed in this chapter are more reflexive than others, but they all illustrate a concern with bringing the personal experiences of the researcher into the study.

One does not, however, need to be female, or even committed to feminist politics, to draw on similar techniques in conducting critical research. If you have suffered from discrimination or prejudice, and want to do political research, you might find it interesting to write about your own autobiography, as well as the emotions you experienced in interviewing people with similar experiences. There are still many institutions where undergraduates are strongly discouraged from writing in the first person, and the curriculum reflects what a feminist would describe as male, positivist values. You can, however, only conduct research critically from a feminist perspective if you are willing to talk about your own experiences of sexism, racism or other forms of discrimination, through belonging to an 'oppressed' group.

Further reading

General reading on feminism

A common failing in students who want to do feminist research is that they have not read any of the key texts which inspired many women in the 1960s and 1970s to become feminists. I would recommend, at the very least, reading some of the following:

De Beauvoir, S. (1974) *The Second Sex*. Vintage, New York.
Friedan, B. (1974) *The Feminine Mystique*. Dell, New York.
Firestone, S. (1970) *The Dialectic of Sex*. Bantam, New York.
Millet, K. (1970) *Sexual Politics*. Doubleday, Garden City, NY.

Other introductory texts

Tong, R. (1993) *Feminist Thought: a Comprehensive Introduction*. Routledge, London.
Carden, M. (1974) *The New Feminist Movement*. Russell Sage, New York.

For discussion of the problems faced by the movement since the 1970s

Segal, L. (1987) *Is the Future Female? Troubled Thoughts on Contemporary Feminism*. Virago, London.
Faludi, S. (1992) *Backlash: the Undeclared War against Women*. Chatto and Windus, London.

Some texts on feminism and methodology

Fonow, M. and Cook, J. (1991a) *Beyond Methodology: Feminist Scholarship as Lived Research*. Indiana University Press, Bloomington, IN.
Reinharz, S. (1992) *Feminist Methods in Social Research*. Oxford University Press, New York.
Harding, S. (ed.) (1987) *Feminism and Methodology*. Open University Press, Milton Keynes.

Some collections

Stanley, L. (ed.) (1990) *Feminist Praxis*. Routledge, London.
Ribbens, J. and Edwards, R. (eds) (1998) *Feminist Dilemmas in Qualitative Research: Public Knowledge and Private Lives*. Sage, London.
Wolf, D. (ed.) (1996) *Feminist Dilemmas in Fieldwork*. Westview, Colorado.

EXERCISE

This exercise is intended for female students who already have a commitment to feminist politics. You should identify a group of women working in a particular occupation (they could, for example, be university lecturers), where you know that women are paid less than men, and are unrepresented in senior positions. Conduct an unstructured interview focusing on the career hopes of the women, and how they view the significance of gender in determining their prospects.

When writing up the interviews, consider how your own gender helped in establishing rapport (did you share experiences?). Did the interviewees share your own political assessment of their position at work? If not, your account should discuss the contrast between your views as a feminist, and how they understand their position in society, drawing upon ideas and concepts from the feminist studies reviewed in this chapter.

8

Postmodern Ethnography

CONTENTS

The most recent intellectual movements that have had an impact across the human sciences are those of postmodernism and poststructuralism. Postmodernism is the belief that we are entering a new era of world history that is significantly different from the modern era. Poststructuralism is a philosophical movement that makes the rather more radical claim that the assumptions we have held about truth and knowledge in the past are mistaken: it is an attempt to disrupt, and reinvigorate, our appreciation and understanding of reality. The two terms are often used interchangeably, which is understandable given that poststructuralist thinkers such as Michel Foucault and Jacques Derrida represent a dramatic break with previous ways of conceptualizing society.

This chapter begins by trying to explain why some intellectuals believe that we are entering a new period in human history, and discusses the implications of poststructuralist ideas for research methods. It then examines how these ideas have become important in anthropology and symbolic interactionism as researchers have become more self-conscious about the difficulty of representing reality in ethnographic texts. The chapter then looks at four experimental studies that have been described as 'postmodern' ethnographies. It concludes by considering how the other traditions I have reviewed in this book have responded to postmodernism. They are all extremely critical of this latest development in social science.

The significance of postmodernism

Although the cultural and intellectual impact of postmodernism may be on the wane, there is no denying that it has been the most vigorous force in intellectual life in the past twenty years, and has also had some degree of impact on wider culture. There are very few Marxists around in universities these days, but there are many people, both old and young, who have embraced postmodernism. Whole fields, such as cultural studies, have grown up fuelled by theoretical debates and ideas from French poststructuralist philosophers and cultural critics such as Jean-Jacques Lyotard, Jean Baudrillard, Gilles Deleuze, Felix Guattari, Jacques Derrida and Michel Foucault. In sociology, Foucault has replaced Marx as the theorist most taught on the undergraduate curriculum, and terms like 'discourse' and 'power/knowledge' have replaced 'capital', 'class struggle' and 'the dialectic' as the common currency of left-wing intellectuals.

In its most radical forms, postmodernist thought claims that the world has changed so profoundly that not only is there no chance of a political revolution of the type envisaged by Marx, but intellectuals have become irrelevant in an affluent society in which no one can imagine an alternative to capitalism (see, for example, Baudrillard 1988; Bauman 1992). This argument was also advanced by the Frankfurt School during the 1960s, but the young people who became involved in political protest during that period, partly as a result of reading books such as Herbert Marcuse's *One Dimensional Man* (1964), were fighting for a better world. Today, there is very little radicalism or political idealism around. The popularity of postmodernism on university campuses in America and Europe probably has a lot to do with the disillusion experienced by middle-aged, left-wing intellectuals following the collapse of communism (see Horowitz 1993). My own view, however, is that it is contemporary youth, the Generation X described in Douglas Coupland's novels, who are most receptive to postmodernism. It speaks to people who do not believe in ideologies or grand narratives, and are either happy with the world as it is, or cynical about the prospects for changing deeply entrenched institutions and ways of thinking through political action.

Poststructuralism and method

Perhaps the most controversial argument put forward by poststructuralists is that there is no such thing as absolute truth. This is mainly directed against a central assumption held by philosophers and political theorists since the eighteenth century: the idea that human beings, through exercising their free will, guided by reason, can produce a better society. Enlightenment thinkers such as Montesquieu, Voltaire, Diderot, Comte, Rousseau and Montaigne promoted this idea at a time when the medieval world, based on religious authority and the dominance of hereditary elites, was in the process of being transformed by what we have come to call capitalism. It also, however, has considerable implications for understanding method in the social sciences. I will now explain some of the implications through discussing the terms 'archaeology/genealogy' and 'deconstructionism'. These should be understood not as additional methods one can use in empirical enquiry, but as part of a philosophical assault against the very idea of method, as it is understood by positivist, realist and interpretive traditions.

Archaeology and genealogy

Although Foucault is sometimes presented to students as a leftist thinker who offered a similar view of society to Marx, in fact there are profound and irreconcilable political and philosophical differences between the two thinkers. Marx belongs to the tradition of critical theory reviewed in Chapter 6: he believed that reason and science can be used to produce a better world. Foucault, on the other hand, was a critic of this tradition, which he saw as delusory and dishonest: knowledge, in his view, was always a means of exercising power. Whereas Marx believed that there would ultimately be a proletarian revolution, Foucault was far more pessimistic about the prospects of change. Power was not concentrated into the hands of any one group or class but spread evenly in institutions and practices such as schooling, medicine, the criminal justice system and psychiatry. In a similar fashion to Max Weber and members of the Frankfurt School, he viewed the rise of the state as a sinister development that reduced human freedom. There was no means of challenging power, since it was everywhere. The only source of resistance would come from local struggles waged by groups like prisoners or homosexuals on the margins of society, which would never result in a transformation of society as a whole.

In advancing these arguments, Foucault employed a method which he describes in his early work as 'archaeology' but later came to describe as 'genealogy'. Since these are often recommended as postmodern methods (see, for example, Kendall and Wickham 1999 and Scheurich 1997), it is important to understand that they cannot really be separated from his project of critiquing Enlightenment thought. They are best understood as methods of philosophical critique and argument, rather than methods which produce empirical findings.

An 'archaeology' is an investigation into the dominant cultural and philosophical assumptions of a particular historical period. Foucault used it to show that ideas and concepts we take for granted are, in fact, historically situated: there is no such thing as absolute or transcendental knowledge. A 'genealogy' involves showing how the growth of any body of knowledge always involves the exercise of power. In historical studies such as *Madness and Civilisation* (1967) and *Discipline and Punish* (1977), Foucault showed not only that current ways of dealing with the insane or criminals are historically contingent, but that what appear to be liberal or progressive measures are part of a broader process in which we have lost our freedom.

Foucault's objective in using these philosophical methods was, therefore, to advance a controversial and deeply pessimistic critique of the modern world. His later writings about 'biopower' and 'governmentality' also suggest that social scientific methods, including the social survey but also the various techniques used by qualitative researchers, can be viewed as tools used by the state, and professional occupations, to regulate and control human populations. The methods courses you are taking at college are, if you like, part of the problem rather than the solution from a Foucauldian perspective, because they teach an instrumental way of thinking about human beings, and are intended to give you technical skills which serve the needs of government.

Deconstructionism

The other method which has become associated with poststructuralism is 'deconstructionism', which has become part of everyday language in Western societies, in the sense of a technique used to find different or alternative meanings in literary texts or films (see Denzin 1994). The originator of the term, Jacques Derrida, was engaged in a more ambitious project. He set out to challenge the assumption, widely held in Western thought, that it is possible to represent the world objectively using language. Derrida regards this view of language as repressive, in the same way as the exercise of reason results in governments building prisons, or the growth of psychiatry as an occupation. He wants to free intellectuals from the feeling that they have to think in a logical, rational or coherent way about human activities.

A key principle of conventional literary criticism, but also of how we read texts in any area of social life, is that it is possible to find a true or objective meaning. One strategy we often adopt if we are unclear about the meaning of a word, or a passage, is to consider what the author must have meant. We might consult other documents or texts relating to that subject, or interview people who knew the author, or even interview the author if this is possible. Our assumption in doing so is that there is a meaning to be found, and that it comes from what was in the author's mind. Derrida challenges this view through suggesting that the meaning does not exist outside the text, but is the product of how it is interpreted by different audiences (see also Fish 1982).

Deconstructionism as a technique of literary criticism involves going through a text and identifying inconsistencies. Cuff et al. describe this in the following terms:

> The operation of deconstruction works in the opposite way to conventional attempts to identify a coherently structured text, unified under its title and the name of the author. The conventional direction seeks out as much internal consistency as possible, trying to bring all aspects of the text within the same scheme. Its obverse, deconstruction, cultivates incongruities and paradoxes, highlighting the ways texts are internally divided amongst themselves, showing how one part of the text counteracts the effect ostensibly found in another, and revealing especially where aspects of the text resist, confound and unravel the order which seeks to impose itself upon the text. (1998, p. 291)

The objective is to show not only that a text can be interpreted in different ways, but that one can never establish a final meaning (which is encapsulated in the concept of *différance*). More fundamentally, Derrida wants to challenge our desire to find coherence, which stems from exactly the same worship of reason which has reduced human freedom in other areas of social life.

Poststructuralism and ethnography

Although poststructuralism and postmodernism are widely taught as bodies of theory in the social sciences, it would be fair to say that they have only had a limited impact on the way in which academics conduct research, or on courses in research methods. Very few researchers now pursue archaeological or genealogical investigations in the way Foucault intended. Deconstructionism has enjoyed some success as a specialist method in literary criticism, but has not taken root in the social sciences. The only subfield in sociology in which relativism is taken seriously is the sociology of scientific knowledge, which, despite courting controversy in a sustained attempt to undermine the authority of science, has only had a limited effect on the rest of the discipline (see, for example,

Woolgar 1988a; and for a critical response Sokal and Bricmont 1997). One might argue that this is hardly surprising: this way of thinking is antithetical to the very idea of social science, if this is motivated by a desire to improve the world through conducting empirical research.

Poststructuralism has received the warmest welcome from researchers in the interpretive tradition who conceptualize social life in terms of meaningful action, and are opposed to the positivist view, put forward by Emile Durkheim, that one should use methods from natural science in studying human beings (see my summary of this debate in Chapter 1). There are some important exceptions, and I will be reviewing the arguments of symbolic interactionists in the Chicago School tradition, and ethnomethodologists, who have an equal hostility towards positivism and poststructuralism, at the end of this chapter. There are two groups of American ethnographers who have been most receptive to poststructuralism, and have even developed new methods to promote the idea that there is no such thing as truth. The first is a group of anthropologists, and literary critics, associated with James Clifford and George Marcus in Rice University, who published the influential collection *Writing Culture* (1986). The second is a group of sociologists in what might be called the extreme anti-positivist wing of the symbolic interactionist tradition. These include ethnographers and cultural analysts associated with the programmes taught by Norman Denzin of the University of Illinois, Arthur Bochner and Carolyn Ellis of the University of South Florida, Andrea Fontana of the University of Nevada–Las Vegas, and Laurel Richardson of the Ohio State University. They have questioned the authority of classic texts, and promoted new forms of ethnographic writing. Some symbolic interactionists have gone further, and experimented with new ways of presenting data about lived experience, such as highly reflective autobiographical accounts and performance texts.

Questioning the authority of classic texts

The most usual way of reading an ethnographic text is to see it as reporting factual information about the world. Anthropologists have always presented their work in scientific terms: making discoveries about primitive peoples and reporting these to governments, or general and academic audiences interested in different cultures back home. Similarly, the ethnographers in the first and second Chicago Schools, whom I introduced in Chapter 2, also presented their findings as a straightforward naturalistic representation of what was happening in different social worlds. Herbert Blumer may have been a vigorous opponent of the inappropriate use of quantitative methods to study human beings, but he still believed that one could produce objective findings through ethnographic research.

Once poststructuralist ideas started to become popular in American universities, it was only a matter of time before this positivist understanding of ethnography came under attack. The main tactic has been to examine classic studies, and question the way they represent reality. The contributors in *Writing Culture* examine particular texts, such as Bronislaw Malinowski's (1961) *Argonauts of the Western Pacific* or Edward Evans-Pritchard's (1940) *The Nuer*, and show how they represent a biased or partial account of social reality. James Clifford, in the introduction, argues that they should be viewed not as contributions to science, but as 'ethnographic fictions':

> To call ethnographies fictions may raise empiricist hackles. But the world as commonly used in recent textual theory has lost its connotation of falsehood, of something merely opposed to truth. It suggests the partiality of cultural and historical truths, the ways they are systematic and exclusive. Ethnographic writings can properly be called fictions in the sense of 'something made up or fashioned', the principal burden of the word's Latin root, *fingere*. But it is important to preserve the [additional] meaning not merely of making, but also of making up, of inventing things not actually real. (Clifford and Marcus 1986, p. 6)

Perhaps the clearest systematic critique of realist ethnography can be found in a review article by George Marcus and Dick Cushman (1982). They identify a number of shortcomings in early anthropological studies. One of these is that 'the existence of the individual was usually suppressed in professional ethnographic writing' (1982, p. 32). This has some similarities to the critique made by Edward Said (1985) against 'Orientalism': the tendency of Western writers and intellectuals during the colonial period to portray people in Asia, Africa and the Middle East as an undifferentiated mass sharing cultural defects such as passivity and the inability to engage in rational thought. Another is that the ethnographer, who produced the account, was usually absent 'as a first person presence in the text'. Instead, they note the 'dominance . . . of the scientific (invisible or omniscient) narrator who is manifest only as a dispassionate, camera-like observer' (1982, pp. 31–2).

Symbolic interactionists, who have taken up poststructuralist ideas, have also questioned the authority of their own 'sacred' texts. One of the best known studies in the Chicago School tradition (although it was written by an anthropologist unconnected with Chicago) is William Foote Whyte's (1943) *Street Corner Society*. This ethnography compares the lives and perspectives of two groups of young men, the corner boys and the college boys, in an Italian American community called 'Corner-ville'. One reason for its enduring appeal lies in the fact that, unlike the early anthropological studies criticized by Marcus and Cushman, it vividly conveys a sense of the lives and personalities of particular individuals. A central character in the ethnography is Doc, the gang leader who befriended Whyte and collaborated with him in writing the study.

Forty years after the publication of *Street Corner Society*, Whyte's findings and methods were criticized in a 1992 special issue of the *Journal of Contemporary Ethnography*. The centrepiece was an article by W.A. Marianne Boelen, who had grown up in the real Cornerville, and claimed that he had misrepresented it as a slum run by racketeers. She also claimed that Doc had been seriously embarrassed by the publication of Whyte's book, so much so that he lost the position of leader in his gang, and eventually suffered a 'nervous breakdown'. Her source for this was not Doc himself, who had died in 1967, but his sons who believed that *Street Corner Society* had destroyed his life.

This was a realist critique in the sense that Boelen claimed that she knew the true facts about Cornerville which had been distorted by Whyte. However, an article by Laurel Richardson in the same issue (1992; reprinted in Richardson 1997) went further in using the dispute between the two accounts to question the authority of all ethnographic texts. It is now impossible to know which is the real Cornerville, or how Doc's life was affected by *Street Corner Society*. Richardson, however, argues that, in a sense, this does not matter, since all ethnographies necessarily use 'fiction-writing techniques' in portraying social reality. Two examples are that Whyte gives real people fictional names, and includes what appear to be 'verbatim quotes' from his 'characters', even though 'he tells us in his appendix that he did not take notes in the field and tape-recordings were not used' (1997, p. 110).

Boelen also claims that Whyte invented the famous episode in the bowling alley in which Doc always managed to win. This is a potentially damning charge for those who view ethnography as a scientific pursuit. It is, of course, impossible to prove what really happened. One can imagine, however, that if Whyte now admitted that he had made up large parts of *Street Corner Society*, then this would seriously undermine its authority as an ethnographic text. By contrast, Richardson, as a poststructuralist, is not concerned about whether or not ethnography lives up to the standards set in natural science:

> Could he have 'invented scenes' such as the bowling alley one, which Boelen's informants say never happened? Perhaps he could; perhaps he did. But does it matter if he did? Is 'scene building' much different from naming characters and quoting them? Do any of these fictional techniques detract from the general sociological points that Whyte wishes to make; or is it conversely because of these techniques that he was able to make his points and generate an abundance of research projects in his wake? (1997, p. 110)

It will be apparent that Marcus and Cushman in anthropology and Richardson in symbolic interactionism are not suggesting that we should no longer read classic texts (see also Clough 1992). Instead, they are questioning the idea that ethnography should be understood as a science. They want us to read studies more critically, and to appreciate the different stories that could have been told, and the literary devices employed to produce what appears to be a factual or objective account. This critique often becomes a political complaint that the voices of native peoples or women or ethnic minorities are being suppressed. However, underlying this is a poststructuralist concern with challenging the idea of truth: there are no true accounts, only different ways of interpreting reality.

New forms of ethnographic writing

In addition to critiquing classic texts, ethnographers influenced by post-structuralism have tried to move beyond realism as a representational genre either by focusing on the role of the author in collecting data, or allowing a range of voices to speak through the text. These two techniques are called 'dialogic' and 'polyphonic' ethnography (Clifford 1988).

Although there is nothing new about first person accounts in either anthropology or symbolic interactionist ethnography, they are usually published as methodological appendices or retrospective essays about the research process. What John Van Maanen (1988) calls 'confessional texts', such as Malinowski's (1967) fieldwork diaries, often cause a stir in the same way as allegations that an ethnographer has invented data; they do not, however, challenge realism. Poststructuralists, on the other hand, argue that *all* ethnography should be conceptualized and written as a first person account (see, for example, Clifford 1988; Marcus and Fischer 1986, Chapter 3). The first text to do this, which explicitly drew on poststructuralist ideas, was Paul Rabinow's (1977) retrospective account about his experiences in Morocco. This describes how he developed a partial and limited understanding of a different culture through developing a relationship with a particular informant, and how he came to question his own cultural assumptions during the fieldwork.

Another experimental form of writing ethnography is the 'polyphonic' or 'multivocal' text, a method which is partly inspired by the writings of Michel Bakhtin, the Russian literary theorist, now recognized to have been an early poststructuralist. According to Denzin, Bakhtin 'anticipates the postmodernist text – a text based on a parralax of discourses in which nothing is ever stable or capable of firm and certain representation' (1997, p. 36). The central idea is that, instead of imposing his or her authority on a text as an impersonal narrator, the author should withdraw and let the subjects speak for themselves. This is again not a completely new development in that even a conventional ethnographer, like Evans-Pritchard, considered publishing a book 'composed entirely of quotations' (Clifford 1988, p. 47). One can, however, see how publishing an ethnography, in which there is a dialogic interplay of voices rather than an objective 'third person' narrator, would appeal to post-structuralists.

Beyond ethnography

Arguably the most radical developments have taken place due to the popularity of cultural studies programmes in American universities since the 1980s. These celebrate ethnic and cultural diversity, but also subvert or challenge traditional disciplinary boundaries between the humanities and social sciences. Norman Denzin in his book *Interpretive Ethnography: Ethnographic Practices for the 21st Century* (1997) suggests that it might be necessary to find new ways of doing ethnography in a postmodern world.

One of these methods, the performance text, requires students to write poems and plays which incorporate multiple voices, and perform these as part of their studies (Becker et al. 1989). This involves collecting qualitative data, using conventional methods, but fashioning this into a theatrical performance. It will often incorporate different perspectives or 'multiple tellings' of the same event (in the manner of the Japanese film *Rashomon*). The audience can also be brought into the performance by inviting them to share in the dilemmas faced by the characters, and offer their own solutions (see Denzin 1997, Chapter 4).

Another increasingly popular way of presenting data is for sociologists to write autobiographical accounts, particularly ones that focus on key emotional experiences or 'epiphanic moments' (Denzin 1989b; Ellis and Flaherty 1992). Both devices challenge the realist view that it is possible to represent the world objectively. In the case of the performance text, one suspects that the goal is to annoy professional colleagues, still very much in the majority, who believe that sociology should be a science. This has much in common with the various attempts of avant-garde artists and novelists to shock audiences through defying realist conventions.

Four experimental ethnographies

A central principle which has informed this introductory text is that one can learn most about qualitative research from reading actual studies. This is true for all the traditions which I have reviewed in the sense that a general summary of their epistemological assumptions, or methodological preferences, cannot do justice to the diversity of empirical work in that field. You also stand little chance of producing good work without immersing yourself in the previous literature. This does not mean slavishly trying to copy particular methods of presenting data or literary techniques, although imitation and recycling have always been central to artistic work. Instead, it requires becoming sensitive to the theoretical, aesthetic and political choices made by researchers in different traditions.

In the case of postmodern ethnography, there are still only a relatively small number of 'experimental' studies, and some of these are now quite old. The celebratory claim that we are about to enter a new era in ethnographic writing, what Denzin (1997) describes as the 'sixth moment', seems decidedly premature. On the other hand, they all provoke reflection about both the purpose and practice of ethnography. I have chosen to examine four studies, which are informed by poststructuralist ideas about representation. Vincent Crapanzo's (1980) *Tuhami* is a 'dialogic' ethnography based on anthropological fieldwork in Morocco. Susan Krieger's (1983) *The Mirror Dance* is one of the few examples in symbolic interactionism of a 'polyphonic' ethnography. Carolyn Ellis's (1995) *Final Negotiations* is an autobiographical account about the lengthy illness and death of her partner. Finally, 'Laura May' is a poem by Laurel Richardson, based on interviewing an unmarried working class mother.

Tuhami: a dialogic ethnography

This study by Vincent Crapanzo (1980) tells the story of an illiterate Moroccan worker called Tuhami, who is visited by demons and saints in his dreams, and believes that he is married to a she-devil called 'A'isha Qandisha. It is not, however, simply a realist account of the beliefs of someone who belongs to a different culture. Instead, Crapanzo presents his findings in the form of the dialogue which took place between himself and Tuhami. The ethnography documents their encounter, and focuses on the interpretive difficulties involved in making sense of a different culture, and the emotional effects of fieldwork.

Crapanzo met Tuhami, whom he paid for his time, about once a week between March and November 1968 in the house of his Moroccan research assistant Lhacen. Tuhami was known locally as someone who knew a lot about 'magic and healing, the lives of saints, [and] the ways of demons' (1980, p. 12). Crapanzo was originally interested in learning about how Moroccans viewed religious brotherhoods such as the Hamadsha. However, it immediately became apparent that Tuhami wanted to tell his life-story, although in a highly allegorical and fantastical way. Crapanzo became increasingly affected personally, and believed that Tuhami also changed during their meetings:

> As Tuhami's interlocutor, I became an active participant in his life history, even though I rarely appear directly in his recitations. Not only did my presence, and my questions, prepare him for the text he was to produce, but they produced what I read as a change of consciousness in him. They produced a change of consciousness in me, too. We were both jostled from our assumptions about the nature of the everyday world and ourselves and groped for common reference points within this limbo of exchange. My research on the Hamadsha and my concern with Tuhami's personal history provided a frame, at least a cover (perhaps more for me than for Tuhami), for our interchange. (1980, p. 11)

Although there is a section providing background information about Moroccan society and religious beliefs that become relevant later, we learn about Tuhami through the stories and recollections he tells Crapanzo. These are presented so that we are put in the position of the anthropologist faced with several contradictory versions of the same event (the *Rashomon* effect), but can also see Crapanzo attempting to make sense of Tuhami's words through drawing on his knowledge of Moroccan culture and society. It is also often unclear whether Tuhami is talking about supernatural beings, such as demons and saints, or real people: they are either equally real to him, or he is talking about the world allegorically. His greatest complaint about these demons is that they have prevented him from marrying, but he is unable, or perhaps unwilling, to escape from their influence.

Towards the end of this ethnography, a remarkable and unexpected thing happens. The reader suddenly starts to realize (although this may just be my own response to the text) that what Tuhami has been saying is deeply sad. The clues were there at the beginning in that Crapanzo tells us that people visited by the she-demon 'were all peculiar in their way – loners, sexual inadequates, physical misfits, eccentrics, or men who for one social reason or another were unable to marry' (1980, p. 5). We were also told that Tuhami had been abandoned by his father, which is particularly stigmatizing in a culture where a son is seen as entirely a product of 'his father's seed', with the mother only being 'its receptacle' (1980, p. 38). Nevertheless, it is only through reading the various chapters that one comes to see Tuhami as a human being; and, at the same time, to share Crapanzo's growing realization that this has become (or perhaps was all along) a therapeutic encounter. He has, in effect, become a psychoanalyst, deeply involved with his patient on an emotional level, rather than a dispassionate scientist investigating another culture.

Another interesting feature of this ethnography is the way Crapanzo acknowledges the presence of Lhacen, his Moroccan fieldwork assistant. Lhacen is what might be described as a background character in that we never hear him speaking, although Crapanzo tells us that they had lengthy discussions about Tuhami, and he was present as a silent observer at every meeting. He had a crucial role in the early stages of the encounter:

> In those first meetings, Lhacen mediated my relationship with Tuhami. I was still new to Morocco. I was caught in a whirl of the unfamiliar. I was without anchor and did not have the confidence that comes with knowing the rules of social comportment and cultural evaluation. I was determined not to succumb to the easy aloofness of the total stranger. I felt awkward, confused, lonely even in the presence of my wife, and occasionally afraid. I was terrified of failure and everything that failure symbolized for me, and I gave expression to this terror most notably in terms of a loss of rapport with the best of my informants. (1980, p. 146)

Most conventional texts do not reveal the extent to which anthropologists rely on local research assistants, or on the emotions they experience during their fieldwork, although these are sometimes discussed in 'confessional' accounts. Crapanzo, on the other hand, believes that this should be a central part of ethnographic writing. In the concluding chapter, he observes that he 'made use of "ethnographic distance" and various theoretical positions, most notably the psychoanalytic' during the fieldwork, 'to distance myself and to defend myself from an onslaught of presumably intolerable emotions' (1980, p. 139). He reveals at one point that he had also grown up without a father, and that there was a kind of mutual therapy taking place during the meetings.

This summary might suggest that, despite acknowledging his difficulties in understanding a different culture, and the emotional impact of his stay in Morocco, Crapanzo has still constructed a realist account in that we are left with his interpretation of Tuhami's 'illness'. The narrative voice may be 'limited, masked, devoid even of a constant perceptual and theoretical vantage-point' (1980, p. 11), but it is still clearly a work by a particular author making use of a set of theoretical resources, and literary devices, in writing about someone who cannot talk back. This is not intended as a criticism of Crapanzo's study, but illustrates the difficulties that arise in trying to construct a truly democratic ethnography along poststructuralist principles. As James Clifford has observed, 'while ethnographies cast as encounters between two individuals may successfully dramatize the intersubjective give-and-take of fieldwork and introduce a counterpoint of authorial voices, they remain *representations* of dialogue' (1988 p. 43; see also Tyler 1987). One can, however, agree that this kind of text does make one think critically about realism, and the role of the researcher in ethnographic research.

The Mirror Dance

This ethnography by Susan Krieger (1983) is based on research conducted while she was a visiting professor at an American Midwestern university in the late 1970s. During her stay there, she became a member of a community of about a hundred lesbian women who met regularly at each other's houses, visited gay bars, and organized sporting activities and cultural events. She kept a journal of her own feelings and experiences, and also conducted seventy-eight interviews with different women at the end of the year which resulted in 'four hundred pages of single-typed interview notes' (1983, p. ix). The theme she wished to address, and which she had experienced at first hand, are the pressures on individuals to conform in this social group.

Krieger had already experimented with presenting ethnographic data as a 'multiple person stream of consciousness narrative', influenced partly by reading Virginia Wolf's novel *The Years* which tells 'an intergenerational family saga' through interweaving a number of related stories. She had developed this approach while writing a book called *Hip Capitalism* (1979), which documents the changes that took place in an underground radio station at the end of the 1960s, when it was acquired by a corporation and was eventually forced to become 'commercial'. Instead of trying to explain how this shift had taken place, she decided to tell the story 'almost entirely by paraphrasing from my interview and documentary evidence' and determined that 'I would allow myself no analytic or theoretical commentary in the body of the text' (1983, p. 187).

Her objective in *The Mirror Dance* was to go even further by completely eliminating her own presence:

> The main difference between this second case and the first . . . was that, in this new study, I attempted to be even more strict in my method than I had been before. I paraphrased my data even more closely and used my interview notes as the only source for writing up my account . . . I added very little of my own wording to my text beyond crediting paraphrased passages to different speakers and identifying when speakers changed. I, therefore, became almost absent as a narrator. I was 'painting a picture' this time, and a modern abstract one at that, rather than 'telling a story' as I had done before. My desire was to have the voices and language of the women I had interviewed provide their own systematic self-reflection, to have them suggest in their own terms the form of a pattern that might explain the problems of individuality the community posed for its members. I could orchestrate these women's voices, with all the care for a faithful grasp of their situation and its meanings that I could manage, but my rule was that I should do little more. (1983, p. 191)

Krieger's experiment has received a mixed critical reaction, in that some readers have complained that there is too little authorial voice (so the study has become flat and uninteresting), and others have argued that she has imposed her own views on her respondents by the way she has edited the interviews (1983, pp. 192–3). These criticisms can be assessed through considering the following extract from the start of Chapter 4, which is called 'The Web of Talk'. It gives a good idea of how qualitative data is presented throughout the study, although some of the individual third person contributions by women run to several paragraphs, or even whole chapters:

> There was this hotline that went around all the time, that kept the community together, felt Shelah. People were always talking about each other. It was not necessarily malicious, said Chip, but it was what traditionally was known as gossip. Things just went like wildfire, Leah observed. Gossip just spread really quickly, particularly with some people. There was a lot of gossip, said Emily. It was not ill-intentioned. It was Hollywood-style gossip, infatuation – 'Last night she was seen with her'. She made hopeless attempts to control it sometimes.
> Privacy? In this community? There was none, felt Jessica. You came into this community, said Martha, and at first you didn't want everyone to know your business. (1983, p. 25)

One problem you might have with this style of writing, from a literary point of view, is that we never learn that much about particular characters. In the best symbolic interactionist ethnographies, or even in dialogic experiments such as *Tuhami*, one comes to know individuals like Tally or Tuhami quite well. This is also the case in *Hip Capitalism*, in that much of the dramatic interest of the story comes from colourful characters such as the 400 pound Tom Donahue, the 'Big Daddy' of the station, and the authoritarian programme director Thom O'Hair, the 'Montana Banana' (1983, p. 189). The seventy women interviewed for this study are, however, presented as a series of disembodied voices. Krieger is trying to portray a community rather than the narratives of particular individuals, and is interested in presenting an 'interplay of voices that echo, again and again, themes of self and community, sameness and difference, merger and separation, loss and change' (1983, p. xvii).

There is, of course, no obligation to make things easy for the reader, or even to be readable, if you employ an experimental technique, provided that you can justify your style of presenting data on epistemological grounds. *The Mirror Dance* is often cited as an example of a radical 'polyphonic' work which challenges realist ideas about representation. The difficulty here is that Krieger is still present in an introductory chapter, in which she explains her theoretical interests in identity and community, and in the methodological appendix. The data is also still presented under thematic chapter headings such as 'parties and gatherings' or 'mothers and children'. Even within particular chapters, the reader is always aware that someone must have organized the materials, and decided which characters get the chance to speak.

Final Negotiations

This autobiographical account by Carolyn Ellis (1995) tells the story of how she met her partner Gene Weinstein in 1975, and how the relationship developed as his health gradually deteriorated and he died nine years later from emphysema, a painful and debilitating illness which prevents oxygen from reaching the lungs. Most of the book, some 300 pages, is a straightforward narrative, but there is also a short introduction, and a forty page methodological appendix, although it is not described as such, about the process of writing the book, which took her nine years to complete.

These sections describe how she made use of a journal she kept during the last year of the illness, how she recollected previous events by using memory recovery techniques, such as 'method acting', and how she edited the book down from 700 to 300 pages by focusing on key moments in the relationship. She experimented with different ways of representing her experience, but, in the end, chose to write a narrative, without academic citations or an attempt to address the illness in terms of theoretical categories or themes. This was because she had become dissatisfied with 'the constraints of detached social-science prose and the demand to write in an authoritative and uninvolved voice' (1995, p. 6). Instead, she wanted to write a text that would be more than a dry, scientific account:

> How you, as a reader, respond to my story as you read and feel it, is an important part of this work. Some of you may prefer to feel with me, as in watching a true-to-life movie; some may be reminded of and feel for the parallels in your own relationships, as in reading an engaging novel; some may prefer cognitively processing the feelings expressed, closer to a traditional social science reading. My goal is to engage you in aspects of relationships that usually are neglected or overlooked in social-science inquiry. (1995, p. 4)

One American reviewer has reported that several of his students were moved to tears by the book: most either 'could not put the book down', or 'could not finish it because the descriptions of Gene's dying process were too graphic and emotionally difficult for them to read' (Karp 1996, p. 294). I suspect that most British readers would not respond in this way; but one can appreciate why someone who has experience of caring for a dying relative could be moved.

Two critical points seem worth making about this type of autobiographical account. The first concerns the extent to which autobiography should be seen as a general method in social science, or whether it is best understood as a form of therapy for people who have experienced serious traumas. One could not, for example, imagine that if you kept a journal about day-to-day events at work, or perhaps about relationships with family and friends, it would produce an interesting narrative. There is a satisfying beginning, middle and end to *Final Negotiations*, which stems from the fact that it is about the course (in symbolic interactionist terms, one might say the career) of an illness and a relationship, but also the fact that she has worked through her grief by writing the book. She has started a new relationship with Art Bochner, and together they have developed new techniques for helping others to talk about their emotions through performing 'personal stories' about traumatic events (Ellis and Bochner 1992). Where would the stories come from if you were writing about everyday life?

The same objection I have already raised in relation to *Tuhami* and *The Mirror Dance* also seems relevant to this autobiographical account, in that Ellis is telling a realist story, and asking us to believe that the events she reports did take place. She does, however, recognize that, from a post-structuralist point of view, there can never be one story, or a simple ending: there can only be multiple interpretations of events. In the end, she decided against ending the book by including 'a conversation with Art my current partner, or alternatively, to record a group of social scientists conversing about the meaning of my story'. She also considered but rejected the idea of ending with 'a conversation between myself and Gene, who would "return from death" to talk to me about what these texts mean', and perhaps give an orthodox social scientific response to the narrative (1995, pp. 329–30). My own view is that this kind of dialogue would be most effective, as a means of advancing a poststructuralist critique of conventional social science, if it resulted in the reader completely reinterpreting the text: but, of course, that is never really possible since the author always has the last word.

Louisa May: poetry as ethnography

'Louisa May's Story of Her Life' is a hundred line poem, composed by Laurel Richardson, based on a tape-recorded interview with an unmarried mother from a Southern rural background (Richardson 1997, Part 4). It is written as a first person narrative, interspersed with italicized comments, which reveal that she is being interviewed. Louisa May's story is that she grew up in the South, got married, had a miscarriage, got divorced, and is now pregnant by another man who lives a hundred miles away. She does not want to marry him, since she does not want a split family, and is happy with her life as a single mother.

The poem is not especially remarkable as literature. It is, in my admittedly unqualified opinion, neither truly awful nor a brilliant evocation of someone else's life. The first ten lines are worth supplying, so that you can judge for yourself:

> The most important thing
> to say   is that
> I grew up in the South.
> Being southern shapes
> aspirations   shapes
> what you think you are
> and what you think you're going to be.
>
> *(When I hear myself, my Ladybird*
> *kind of accent on tape, I think, O Lord,*
> *You're from Tennessee.)*
>
> (1997, p. 131)

Richardson began her academic career as a feminist, doing empirical research of a similar kind to the interview studies reviewed in the previous chapter. Over the years, however, she became increasingly dissatisfied:

> I realized there were few substantive (not theoretical or methodological) sociology texts that I enjoyed reading or could point to as models for my students . . . Even when the topic was ostensibly riveting, the writing style and reporting conventions were deadening. Nearly every time sociologists broke out into prose, they tried to suppress (their own) life: passive voice, absent

narrator; long, inelegant, repetitive authorial statements and quotations; 'cleaned up' quotations, each sounding like the author; hoards of references; sonorous prose rhythms, dead or dying metaphors; lack of concreteness or overly detailed accounts; tone deafness; and most disheartening, the suppression of narrativity. (1997, p. 148)

Richardson also describes writing the Louisa May poem as a personal breakthrough: it did not simply introduce narrative techniques (such as establishing a plot or character) into an ethnography, but broke completely with social science by turning her data into a poem. Inevitably, the response at conferences was mixed, and she subsequently wrote a short play (1997, pp. 158–63) dramatizing what happened when she carelessly, or perhaps deliberately, skipped a line in reading out the poem, so there was a discrepancy with the written text (her parenthetical comments on the proceedings are in italics).

Most of the male characters complain that her findings must be inaccurate or unreliable, since she refuses to supply the tape-recording ('*reliability – validity – cannot accept your findings – inaccuracy – reliability – validity – cannot accept your findings – cannot accept your findings*'). Some women in the audience believe that she must be talking about her own experience of getting divorced ('*I'm stunned*'). The most perceptive people there recognize that the slip is intended to problematize the issue of representation ('*Mmm . . . Would someone have commented about a "slip" in a prose text? Would anyone at a sociology conference question the difference between an oral and written rendition of an interview snippet?*').

Assessing postmodern ethnography

Postmodern ethnography is the newest of the traditions I have reviewed in this book, and is still the subject of lively critical assessment, especially in the field of symbolic interactionism, where enthusiasts such as Norman Denzin and Laurel Richardson have deliberately set out to provoke a response, through criticizing what they describe as the 'boring' work of established researchers. In this concluding section, I would like to review some responses which either have been, or might be, advanced by Chicago School ethnography, grounded theory, ethnomethodology, the critical tradition, and what might be called radical poststructuralism. This provides an opportunity to review some of the epistemological positions that I have discussed in this book, which inform different ways of doing qualitative research.

Chicago School ethnography

Some symbolic interactionists, who are continuing the tradition of the Chicago School, have mounted scathing attacks on what they see as the rampant subjectivism of postmodernists. Herbert Gans has, for example, complained about the new vogue for 'autoethnographic' work in which researchers write about their own experiences:

> Even if it is well meant and well done, this kind of ethnography has nothing to do with analyzing what people do with and to each other in their groups and networks, or how institutions and communities function or malfunction. Abandoned also is the effort to use sociology and years of intensive field research to report to readers about parts of society about which they know only stereotypes. At times, it is difficult not to suspect that some ethnographers are avoiding the hard work that fieldwork entails, even if not deliberately. Although others are using ethnography as a synonym for autobiography, a few are simply engaged in ego trips, whether or not they know it. (1999, p. 542)

From this perspective, fieldwork should be a science concerned with addressing 'lived experience' based on spending long periods of fieldwork in different social settings (see Chapter 2). Once ethnographers start writing about themselves, or giving up research in favour of fiction, then they turn their backs on the world, and lose the capacity to contribute to public debate about social problems.

Grounded theory

So far as I am aware, researchers in the grounded theory tradition have ignored postmodern ethnography. As I demonstrated in Chapter 3, Anselm Strauss and Barney Glaser believed that symbolic interactionism should move in a positivistic direction, by developing systematic procedures for collecting and analysing data. The two traditions represent opposite wings of a spectrum within symbolic interactionism between positivism and interpretivism, with Chicago School ethnography occupying the middle ground. It is interesting to note that grounded theory has been successful, and is taught in one form or another on many social science programmes, precisely because of this strategic accommodation with positivism. Quantitative researchers, incidentally, continue to dominate departments of social science in America, and have, if anything, tightened their grip in the computer age. Ethnographers, whether they are new or old, are most likely to be working in smaller, less prestigious institutions.

Ethnomethodology

There are superficial similarities between ethnomethodology and poststructuralism, in that many people viewed the former as a kind of radical subjectivism (see, for example, Meehan and Wood 1975) when it became fashionable for a few years at the end of the 1960s. It is still often associated with the idea that there is no absolute truth, only different ways of interpreting or constructing the social world. This, however, is a considerable misreading, since ethnomethodologists place considerable emphasis on respecting the character of the everyday world as it is perceived and experienced by its members. There is nothing subjectivist about Lawrence Wieder's study of the convict code which I summarized in Chapter 4, or ethnographies which address how people in different occupations understand and accomplish their day-to-day work.

Perhaps the best ethnomethodological critique of postmodern ethnography is a paper by Egon Bittner (1973), which was written before the term was even invented. He noted that the critique of positivism at the time seemed to result in 'studies of a loose, impressionistic and personal nature' which did not address 'those traits of depth, stability and necessity that people recognize as actually inherent in the conditions of their existence' (1973, pp. 117, 123). Bittner felt that the reasons for this 'abortive phenomenology' lay in the fact that fieldworkers dip into different social worlds, which encourages a relativist viewpoint. He did not, however, predict that this shift 'from the object to the subject' would be taken a stage further by contemporary researchers who only want to write about their own experiences and feelings, and contest the whole idea of 'objectivity' (1973, p. 122).

The critical tradition

Although there is little, if any, political content in the four experimental ethnographies I have reviewed in this chapter, and I have tended to question the extent to which poststructuralism is compatible with left-wing politics, there are still close ties between poststructuralists and critical theorists. Robert Prus has observed, perceptively, that cynical, relativist and anti-scientific viewpoints appeal to anti-establishment intellectuals:

> For those concerned with exploitation, power and empowerment (from a Marxist, 'critical' or 'cultural studies' perspective) postmodernism offers a powerful rhetorical weapon that might be used not only to challenge disfavored situations, practices and people, but also to change (in activist manners) the prevailing social orders. (1996b, p. 218)

Although I have not given it much emphasis in this chapter, one could argue that most programmatic statements advocating postmodern ethnography are also sympathetic towards critical theory, even though they have opposing epistemological assumptions. To give one example, George Marcus promotes dialogic methods in anthropology, but also admires Paul Willis's *Learning to Labour*, and Marxist anthropological studies such as Michael Taussig's (1980) *The Devil and Commodity Fetishism in South America* or June Nash's (1979) *We Eat the Mines and the Mines Eat Us* (see Marcus 1986; Marcus and Fischer 1986). This feeling may, of course, be reciprocated, but at least some critical anthropologists have criticized postmodernism for not addressing the economic, social and political structures which produce Third World poverty (Polier and Rosebery 1989). Feminists have also been highly critical of postmodern ethnography (see Mascia-Lees et al. 1989; Wolf 1992). The argument here is that insights from postmodernism about difference should be combined with a realist understanding of the structures which oppress women.

Radical poststructuralism

The last word on postmodern or poststructuralist ethnography is, perhaps, best left to the poststructuralists themselves. One cannot imagine Derrida finding much of interest in this literature, since there is very little philosophical content, and the critique of representation and meaning is not pushed very far (see Watson 1987). The four experimental ethnographies I have discussed, which are often cited as the best and most radical examples of work in this genre, all seem to be informed by realist epistemological assumptions, despite the fact that the authors are committed to the poststructuralist position that there is no such thing as truth, and wish to break completely with positivist social science. This even applies to Richardson, who critiques the idea of representation in ethnography while presenting a realist account of her battles with various departmental heads.

Writers in the sociology of science have, arguably, taken poststructuralism more seriously by writing relentlessly reflexive accounts, questioning the idea of a coherent text, and deconstructing the author (see, for example, Ashmore 1989; Woolgar 1988b). Most have either given up or become tired of these experiments, and it may be that intellectuals are beginning to tire of poststructuralism and postmodernism more generally. It is, after all, hard mounting a sustained challenge to positivism, given its deep roots in Western intellectual culture.

Further reading

Some introductions to poststructuralism and postmodernism

Cuff, E.C., Sharrock, W.W. and Francis, D. (1998) *Perspectives in Sociology*, 4th edn. Routledge, London, Chapters 10-12.

Best, S. and Kellner, D. (1991) *Postmodern Theory: Critical Interrogations.* Macmillan, London.

Sarup, M. (1993) *An Introductory Guide to Post-Structuralism and Postmodernism.* Harvester Wheatsheaf, London.

Postmodernism and ethnography

Clifford, J. and Marcus, G.E. (1986) *Writing Culture: the Poetics and Politics of Ethnography*. University of California Press, Berkeley, CA.

Marcus, G. and Cushman, D. (1982) 'Ethnographies as texts', *Annual Review of Anthropology*, 11: 25–69.

Marcus, G. and Fischer, M. (1986) *Anthropology as Cultural Critique: an Experimental Moment in the Human Sciences*. University of Chicago Press, Chicago.

Fontana, A. (1994) 'Ethnographic trends in the postmodern era', in D. Dickens and A. Fontana (eds), *Postmodernism and Social Inquiry*. UCL Press, London, pp. 203–23.

Denzin, N. (1997) *Interpretive Ethnography: Ethnographic Practices for the 21st Century*. Sage, London.

EXERCISES

1   Critically examine any text that you have produced, or any ethnography that you admire, from a postmodern perspective.

2   Write a short poem based on conducting a life-history interview with someone from a different class or ethnic background, and recite it to your class. Alternatively, write and perform a short play based on a debate in which you have participated about postmodernism in a research methods seminar. In each case, you should also write a statement discussing the implications for conventional ethnography.

Part III

CONCLUSION

9

The Craft of Qualitative Research

CONTENTS

This book has introduced a number of research traditions that use qualitative methods, such as interviewing, ethnographic fieldwork and discourse analysis, to investigate the social world. In the first part, I looked at the interpretive traditions of Chicago School ethnography in symbolic interactionism, grounded theory, dramaturgical analysis, ethnomethodological ethnography and conversation analysis. In the second part, I examined a range of critical traditions, including Marxist and feminist varieties of qualitative research, critical discourse analysis and postmodern ethnography.

In each case, I have tried to explain the epistemological and theoretical assumptions of the tradition, and have shown how these have informed the work of particular researchers through discussing a number of case studies. I hope that you take away a sense that there is much of interest taking place in all these fields, and that you will be encouraged to follow up the references at the end of each chapter which direct you to more specialized introductions and readings. I particularly hope that you will read some of the actual studies, and will try out the different ways of presenting and analysing qualitative data that you find there in your own work.

In this concluding chapter, I want to consider some of the practical issues that arise in doing research. I will begin by offering some advice on how to write undergraduate projects and dissertations. I will also outline what is involved in becoming a qualitative researcher, from doing a PhD to publishing academic books and articles, and applying for grants from funding bodies to pursue applied projects.

Undergraduate projects and dissertations

Most social science degrees in the United Kingdom require students to do empirical research. Ideally, any programme should include modules on quantitative and qualitative methods running through the first and second years. In the third year, there is also often the opportunity to write a 10,000 word empirical dissertation.

Learning how to think theoretically

The main argument I have advanced in this book is that methods courses should not simply be viewed as an opportunity to learn a set of techniques, such as how to use SPSS-X in the case of quantitative research, or a data analysis package like NUD•IST for a qualitative project. They should also allow you to appreciate the epistemological and theoretical assumptions of different research traditions. To use an analogy with the entertainment industry, one would not get very far in learning how to make films simply by learning technical skills such as how to frame shots or light a set. Instead, film students also learn the language of cinema as an artistic medium: how to appreciate, work within and even subvert different representational genres.

The magistrates' courts revisited

One way to explain the distinction between method and methodology is to return to the example of the magistrates' courts. At the start of Chapter 1, I reviewed a range of qualitative methods that you could use in studying your local courts (or any other social setting). The five methods I discussed were observation, interviewing, ethnographic fieldwork, discourse analysis and textual analysis. Having read the rest of the book, it should be possible to appreciate that each of the research traditions I have reviewed employs these methods, but that they write about the world in different ways.

One can collect and analyse qualitative data in the lower courts from a Marxist, feminist, symbolic interactionist or ethnomethodological perspective (see, for example, Blumberg 1969; Carlen 1976; Eaton 1986; Travers 1997). There are, as far as I know, no poststructuralist studies, but it is easy to imagine how one might write about legal hearings from this theoretical perspective. A central theme would be that one can never establish the truth through the legal process: all one gets are different versions of events, which can never tell us what 'really' happened. Research methods courses should teach students how to analyse and interpret qualitative data using ideas and concepts from these traditions: there should be a close link between theory, substantive topics and method throughout the undergraduate degree.

There may be objections here that the type of methods course I am proposing is unworkable, since it is difficult to imagine undergraduates doing more than collecting and writing about data in a positivist framework. It makes no sense, however, to treat undergraduates, or even school students, as second class citizens who are taught a watered down form of research practice on methods courses, while expecting them to engage with complex methodological debates and issues in the rest of the curriculum. In my view, methods courses should not simply teach a set of techniques but offer an opportunity to experiment with different ways of representing reality.

Becoming a qualitative researcher

If you enjoy your undergraduate degree, it may be that you will want to continue your studies, and perhaps go on to teach your subject by working in higher education. If so, you will need to obtain a doctorate, and learn how to produce work that will satisfy the standards set by other academics in your field. You may also want to use your research skills to address problems of interest to government and industry.

Writing a doctorate

The usual route towards becoming an academic is to do a PhD which, in the United Kingdom, involves writing an 80,000 word dissertation over a three year period. The first year is spent reading the literature, and developing a theoretical position. The second year is spent collecting data, and the final year writing up the dissertation. This is assessed by an external examiner who decides whether you have produced an original piece of research, and understand theoretical debates and arguments relating to that topic in the discipline.

I suggested in the preface that becoming a sociologist usually involves being trained in a craft tradition in which individual researchers share a set of theoretical and epistemological assumptions. Your best chance of doing developed work as a grounded theorist, conversation analyst, critical discourse analyst or postmodern ethnographer lies in studying with people working in these traditions. In symbolic interactionist terms, this may not actually require meeting people in the flesh, since this may not always be possible, but will mean treating theorists and researchers in that tradition as your reference group (Shibutani 1961). You will find this happening naturally as you get drawn into the literature, and become interested in the specialist debates that take place there about methodological issues.

Submitting papers to journals

Having obtained a PhD, the next step is to obtain a lecturing or research post, and to submit articles for publication in academic journals. It is possible, at least in theory, to publish qualitative research in most main-stream journals across a range of disciplines. In practice, however, there is a tendency for people working in particular traditions to publish in the specialist journals which I have identified in different chapters.

Submitting a paper to a journal means that you will receive feedback from at least two reviewers: some of the comments may be misinformed and unhelpful, but you should also receive some useful comments which will help you to improve the quality of your work. You can obtain a great deal of pleasure from trying to produce work that meets the standards set by other academics working in that field. On the other hand, it can be a frustrating business trying to get work published, especially since the reviewing process can be quite slow. One useful tip for the novice is that you should be psychologically prepared to receive a lot of rejections. The practical way to cope with this is to attempt to address or respond to the criticisms, and immediately submit the paper elsewhere.

Finding a publisher for a monograph

Most qualitative researchers in the fieldwork tradition prefer to publish books rather than journal articles. This is because one can include a lot more data in a monograph, and it offers more freedom, and oppor-tunities for creativity, in the way you can write about and present data. One technique which I employed in *The British Immigration Courts* (1999) was to contrast a number of different perspectives on immigration con-trol, in a way which was intended to make the reader think more critically about this political issue. This would not have been possible in an 8000 word journal article.

If you have written an ethnography, you will ideally be looking for a publishing firm that is willing to publish it as a reasonably priced paperback. Here you will meet one of the new realities of mass higher education. Undergraduate students no longer have the money to buy specialist texts, so most monographs are only published in expensive hardback editions which are expected to sell only a few hundred copies to academic libraries.

The largest commercial academic publishers no longer publish mono-graphs of any kind, and even the smaller presses, including university presses in America, are often reluctant to take risks in publishing a book that may only interest a small readership. There are only a couple of companies worldwide which specialize in publishing ethnographic monographs, and these have a preference for particular research traditions. As in many other areas in life, having a patron or being on the inside of particular networks always helps. Do not despair, however, if your manuscript keeps being returned: if you persevere, and try every available avenue, you should eventually get published.

New forms of publication

One technological development which may eventually revolutionize academic publishing is the internet, which makes it possible to obtain information anywhere in the world through a computer screen. So far there is little indication that more qualitative research is being published on websites, despite the fact that fewer manuscripts are being accepted by conventional publishers. There is also little indication that researchers are taking up the opportunities offered by these technologies to include audio and video clips, or do interesting things with hyperlinks, even though these techniques are already being used by some American e-novelists (although these mainly publish on CD-ROM).

A conventional cloth-bound or paperback book still feels like a more satisfying and tangible cultural product than obtaining a printout from a website, or reading text on a computer screen. It is also still the best way of reaching a large audience through libraries or bookshops. On the other hand, the internet should make it easier to get ethnographies published, and may encourage more qualitative researchers to present visual and audio data as part of an ethnographic account.

Doing applied research

The main source of funding in Britain for social scientists is the Economic and Social Research Council, which supports research which improves either the efficiency and effectiveness of public sector organizations or the performance of the economy. The statement in a grant application should include an introduction to your research question, and details of how you are proposing to collect and analyse the data. You are also required to state how your project represents 'value for money', and show how you intend to communicate your findings to non-academic audiences. If you are doing an ethnography of some institution, such as a school or hospital, you also need to demonstrate that you have their permission to conduct the study (unless, that is, you are planning to collect data covertly). Obtaining access is, therefore, as important as obtaining funding: each stage of the project will involve writing letters or statements explaining why you want to conduct this piece of research, and how it will benefit that institution and wider society.

Your key argument, as a qualitative researcher, will always be that conducting an ethnographic study offers a rich and detailed account of what happens inside a particular institution which can address practical questions of interest to managers and practitioners. Quantitative studies are good at giving an overview of some phenomenon, or identifying a problem that needs investigating. The qualitative researcher can go further by describing what people are doing on the ground.

Some organizations you approach may be suspicious of your motives, or regard qualitative methods as a 'soft' variety of research. You will find, however, that many people in positions of responsibility are already familiar with your objectives, and sympathetic towards the practical and political problems that will inevitably arise. The objective of any applied research project should not simply be to publish academic books or articles. You will also need to produce findings which are useful to the organization which has commissioned the research, or which succeed in generating debate about public policy by reaching a wider audience through the mass media. Part of the craft of qualitative research lies in learning how to address these different audiences.

Contemporary challenges

It would be dishonest to end this book without acknowledging that these are difficult times for qualitative researchers, and for intellectuals in general, owing to the fact that resources per student have declined in most Western countries as their higher education systems have expanded. There can be no doubt that the quality and interest of many of the studies I have reviewed was made possible by the fact that qualitative research was generously funded by universities and funding agencies. Today, there is less money, or at least what money there is has to be spread more thinly. Ironically, the larger numbers who now have the opportunity to enter higher education mean that there are fewer opportunities to engage in scholarship and research.

This has less to do with a shift in the *Zeitgeist* (see Bauman 1992) than with the problems all countries in the developed world face in funding public services. The hard sciences often have as much cause for complaint as the humanities and social sciences that not enough money is being spent to recruit bright young people into academic life, or to give them the time to produce research of high quality. A further difficulty in Britain is the time taken up by the highly bureaucratic and expensive Research Assessment Exercise, which was created partly out of a need to ration scarce resources among growing numbers of 'research-active' academics.

On a more positive note, more people are doing social science degrees in higher education than ever before, and many of these take courses in qualitative research methods. There may no longer be a mass general audience for qualitative monographs, but there is a mass audience in universities. There are also new, cheap ways of disseminating information through the internet. Although it may prove difficult matching the achievements of the past, there is no shortage of things to write about.

Bibliography

Anderson, E. (1976) *A Place on the Corner*. University of Chicago Press, Chicago.

Anderson, N. (1923) *The Hobo*. University of Chicago Press, Chicago.

Anderson, R.J., Hughes, J.A. and Sharrock, W.W. (1989) *Working for Profit: the Social Organisation of Calculation in an Entrepreneurial Firm*. Avebury, Aldershot.

Ashmore, M. (1989) *The Reflexive Thesis: Righting the Sociology of Scientific Knowledge*. University of Chicago Press, Chicago.

Atkinson, J.M. and Heritage, J. (eds) (1984) *Structures of Social Action: Studies in Conversation Analysis*. Cambridge University Press, Cambridge.

Atkinson, P., Coffey, A. and Delamont, S. (1999) 'Ethnography: post, past and present', *Journal of Contemporary Ethnography*, 28 (5): 460–71.

Ball, D. (1967) 'An abortion clinic ethnography', *Social Problems*, 14: 293–301.

Baudrillard, J. (1988) *Selected Writings*. Polity, Cambridge.

Bauman, Z. (1992) 'Is there a postmodern sociology?', in Z. Bauman, *Intimations of Postmodernity*. Routledge, London, pp. 93–113.

Becker, H.S. (1951) 'Role and career problems of the Chicago public-school teacher'. PhD dissertation, University of Chicago.

Becker, H.S. (1963) *Outsiders*. Free Press, New York.

Becker, H.S. (1967) 'Whose side are we on?', *Social Problems*, 14: 239–47.

Becker, H.S. (1982) *Artworlds*. University of California Press, Berkeley.

Becker, H.S., Hughes, E.C., Geer, B. and Strauss, A.L. (1961) *Boys in White: Student Culture in a Medical School*. University of Chicago Press, Chicago.

Becker, H.S., Hughes, E.C. and Geer, B. (1968) *Making the Grade: the Academic Side of Student Life*. Wiley, New York.

Becker, H.S., McCall, M.M. and Morris, L.V. (1989) 'Theatres and communities: three scenes', *Social Problems*, 36: 93–116.

Best, S. and Kellner, D. (1991) *Postmodern Theory: Critical Interrogations*. Macmillan, London.

Beynon, H. (1973) *Working for Ford*. Penguin, Harmondsworth.

Bhaskar, R. (1978) *A Realist Theory of Science*, 2nd edn. Harvester Press, Sussex.

Billig, M. (1992) *Talking of the Royal Family*. Sage, London.

Birdwhistell, R.L. (1970) *Kinesics and Context: Essays on Body Motion Communication*. University of Pennsylvania Press, Philadelphia.

Bittner, E. (1973) 'Objectivity and realism in sociology', in G. Psathas (ed.), *Phenomenological Sociology*. John Wiley, New York, pp. 109–25.

Blumberg, A. (1969) 'The practice of law as a confidence game', in V. Aubert (ed.), *The Sociology of Law*. Penguin, Harmondsworth, pp. 321–31.

Blumer, H. (1933) *Movies and Conduct*. Macmillan, New York.

Blumer, H. (1969) 'Sociological analysis and the variable', in H. Blumer, *Symbolic*

Interactionism: Perspective and Method. University of California Press, Berkeley, CA, pp. 127–39.

Blumer, H. (1972) '"Action" vs. "interaction"', *Society*, 9: 50–3.

Blumer, H. and Hauser, P. (1933) *Movies, Delinquency and Crime.* Macmillan, New York.

Boden, D. and Zimmerman, D.H. (1991) *Talk and Social Structure: Studies in Ethnomethodology and Conversation Analysis.* Polity, Cambridge.

Boelen, W.A.M. (1992) 'Street Corner Society: Cornerville revisited', *Journal of Contemporary Ethnography*, 21: 11–51.

Bourdieu, P. et al. (2000) *The Weight of the World: Social Suffering in Contemporary Society.* Polity, Cambridge.

Bowers, J., Button, G. and Sharrock, W.W. (1995) 'Workflow from within and without: technology and co-operative work on the print industry shopfloor', in *Proceedings of the Fourth International Conference on Computer Supported Co-operative Work.* Stockholm, Sweden, pp. 51–66.

Breitman, G. (1965) *Malcolm X Speaks.* Grove Weidenfeld, New York.

Bryman, A. (1988) *Quantity and Quality in Sociological Research.* Unwin Hyman, London.

Burawoy, M. (ed.) (1991) *Ethnography Unbound: Power and Resistance in the Modern Metropolis.* University of California Press, Berkeley.

Burns, T. (1992) *Erving Goffman.* Routledge, London.

Cameron, D. (1995) *Feminism and Linguistic Theory.* Macmillan, London.

Cameron, D., Frazer, E., Harvey, P., Rampton, B. and Richardson, K. (1992) *Researching Language: Issues of Power and Method.* Routledge, London.

Carden, M. (1974) *The New Feminist Movement.* Russell Sage, New York.

Carlen, P. (1976) *Magistrates' Justice.* Martin Robertson, Oxford.

Chouliaraki, L. and Fairclough, N. (1999) *Discourse in Late Modernity: Rethinking Critical Discourse Analysis.* Edinburgh University Press, Edinburgh.

Cicourel, A. (1968) *The Social Organization of Juvenile Justice.* Wiley, New York.

Cicourel, A. and Kitsuse, J. (1963) *The Educational Decision-Makers.* Bobbs-Merrill, Indianapolis.

Clifford, J. (1988) 'On ethnographic authority', in J. Clifford, *The Predicament of Culture: Twentieth Century Ethnography, Literature and Art.* Harvard University Press, Cambridge, pp. 21–54.

Clifford, J. and Marcus, G.E. (1986) *Writing Culture: the Poetics and Politics of Ethnography.* University of California Press, Berkeley, CA.

Clough, P.T. (1992) *The End(s) of Ethnography.* Sage, Newbury Park, CA.

Coffey, A. (1999) *The Ethnographic Self.* Sage, London.

Crapanzo, V. (1980) *Tuhami: Portrait of a Moroccan.* University of Chicago Press, Chicago.

Cressey, P. (1932) *The Taxi-Dance Hall.* University of Chicago Press, Chicago.

Cuff, E.C., Sharrock, W.W. and Francis, D. (1998) *Perspectives in Sociology*, 4th edn. Routledge, London.

Daly, M. (1978) *Gyn/Ecology: The Metaethics of Radical Feminism.* Beacon Press, Boston.

De Beauvoir, S. (1974) *The Second Sex.* Vintage, New York.

Denzin, N. (1989a) *The Research Act*, 3rd edn. Prentice-Hall, Englewood Cliffs, NJ.

Denzin, N. (1989b) *Interpretive Interactionism.* Sage, Newbury Park, CA.

Denzin, N. (1994) 'Postmodernism and deconstructionism', in D. Dickens and A. Fontana (eds), *Postmodernism and Social Inquiry.* UCL Press, London, pp. 182–202.

Denzin, N. (1997) *Interpretive Ethnography: Ethnographic Practices for the 21st Century.* Sage, London.

Devine, F. and Heath, S. (1999) *Sociological Research Methods in Context.* Macmillan, Basingstoke.

Dey, I. (1993) *Qualitative Data Analysis: a User-Friendly Guide for Social Scientists.* Routledge, London.

Diamond, T. (1992) *Making Grey Gold: Narratives from Inside Nursing Homes.* University of Chicago Press, Chicago.

Donovan, F. (1920) *The Woman Who Waits.* Goreham, Boston.

Donovan, F. (1929) *The Saleslady.* University of Chicago Press, Chicago.

Drew, P. and Heritage, J. (1992) *Talk at Work: Interaction in Institutional Settings.* Cambridge University Press, Cambridge.

Drew, P. and Wooton, A. (eds) (1988) *Erving Goffman: Exploring the Interaction Order.* Polity, Cambridge.

Duneier, M. (1999) *Sidewalk.* Farrar, Strauss and Giroux, New York.

Durkheim, E. (1951) *Suicide.* Free Press, New York.

Durkheim, E. (1985) 'The rules of sociological method', in K. Thompson (ed.), *Readings from Emile Durkheim.* Routledge, London, pp. 63–90.

Dworkin, A. (1981) *Our Blood: Prophecies and Discourses on Sexual Politics.* Putnam, New York.

Eaton, M. (1986) *Justice for Women? Family, Court and Social Control.* Open University Press, Milton Keynes.

Ellis, C. (1995) *Final Negotiations: a Story of Love, Loss and Chronic Illness.* Temple University Press, Philadelphia.

Ellis, C. and Bochner, A. (1992) 'Telling and performing personal stories: the constraints of choice in abortion', in C. Ellis and M.G. Flaherty (eds), *Investigating Subjectivity: Research on Lived Experience.* Sage, Newbury Park, CA, pp. 70–101.

Ellis, C. and Flaherty, M.G. (1992) *Investigating Subjectivity: Research on Lived Experience.* Sage, Newbury Park, CA.

Emerson, R., Fretz, R. and Shaw, L. (1995) *Writing Ethnographic Fieldnotes.* University of Chicago Press, Chicago.

Engestrom, Y. and Middleton, D. (1996) *Cognition at Work.* Cambridge University Press, Cambridge.

Evans-Pritchard, E. (1940) *The Nuer.* Oxford University Press, Oxford.

Fairclough, N. (1989) *Language and Power.* Longman, London.

Fairclough, N. (2000a) 'Language and neo-liberalism', *Discourse and Society,* 11 (2): 147–8.

Fairclough, N. (2000b) *New Labour, New Language.* Routledge, London.

Faludi, S. (1992) *Backlash: the Undeclared War Against Women.* Chatto and Windus, London.

Fanon, F. (1963) *The Wretched of the Earth.* Grove, New York.

Fine, G. (1995) *A Second Chicago School? The Development of a Postwar American Sociology.* University of Chicago Press, Chicago.

Firestone, S. (1970) *The Dialectic of Sex.* Bantam, New York.

Fish, S. (1982) *Is There a Text in This Class?* Harvard University Press, Cambridge.

Flick, U. (1998) *An Introduction to Qualitative Research.* Sage, London.

Fonow, M. and Cook, J. (eds) (1991a) *Beyond Methodology: Feminist Scholarship as Lived Research.* Indiana University Press, Bloomington, IN.

Fonow, M. and Cook, J. (1991b) 'Back to the future: a look at the second wave of epistemology and method', in M. Fonow and J. Cook (eds), *Beyond Methodology: Feminist Scholarship as Lived Research.* Indiana University Press, Bloomington, pp. 1–15.

Fontana, A. (1994) 'Ethnographic trends in the postmodern era', in D. Dickens and A. Fontana (eds), *Postmodernism and Social Inquiry.* UCL Press, London, pp. 203–23.

Foucault, M. (1967) *Madness and Civilisation: a History of Insanity in the Age of Reason.* Tavistock, London.

Foucault, M. (1977) *Discipline and Punish: the Birth of the Prison*. Tavistock, London.

Friedan, B. (1974) *The Feminine Mystique*. Dell, New York.

Gans, H. (1999) 'Participant observation in the Era of "Ethnography"', *Journal of Contemporary Ethnography*, 28 (5): 540–8.

Gardner, C.B. (1995) *Passing By: Gender and Public Harassment*. University of California Press, Berkeley.

Garfinkel, H. (1984a) 'Some rules of correct decisions that jurors respect', in H. Garfinkel, *Studies in Ethnomethodology*. Polity, Cambridge, pp. 104–15.

Garfinkel, H. (1984b) 'Common-sense knowledge of social structures: the documentary method of interpretation in lay and professional fact-finding', in H. Garfinkel, *Studies in Ethnomethodology*. Polity, Cambridge, pp. 76–103.

Garfinkel, H., Lynch, M. and Livingston, E. (1981) 'The work of a discovering science construed from materials from the optically discovered pulsar', *Philosophy of the Social Sciences*, 11: 67–78.

Geuss, R. (1981) *The Idea of a Critical Theory: Habermas and the Frankfurt School*. Cambridge University Press, Cambridge.

Glaser, B. and Strauss, A. (1965) *Awareness of Dying*. Aldine, Chicago.

Glaser, B. and Strauss, A. (1967) *The Discovery of Grounded Theory*. Aldine, Chicago.

Goffman, E. (1959) *The Presentation of Self in Everyday Life*. Penguin, Harmondsworth.

Goffman, E. (1961a) *Asylums*. Penguin, Harmondsworth.

Goffman, E. (1961b) *Encounters: Two Studies in the Sociology of Interaction*. Bobbs-Merrill, Indianapolis.

Goffman, E. (1963) *Behavior in Public Places: Notes on the Social Organization of Gatherings*. Free Press, New York.

Goffman, E. (1970) *Strategic Interaction*. Basil Blackwell, Oxford.

Goffman, E. (1971) *Relations in Public: Microstudies of Public Order*. Basic, New York.

Goffman, E. (1974) *Frame Analysis: an Essay on the Organization of Experience*. Harper and Row, New York.

Goffman, E. (1983) 'The interaction order', *American Sociological Review*, 48: 1–17.

Goffman, E. (1989) 'On Fieldwork' (transcribed and edited by L. Lofland), *Journal of Contemporary Ethnography*, 18 (2): 123–32.

Goode, D. (1994) *A World without Words*. Temple University Press, Philadelphia.

Goodwin, M.H. (1990) *He-Said-She-Said: Talk as Social Organization among Black Children*. Indiana University Press, Bloomington.

Gouldner, A.W. (1962) 'Anti-minotaur: the myth of a value-free sociology', *Social Problems*, 9: 199–213.

Gubrium, J. (1992) *Out of Control: Family Therapy and Domestic Order*. Sage, Newbury Park, CA.

Gubrium, J. and Holstein, J. (1997) *The New Language of Qualitative Method*. Oxford University Press, Oxford.

Halfpenny, P. (1979) 'The analysis of qualitative data', *Sociological Review*, 21 (1): 799–825.

Hall, S., Critcher, C., Jefferson, T., Clarke, J. and Roberts, B. (1978) *Policing the Crisis: Mugging, the State and Law and Order*. Macmillan, London.

Hammersley, M. (1989) *The Dilemma of Qualitative Method: Herbert Blumer and the Chicago Tradition*. Routledge, London.

Hammersley, M. (1991) *Reading Ethnographic Research*. Longman, London.

Hammersley, M. (2000) *Taking Sides in Social Research*. Routledge, London.

Hammersley, M. and Atkinson, P. (1995) *Ethnography: Principles and Practice*, 2nd edn. Routledge, London.

Harding, S. (ed.) (1987) *Feminism and Methodology*. Open University Press, Milton Keynes.

Harper, R. (1987) 'The fate of idealism in accountancy', in *Proceedings of the Third Conference on Multi-Disciplinary Approaches to Accountancy*, Vol. 3–4, Manchester University, pp. 1–10.

Harper, R. (1998) *Inside the IMF*. Academic Press, London.

Harper, R., Randall, D. and Rouncefield, M. (2000) *Organisational Change in Retail Finance: an Ethnographic Perspective*. Routledge, London.

Harvey, L. (1990) *Critical Social Research*. Unwin Hyman, London.

Hayner, N. (1936) *Hotel Life*. McGrath, College Park, MD.

Heath, C. (1997) 'The analysis of activities in face to face interaction using video', in D. Silverman (ed.), *Qualitative Research: Theory, Method and Practice*. Sage, London, pp. 183–200.

Heath, C. and Luff, P. (1996) 'Convergent activities: line control and passenger information on the London Underground', in Y. Engestrom and D. Middleton (eds), *Cognition at Work*. Cambridge University Press, Cambridge, pp. 96–129.

Heritage, J. (1984) *Garfinkel and Ethnomethodology*. Polity, Cambridge.

Heritage, J. and Greatbach, D. (1991) 'On the institutional character of institutional talk: the case of news interviews', in D. Boden and D. Zimmerman (eds), *Talk and Social Structure: Studies in Ethnomethodology and Conversation Analysis*. Polity, Cambridge, pp. 93–137.

Hester, S. and Eglin, P. (eds) (1996) *Membership Categorization*. University Press of America, Lanham, MD.

Hiller, E.T. (1928) *The Strike*. University of Chicago Press, Chicago.

Hodge, R. and Kress, G. (1993) *Language and Ideology*, 2nd edn. Routledge, London.

Horowitz, I.L. (1993) *The Decomposition of Sociology*. Oxford University Press, Oxford.

Hughes, J. and Sharrock, W.W. (1990) *The Philosophy of Social Research*, 2nd edn. Longman, London.

Hutchby, I. (1992) *Confrontation Talk: Arguments, Asymmetries and Power in Talk Radio*. Lawrence Erlbaum, Hillsdale, NJ.

Hutchby, I. and Wooffitt, R. (1998) *Conversation Analysis: Principles, Practices and Applications*. Polity, Cambridge.

Jaworski, A. and Coupland, N. (eds) (1999) *The Discourse Reader*. Routledge, London.

Karp, D. (1996) 'Review of *Final Negotiations* by Carolyn Ellis', *Journal of Contemporary Ethnography*, 25 (2): 293–6.

Kelly, L. (1988) *Surviving Sexual Violence*. Polity, Cambridge.

Kendall, G. and Wickham, G. (1999) *Using Foucault's Methods*. Sage, London.

Kincheloe, J. and McLaren, P. (2000) 'Rethinking critical theory and qualitative research', in N. Denzin and Y. Lincoln (eds), *The Handbook of Qualitative Research*, 2nd edn. Sage, London, pp. 138–57.

Krieger, S. (1979) *Hip Capitalism*. Sage, Beverley Hills, CA.

Krieger, S. (1983) *The Mirror Dance: Identity in a Woman's Community*. Temple University Press, Philadelphia.

Lee, J.R.E. (1984) 'Innocent victims and evil doers', *Womens' Studies International Forum*, 7 (1): 69–73.

Liebow, E. (1967) *Tally's Corner*. Little Brown, Boston.

Livingston, E. (1987) *Making Sense of Ethnomethodology*. Routledge, London.

Lofland, J. and Lofland, L. (1995) *Analyzing Social Settings*, 3rd edn. Wadsworth, Belmont, CA.

Lynch, M. (1985) *Art and Artefact in Laboratory Science: a Study of Shop Work and Shop Talk in a Research Laboratory*. Routledge, London.

Lynch, M. (1993) *Scientific Practice and Ordinary Action: Ethnomethodology and Social Studies of Science*. Cambridge University Press, Cambridge.

Lynch, M. and Bogen, D. (1994) 'Harvey Sacks' primitive natural science', *Theory, Culture and Society*, 11: 65–104.

Mac an Ghaill, M. (1988) *Young, Gifted and Black: Student–Teacher Relations in the Schooling of Black Youth*. Open University Press, Milton Keynes.

Mac an Ghaill, M. (1994) *The Making of Men: Masculinities, Sexualities and Schooling*. Open University Press, Buckingham.

MacLeod, J. (1976) *Ain't No Makin' It: Aspirations and Attainment in a Low-Income Neighbourhood*. Westview, Oxford.

Mahony, P. and Zmroczek, C. (eds) (1997) *Class Matters: 'Working Class' Women's Perspectives on Social Class*. Taylor and Francis, London.

Malinowski, B. (1961) *Argonauts of the Western Pacific*. Dutton, New York.

Malinowski, B. (1967) *A Diary in the Strict Sense of the Term*. Harcourt Brace, New York.

Manning, P. (1992) *Erving Goffman and Modern Sociology*. Polity, Cambridge.

Marcus, G. (1986) 'Contemporary problems of ethnography in the modern world system', in J. Clifford and G.E. Marcus (eds), *Writing Culture: the Poetics and Politics of Ethnography*. University of California Press, Berkeley, pp. 165–93.

Marcus, G. and Cushman, D. (1982) 'Ethnographies as texts', *Annual Review of Anthropology*, 11: 25–69.

Marcus, G. and Fischer, M. (1986) *Anthropology as Cultural Critique: an Experimental Moment in the Human Sciences*. University of Chicago Press, Chicago.

Marcuse, H. (1964) *One Dimensional Man*. Routledge, London.

Marx, K. and Engels, F. (1967) *The Communist Manifesto*. Penguin, Harmondsworth.

Mascia-Lees, F., Sharpe, P. and Cohen, C. (1989) 'The postmodernist turn in anthropology: cautions from a feminist perspective', *Signs*, 15 (11): 7–33.

Maynard, D. (1984) *Inside Plea-Bargaining: the Language of Negotiation*. Plenum, New York.

Maynard, D. (1991) 'The perspective-display series and the delivery and receipt of diagnostic news', in D. Boden and D. Zimmerman (eds), *Talk and Social Structure: Studies in Ethnomethodology and Conversation Analysis*. Polity, Cambridge, pp. 164–92.

Mead, G.H. (1934) *Mind, Self and Society*. University of Chicago Press, Chicago.

Meehan, A.J. (1997) 'Record-keeping practices in the policing of juveniles', in M. Travers and J. Manzo (eds), *Law in Action: Ethnomethodological and Conversation Analytic Approaches to Law*. Ashgate, Aldershot, pp. 183–208.

Meehan, H. and Wood, H. (1975) *The Reality of Ethnomethodology*. Wiley, New York.

Merton, R. (1967) *On Theoretical Sociology*. Free Press, New York.

Messinger, S., Sampson, H. and Towne, R. (1962) 'Life as theater: some notes on the dramaturgic approach to social reality', *Sociometry*, 14 (2): 141–63.

Miles, M. and Huberman, A. (1994) *Qualitative Data Analysis: an Expanded Sourcebook*. Sage, London.

Millet, K. (1970) *Sexual Politics*. Doubleday, Garden City, NY.

Mills, C.W. (1959) *The Sociological Imagination*. Oxford University Press, New York.

Moerman, M. (1988) *Talking Culture: Ethnography and Conversation Analysis*. University of Pennsylvania Press, Philadelphia.

Nash, J. (1979) *We Eat the Mines and the Mines Eat Us: Dependency and Exploitation in Bolivian Tin Mines*. Columbia University Press, New York.

Nelson, C. (1994) 'Ethnomethodological positions on the use of ethnographic data in conversation analytic research', *Journal of Contemporary Ethnography*, 23: 307–29.

Oakley, A. (2000) *Experiments in Knowing: Gender and Method in the Social Sciences*. Polity, Cambridge.

Pierce, J. (1995) *Gender Trials: Emotional Lives in Contemporary Law Firms*. University of California Press, Berkeley.

Polier, N. and Rosebery, W. (1989) 'Tristes tropes: post-modern anthropologists encounter the other and discover themselves', *Economy and Society*, 18 (2): 245–64.

Pomerantz, A. (1978) 'Compliment responses: notes on the cooperation of multiple constraints', in J. Schenkein (ed.), *Studies in the Organization of Conversational Interaction*. Academic, New York, pp. 79–112.

Pomerantz, A. (1988) 'Offering a candidate answer: an information seeking strategy', *Communication Monographs*, 55: 361–73.

Prus, R. (1989) *Making Sales: Influence as Interpersonal Accomplishment*. Sage, Newbury Park, CA.

Prus, R. (1996a) *Symbolic Interaction and Ethnographic Research*. State University of New York Press, New York.

Prus, R. (1996b) 'Betwixt positivist proclivities and postmodern tendencies', in R. Prus, *Symbolic Interaction and Ethnographic Research*. State University of New York Press, New York, pp. 203–44.

Prus, R. and Styllianos, I. (1980) *Hookers, Rounders and Desk Clerks: the Social Organization of the Hotel Community*. Sheffield, Salem, WI.

Pryce, K. (1979) *Endless Pressure*. Penguin, Harmondsworth.

Psathas, G. (1995) *Conversation Analysis: the Study of Talk-in-Interaction*. Sage, London.

Rabinow, P. (1977) *Reflections on Fieldwork in Morocco*. University of California Press, Berkeley.

Reinharz, S. (1992) *Feminist Methods in Social Research*. Oxford University Press, New York.

Ribbens, J. and Edwards, R. (eds) (1998) *Feminist Dilemmas in Qualitative Research: Public Knowledge and Private Lives*. Sage, London.

Richardson, L. (1992) 'Trash on the corner: ethics and ethnography', *Journal of Contemporary Ethnography*, 21: 103–19.

Richardson, L. (1997) *Fields of Play: Constructing an Academic Life*. Rutgers University Press, New Brunswick, NJ.

Rist, R. (1970) 'Student social class and teacher expectations: the self-fulfilling prophecy in ghetto education', *Harvard Educational Review*, 40 (3): 411–51.

Robillard, A.B. (1999) *Meaning of a Disability: the Lived Experience of Paralysis*. Temple University Press, Philadelphia.

Rock, P. (1979) *The Making of Symbolic Interactionism*. Macmillan, London.

Rosaldo, R. (1980) *Ilongot Headhunting 1883–1974: a Study in Society and History*. Stanford University Press, Stanford.

Ryove, A.L. and Schenkein, J.N. (1974) 'Notes on the art of walking', in R. Turner (ed.), *Ethnomethodology*. Penguin, Harmonsdworth, pp. 265–74.

Sacks, H. (1972) 'On the analyzability of stories by children', in J. Gumperz and D. Hymes (eds), *Directions in Sociolinguistics: the Ethnography of Communication*. Rinehart and Winston, New York, pp. 325–45.

Sacks, H. (1984) 'Note on methodology', in J.M. Atkinson and J. Heritage (eds), *Structures of Social Action: Studies in Conversation Analysis*. Cambridge University Press, Cambridge, pp. 21–7.

Sacks, H. (1987) 'On the preferences for agreement and contiguity in sequences in conversation', in G. Button and J.R.E. Lee (eds), *Talk and Social Organization*. Multilingual Matters, Cleveland, pp. 54–69.

Sacks, H. (1992) 'The baby cried. The mommy picked it up', in H. Sacks, *Lectures on Conversation* (edited by E. Schegloff). Blackwell, Oxford, pp. 252–66.

Sacks, H., Schegloff, E. and Jefferson, G. (1974) 'A simplest systematics for the organisation of turn-taking for conversation', *Language*, 50: 696–735.

Said, E. (1985) *Orientalism*. Penguin, Harmondsworth.

Sarup, M. (1993) *An Introductory Guide to Post-Structuralism and Postmodernism*. Harvester Wheatsheaf, London.

Schegloff, E.A. (1968) 'Sequencing in conversational openings', *American Anthropologist*, 80: 1075–95.

Schegloff, E.A. (1987a) 'Recycled turn beginnings: a precise repair mechanism in conversation's turn-taking organization', in G. Button and J.R.E. Lee (eds), *Talk and Social Organization*. Multilingual Matters, Cleveland, pp. 70–85.

Schegloff, E.A. (1987b) 'Analyzing single episodes of interaction: an exercise in conversation analysis', *Social Psychology Quarterly*, 50: 101–14.

Schegloff, E.A. (1991) 'Reflections on talk and social structure', in D. Boden and D. Zimmerman (eds), *Talk and Social Structure: Studies in Ethnomethodology and Conversation Analysis*. Polity, Cambridge, pp. 44–70.

Scheurich, J. (1997) *Research Method in the Postmodern*. Falmer, London.

Seale, C. (ed.) (1998) *Researching Society and Culture*. Sage, London.

Segal, L. (1987) *Is the Future Female? Troubled Thoughts on Contemporary Feminism*. Virago, London.

Sharrock, W.W. and Anderson, R.J. (1986) *The Ethnomethodologists*. Ellis Horwood, Chichester.

Sharrock, W.W. and Watson, D.R. (1989) 'Talk and police work', in H. Coleman (ed.), *Working with Language: a Multi-Disciplinary Consideration of Language Use in Work Contexts*. Mouton de Gruyer, New York, pp. 431–50.

Shaw, C. (1930) *The Jack-Roller: a Delinquent Boy's Own Story*. University of Chicago Press, Chicago.

Shibutani, T. (1961) *Society and Personality*. Prentice-Hall, Englewood Cliffs, NJ.

Silverman, D. (1993) *Interpreting Qualitative Data: Methods for Analysing Talk, Text and Interaction*. Sage, London.

Silverman, D. (ed.) (1997) *Qualitative Research: Theory, Method and Practice*. Sage, London.

Silverman, D. (1998) *Harvey Sacks*. Polity, Cambridge.

Skeggs, B. (1997) *Formations of Class and Gender: Becoming Respectable*. Sage, London.

Smith, D. (1987) 'A sociology for women', in D. Smith, *The Everyday World as Problematic*. Open University Press, Milton Keynes, pp. 49–104.

Smith, G. (ed.) (1999) *Goffman and Social Organization: Studies in a Sociological Legacy*. Routledge, London.

Sokal, A. and Bricmont, J. (1997) *Intellectual Impostures: Postmodern Philosophers' Abuse of Science*. Profile, London.

Spender, D. (1980) *Man Made Language*. Harper Collins, London.

Spradley, J. (1979) *The Ethnographic Interview*. Holt, Rinehart and Winston, New York.

Stacey, J. (1988) 'Can there be a feminist ethnography?', *Women's Studies International Forum*, 11 (1): 21–7.

Stanley, L. (ed.) (1990) *Feminist Praxis*. Routledge, London.

Stanley, L. (1993) 'On auto/biography in sociology', *Sociology*, 27 (1): 41–52.

Stanley, L. and Wise, S. (1983) *Breaking Out: Feminist Consciousness and Feminist Research*. Routledge, London.

Stanley, L. and Wise, S. (1991) 'Feminist research, feminist consciousness and experiences of sexism', in M. Fonow and J. Cook (eds), *Beyond Methodology: Feminist Scholarship as Lived Research*. Indiana University Press, Bloomington, pp. 265–83.

Strauss, A. (1985) *Qualitative Analysis for Social Scientists.* Cambridge University Press, Cambridge.

Strauss, A. and Corbin, J. (eds) (1997) *Grounded Theory in Practice.* Sage, London.

Strauss, A. and Corbin, J. (1998) *Basics of Qualitative Research: Techniques and Procedures for Producing Grounded Theory,* 2nd edn. Sage, London.

Strauss, A., Fagerhaugh, S., Suczek, B. and Wiener, C. (1985) *The Social Organization of Medical Work.* University of Chicago Press, Chicago.

Suchman, L. (1987) *Plans and Situated Actions: the Problem of Human–Machine Communication.* Cambridge University Press, Cambridge.

Suchman, L. and Jordan, B. (1990) 'Interactional troubles in face-to-face survey interviews', *Journal of the American Statistical Association,* 85: 232–41.

Sudnow, D. (1967) *Passing On: the Social Organization of Dying.* Prentice-Hall, Englewood Cliffs, NJ.

Sudnow, D. (1978) *Ways of the Hand.* Harvard University Press, Cambridge, MA.

Taussig, M. (1980) *The Devil and Commodity Fetishism in South America.* University of South Carolina Press, Chapel Hill.

Ten Have, P. (1999) *Doing Conversation Analysis: a Practical Guide.* Sage, London.

Thomas, W.I. and Znaniecki, F. (1958) *The Polish Peasant in Europe and America.* Dover, New York.

Thrasher, F. (1927) *The Gang.* University of Chicago Press, Chicago.

Todd, A.D. and Fisher, S. (eds) (1988) *Gender and Discourse: the Power of Talk.* Ablex, New York.

Tong, R. (1993) *Feminist Thought: a Comprehensive Introduction.* Routledge, London.

Travers, M. (1997) *The Reality of Law: Work and Talk in a Firm of Criminal Lawyers.* Ashgate, Aldershot.

Travers, M. (1999) *The British Immigration Courts: a Study of Law and Politics.* Policy, Bristol.

Tyler, S. (1987) *The Unspeakable: Discourse, Dialogue and Rhetoric in the Postmodern World.* University of Wisconsin Press, Madison, WI.

Van Dijk, T. (1996) *Discourse Studies: a Multidisciplinary Introduction* (2 volumes). Sage, London.

Van Maanen, J. (1988) *Tales of the Field: on Writing Ethnography.* University of Chicago Press, Chicago.

Vom Lehn, D., Heath, C. and Hindmarsh, J. (2000) 'Exhibiting interaction: conduct and collaboration in museums and galleries', in C. Heath (ed.), *Selected Papers I: Work, Interaction and Technology Group.* The Management Centre, King's College, London, pp. 106–36.

Waller, W. (1930) *The Old Love and the New.* Southern Illinois University Press, Carbondale, IL.

Watson, G. (1987) 'Make me reflexive but not yet: strategies for managing essential reflexivity in ethnographic discourse', *Journal of Anthropological Research,* 43 (1): 29–41.

Watson, R. (1997a) 'Ethnomethodology and textual analysis', in D. Silverman (ed.), *Qualitative Research: Theory, Method and Practice.* Sage, London, pp. 80–98.

Watson, R. (1997b) 'The presentation of victim and motive in discourse: the case of murder interrogations', in M. Travers and J. Manzo (eds), *Law in Action: Ethnomethodological and Conversation Analytic Approaches to Law.* Ashgate, Aldershot, pp. 77–98.

Watson, R. (1999) 'Reading Goffman on interaction', in G. Smith (ed.), *Goffman and Social Organization: Studies in a Sociological Legacy.* Routledge, London, pp. 138–55.

Weber, M. (1949) *The Methodology of the Social Sciences.* Free Press, New York.

Weber, M. (1958) *The Protestant Ethic and the Spirit of Capitalism.* Scribners, New York.

Weinberg, T. (1983) *Gay Men, Gay Selves*. Irvington, New York.

West, C. (1995) 'Women's competence in conversation', *Discourse and Society*, 6 (1): 107–31.

West, C. and Zimmerman, D.H. (1997) 'Women's place in everyday talk: reflections on parent–child interaction', *Social Problems*, 24: 521–9.

Whyte, W.F. (1943) *Street Corner Society*. University of Chicago Press, Chicago.

Wieder, D.L. (1974) *Language and Social Reality*. Mouton, The Hague.

Willis, P. (1977) *Learning to Labour: How Working Class Kids Get Working Class Jobs*. Saxon House, Farnborough.

Willis, P. (2000) *The Ethnographic Imagination*. Polity, Cambridge.

Wirth, L. (1928) *The Ghetto*. University of Chicago Press, Chicago.

Wolf, D. (ed.) (1996) *Feminist Dilemmas in Fieldwork*. Westview, Colorado.

Wolf, M. (1992) *A Thrice Told Tale: Feminism, Postmodernism and Ethnographic Responsibility*. Stanford University Press, CA.

Wooffitt, R., Fraser, N., Gilbert, G.N. and McGlashan, S. (1997) *Humans, Computers and Wizards: Analysing Human–(Simulated)–Computer Interaction*. Routledge, London.

Woolgar, S. (1988a) *Science: the Very Idea*. Routledge, London.

Woolgar, S. (1988b) (ed.) *Knowledge and Reflexivity: New Frontiers in the Sociology of Knowledge*. Sage, London.

Wowk, M. (1984) 'Blame allocation, sex and gender in a murder interrogation', *Women's Studies International Forum*, 7 (1): 75–82.

Zorbaugh, H. (1929) *The Gold Coast and the Slum*. University of Chicago Press, Chicago.

Index